Molière

Updated Edition

Twayne's World Authors Series

French Literature

David O'Connell, Editor

Georgia State University

Portrait of Molière by Pierre Mignard, courtesy of Musée Condé, Château de Chantilly.

Molière

Updated Edition

By Hallam Walker

Davidson College

Twayne Publishers
A Division of G. K. Hall & Co. • *Boston*

842.09
MOLIERE
WALKER, H

Molière, Updated Edition
Hallam Walker

Copyright 1990 by G. K. Hall & Co.
All rights reserved.
Published by Twayne Publishers
A Division of G. K. Hall & Co.
70 Lincoln Street
Boston, Massachusetts 02111

First edition copyright © 1971 by Twayne Publishers, Inc.

Copyediting supervised by Barbara Sutton
Book production by Gabrielle B. McDonald
Book design by Barbara Anderson

Typeset in 11 pt. Garamond
by Compositors Corporation, Cedar Rapids, Iowa

Printed on permanent/durable acid-free paper
and bound in the United States of America

First printing 1990
10 9 8 7 6 5 4 3 2 1

Library of Congress Cataloging-in-Publication Data

Walker, Hallam.
    Molière / by Hallam Walker. — Updated ed.
        p.   cm. — (Twayne's world author series ; TWAS 176. French
    literature)
    Includes bibliographical references.
    ISBN 0-8057-8258-3 (alk. paper)
    1. Molière, 1622–1673—Criticism and interpretation.   I. Title.
    II. Series : Twayne's world authors series ; TWAS 176.   France.
PQ1860.W3   1990
842′.4—dc20   89-24656
                                               CIP

Contents

Foreword: To Read

The publication of Molière's plays
a bit wary of having his comedies
that their true nature would not b
performances. The following adm
to *L'Amour médecin* (Love as the
command in 1665.

It is not necessary to warn you that th
tion. One knows well that comedies a
the reading of this one except by pers
of the live action of the theater *[tout*
would be desirable that these sorts o
ornaments that accompany them in
much more acceptable state. The air
sieur Lully, mingled with the beauty
them, no doubt, graces which are d

Even in the case of a comedy v
advice to visualize the staged per
agination. In the basic sense ima
with the mind's eye, and some ex
cal comedy will be of help. Sho
lines of a scene, keeping a natura
a way incompatible with stagin
being his or her own producer an
she sees them.
In doing this sort of reading o
ter is the time involved. The wl
place within the space of time no
physical action—no more and
upon time. It is a concentratio
presentation of so many words a
troduction, exposition, develo
may be varied, resumed, or mer
in time. If the play is well writ

About the Author

Hallam Walker is professor emeritus of French at Davidson College in North
Carolina. A native of New Jersey, he completed his studies at Princeton Uni-
versity, where he returned to take his doctorate after naval service in World
War II. He taught at branches of the Pennsylvania State University, Wash-
ington and Lee University, and Duke University prior to coming to Davidson
College in 1965. Walker is the author of numerous articles on the French
novel, theater, and poetry, with subjects ranging from Cyrano de Bergerac to
Baudelaire. He has edited Molière's *Le Tartuffe* and been active in the North
American Society for Seventeenth-Century French Literature, the Modern
Language Association of America, and the American Association of Teachers
of French. His current studies center on literary perceptions of the natural
world and their role in environmental policy shaping.

will grasp during the performance just what the themes and structures are all about, catching the repeated elements as they go by rapidly. Note that the action is not to be stopped in the way that one might halt and reread a passage in a novel. Things are happening before the spectator with an impression of the ongoing nature of events in real life. Theater is a becoming in the present, not events of the past recalled. The story or novel is normally narrated in the past tense, but the temporal mode of the theater is totally present. Thus our reading habits must be shaped to this mode.

As the scenes flow by, acted out or read aloud, the reader should be alert to characteristic words or gestures on the part of persons being portrayed. What are their real concerns and how do they project them to the other characters? In Molière's comedies the externals of a miser or a hypochondriac, for example, are riotously heightened for laughs, but one wonders what causes the bizarre behavior and how it impinges upon others. We soon perceive that the signs all point to a struggle for power and control within a family under a tyrannical parent. Love within the family and love between young men and women is at stake. Beneath the gags and farce the audience looks for signs of mounting tensions and resolution of the problems. In Molière's comedies the ending normally brings an accommodation to social norms and a means of coping with the aberrant individual. Like a classical music composition, the play will arrive at a clear ending from which one can look back over the experiencing of the piece and see that the flow of words and gestures has been in a satisfyingly coherent pattern with some real human meaning. Theater is an art that creates a virtual experience of human life; it is as if we lived through the events. To resume the comparison with a piece of fiction, in the novelist's art we are made to feel that we remember a past event. Each literary mode has its own way of augmenting the lives of its audience.

So, we must enter into the reading of the plays without the disposition toward hindsight and reflection that mark the reading of fiction. We should be there in the happening as much as possible and get caught up in a new experience. Then, after the play is over, we can reflect on it as an experience and decide what really went on. All will probably not be crystal clear, no more than things are in life. But the playwright will have selected elements and strung them together to form a pattern in such a way that they should communicate a powerful sense of meaning and wholeness, as opposed to the randomness of everyday life. I hope readers will try this sort of reading of theater.

In the French theater the start of a performance is heralded by the sound of rhythmic tapping behind the scenes, followed by three spaced knocks, then the curtain opens. We should think of this in starting a play and see Molière step up to the footlights.

Preface to the Updated Edition

In the almost two decades since the first publication of this book the flow of print on Molière has continued without pause. The perennial challenge to understand the nature and import of his comedies, combined with the advent of some new critical concepts, has stimulated a variety of interesting interpretations. The last chapter of this study now contains an extensive review of recent books, articles, and staged versions of the plays. The expanded Bibliography lists important studies with brief annotations to guide the reader.

The general trend in work on Molière has been, in my view, a healthy emphasis upon the approach offered by Will G. Moore in his *Molière, a New Criticism* (Oxford: Clarendon, 1949), to see Molière as a great creator of theater. Prior to Moore's book much attention had been given to digging out the playwright's life from his works or to building philosophical systems from them. Current criticism may tend toward a reductionism that explains the plays in terms of one critical theory or toward a personal interpretive essay. All these works, however, confirm the unending fascination of Molière .

The text of this book, an introduction to Molière for the Anglophone student or reader, has been expanded in several areas for this edition. I hope that the problems of interpretation of the plays will stimulate further interest and study. The Bibliography will lead to analyses beyond the scope of this book.

The very nature of this work leads to the assumption that the plays will be read in English. Two problems arise immediately in this event: theater is not experienced as live performance but as written text, and the original language is lost. The second can be dealt with more easily because one may learn French and consult annotated edtions for the sense of difficult passages. The problem of reading plays and not seeing them staged is more serious, which is why I have included the preceding Foreword on how to read a Molière play. A play is not a novel or a story but a special genre with its own rules, and we err if we expect to find in it things foreign to its nature. In short, one should ask the right questions of a piece of theater, following the wishes of Molière, who admonishes his reader to "read with eyes to discover all of the live action of the theater" (*L'Amour médecin*).

I reiterate my thanks to the publishers of the *French Review* and *Romance Quarterly* for permission to use again the materials noted in the original Preface. Permission of the publishers of *L'Esprit créateur* is gratefully acknowledged for my use of material on *Les Fâcheux,* originally published in *Paths to Freedom: Studies in French Classicism in Honor of E. B. O. Borgerhoff.*

Hallam Walker

Davidson College

Preface

With a wealth of studies amassed over three centuries to draw upon for a comprehension of Molière and his theater, yet another treatment of the man and his works needs some justification. This book gives to the reader unfamiliar with Molière a rapid introduction to the career of the playwright as well as summaries and analyses of the plays. It also examines the theatrical and literary values of the comedies with the particular aim of showing their excellence as creations for the stage and as great innovations in the development of world theater.

Since Molière was above all a professional creator of theater, a master of his art, we shall hope to understand something of this mastery through trying to perceive how the works exist on the boards as well as in printed text. The play, a condensed and heightened rendering in gesture and words of life's patterns of spiritual and social movement, challenges our critical acumen to see how the form speaks to us of human realities. The implications of the ideas in the plays are rich and will suggest to each age and mind deeper meanings. Whether or not one infers a philosophy in Molière will depend upon one's viewpoint, and, to give the clearest possible views, we shall look at, behind, and through theatrical forms, hoping to catch a glimpse of the vital spark that animates a highly contrived artwork.

The advent of recent critical approaches to Molière is sufficient reason for this treatment of the author for the general reader. I pass on here some of the stimulating insights given in criticism of Molière in the last two decades. The Bibliography and Notes detail my debts for the ideas.

References are from the edition of Molière's works in the *Bibliothèque de la Pléiade* series (Paris, 1962), with text established and annotated by Maurice Rat. English translations are my own, with stress on natural tone possibly causing some freedom of expression.

The sections on *L'Avare, Dom Juan,* and *Le Bourgeois gentilhomme* appeared in other form in the *French Review,* and parts of the chapter on *Le Misanthrope* were published in the *Kentucky Foreign Language Quarterly.* The permission of the publishers to use this material is gratefully acknowledged.

Hallam Walker

Chronology

1622   Jean-Baptiste Poquelin born in Paris, the eldest of six children of Jean Poquelin, upholstery and rug merchant, and Marie Cressé Poquelin.

1631   Jean Poquelin buys royal post of *tapissier ordinaire du Roi*.

1632–1641   Jean-Baptiste grows up in Les Halles district of Paris. Attends excellent Jesuit school, Collège de Clermont, and also theaters. Meets actress Madeleine Béjart. Liaison with her and theater.

1641   Law degree. Sent to southern France to fill father's post with royal suite.

1643   Founds Illustre Théâtre in Paris with Béjarts. Commitment to theater. Rights to *tapissier* post renounced. Armande, future wife of Molière, born to Madeleine and Count of Modène (?).

1644   Illustre Théâtre fails after several shows and moves. Molière bailed out of debtor's prison.

1645   Start of thirteen years of provincial touring with troupes. Joins Dufresne company with Béjarts and takes charge in a few years. Assumes name of Molière.

1648–1649   At Nantes, Toulouse, Montpellier, and Narbonne. Exact movements obscure, but rough conditions certain.

1650–1651   At Agen and Pézenas. Governor of Languedoc and Prince of Conti patrons of troupe.

1652–1655   In Languedoc, Grenoble, and Lyons. Italian troupe at Lyons a strong influence. Writes *L'Etourdi*.

1656–1658   Travels from South to Rouen. Patronage of king's brother obtained for assault on Paris. Farce succeeds at Louvre. Troupe established at Petit-Bourbon on alternate days with Italian comedians.

1659   Success of early farces and of *Les Précieuses ridicules,* first of new style in comedy.

1660   Troupe transfers to Palais-Royal hall after razing of Petit-

Bourbon for Louvre expansion. Stage on which *Sganarelle* and other Paris plays are produced.

1661   *Dom Garcie de Navarre,* a failure in tragicomedy. *L'École des maris,* great hit, wins commission from financier Fouquet for royal entertainment, *Les Fâcheux. Comédie-ballet* invented for outdoor fête at Fouquet's château. Louis XIV starts personal reign, discharges Fouquet, hires Molière.

1662   Marriage of Molière and Armande, *L'École des femmes* a popular success and target of rivals and prudes.

1663   With royal support, Molière replies to accusations about profession, person, and piety. *La Critique de L'École des femmes* and *L'Impromptu de Versailles.*

1664   *Le Mariage forcé,* ballet romp for Louis. Molière's son has king for godfather. At Versailles fête *La Princesse d'Elide* charms court and *La Tartuffe* shocks church. Start of long controversy on *Tartuffe.*

1665   *Dom Juan,* a popular success but suppressed as immoral.

1666   Molière ill and off stage for three months. *Le Misanthrope* has mixed reception.

1667   *L'Imposteur,* a version of *Tartuffe,* offered but suppressed. *Mélicerte* and *Le Sicilien* created for court ballet.

1668   Royal entertainments, *Amphitryon* and *George Dandin.* In Paris, *L'Avare* not popular. Illness and marital trouble.

1669   A version of *Tartuffe* permitted in Paris. Great success. *Monsieur de Pourceaugnac* created for court.

1670   *Les Amants magnifiques* and *Le Bourgeois gentilhomme* for royal entertainment.

1671   *Psyché,* machine ballet and spectacle, created at Palais-Royal with other authors. *Les Fourberies de Scapin.*

1672   *La Comtesse d'Escarbagnas* for court. *Les Femmes savantes* in Paris. Death of Madeleine Béjart. Marital reconciliation and birth of a son. Professional rivalry with Jean-Baptiste Lully, producer of opera at court.

1673   Lully wins royal favor. Ailing Molière obliged to stage *Le Malade imaginaire* in Paris instead of at court. Stricken in fourth performance, 17 February, and dies. Troupe joins that of Marais to play at Guénégaud theater.

1677   Royal order combines Guénégaud and Hôtel de Bourgogne troupes to form Comédie-Française.

Chapter One
Toward a Life in the Theater

The Scene, Paris

Like any young person fascinated by a career on the stage, Molière must be called stagestruck. Unlike most, he made good. To the dismay of his family, the heir to an upholstery trade with royal patronage declared that he would be an actor, a profession on the edge of respectability. The disappointment of his father in 1645 was only equaled by the initial lack of success of Jean-Baptiste Poquelin, but a long apprenticeship combined with an evident genius was to bring him to a theatrical and literary greatness scarcely ever reached by a comedian. The events of his life are not reviewed extensively because they are presented in other works.[1] An understanding of his growth in theatrical experience will be essential, however, if we are to perceive the interpenetration of a life on the boards and his written creations. Plays tend to have most life for the reader if they are placed in their context of lights and greasepaint as works created for staging. Molière's intentions as an artist are to be respected, and he was determined above all to produce good theater.

Jean-Baptiste Poquelin assumed the stage name of Molière early in his career, but this secular rechristening came only after a fairly staid early existence. In 1622 Jean Poquelin and the former Marie Cressé presented their infant Jean for baptism. Everything augured well for the child who was destined by his parents to carry on the trade in rugs and hangings which had been built up by bourgeois thrift and canniness, enhanced by purveying to royalty, and safely cushioned with investments. With a better education than his father, there was no doubt that the son would outstrip him in wealth and standing. The Collège de Clermont was selected as the best school for Jean-Baptiste, and there he studied under Jesuit teachers not only the usual ancient languages and rhetoric but also the exact sciences and some social graces. An excellent private institution for its day, the Collège was designed to guide the privileged youth of nobility and bourgeoisie toward wholesome and useful lives, always with a distinct upper-class tone. The curriculum also included drama for training in speech and Latin. The boy acquired the ability to read Latin well, he made some useful social contacts, and he developed a taste for the drama in the productions offered by the students on prize days.

The actual intellectual and literary formation of the future playwright must remain largely unknown to us, but his awareness of the main currents of the seminal ideas of his age is likely. A lively intelligence, even casually exposed to the free-thinking physicist Gassendi (not a teacher but a friend), must have been stimulated to learn of the epochal discoveries of Galileo and Kepler. A revolution in scientific and philosophical thought was coming about then, symptomatic of the creativity and inventiveness of the age. It is this sense of possible, indeed necessary, change that Molière could have gleaned from exposure to a mind like Gassendi's. On a simpler level, the boy must have been delighted by the life in a vibrant city being pushed to new achievements by Cardinal Richelieu, for he lived in the midst of it all between the markets and the river.

In 1641 he had finished his studies at Clermont and had taken a law degree, a very casual business at this period. At the age of twenty he traveled to the shores of the Mediterranean in the suite of Louis XIII, taking the place of his father in the post of royal bedmaker, a ceremonial function. The progress of the pompous train of carriages through the south to Narbonne at least familiarized young Poquelin with a country that he was to travel through in rougher style as a wandering actor. Before this could come about, however, he had to receive the necessary nudge to get him out of the upholstered family nest, and such an impulsion evidently came from a woman of considerable charm and theatrical ability, Madeleine Béjart.

Professional and personal liaison with this actress a bit his senior led Poquelin to join, formally, a troupe with which he had done some amateur acting. The elder Poquelin's plans came in for some shuffling because he paid his first son to buy the privilege of being a *valet de chambre* at the court and settled this sinecure upon his second son. The six hundred and thirty livres paid for the post disappeared into the treasury of the Illustre Théâtre, which was established in June 1643. Although the professional and business capabilities of the partners were not bad, financial difficulties plagued the struggling group. Assuming the leadership sometime in the first year, Molière (for he now used the name) took upon himself money worries, as well as the artistic direction of a company probably less illustrious than its billing. Indoor tennis courts served as theaters in those days when only two regular theaters existed in Paris, and the rent of a court offered a financial problem that the cost of props and costumes augmented. Molière moved from one court to another, but a bill from a candlemaker finally proved to be his downfall and he landed in the Châtelet debtor's prison.

Parental aid was given to Molière for his troupe, and then the duke of Orléans permitted his name to be used as patron. An occasional hit swelled the receipts, but the true value of the enterprise for Molière was its lesson of practicality. Artistic and dramatic talent was worthless unless a theater existed in which it could make itself known. The sheer physical requirements of finances, space, facilities, skilled actors, and an audience could never be denied, and the brilliant theatrical career of Molière was constructed as much upon these elements as upon creative literary skill. By 1645 he was well on his way toward becoming a real man of the theater, but a training period still remained. The harsh lessons from the city had to be applied during a tour through the provinces, and anyone who could build a name as actor-manager of a road company in the seventeenth century really proved himself.

Some changes in the troupe were made as a result of experience. The melodramas staged by the Illustre Théâtre in Paris were gradually replaced by plays more in keeping with the troupe's true abilities in comedy. Molière turned to farce and to the tragicomedy, which had a great vogue in the 1630s and 1640s. The public delighted in the latter sort of play in which noble heroes struggled to overcome evil and preserve honor. An inflated style of declamation was much admired, and only the hand of a master playwright like Corneille kept such theater from exaggerating its tendency to bombast. The developing style of Molière would find that sort of writing uncongenial, for his forte was to be an impression of natural ease. This he was on his way to discover.

A Touring Company

The exact conditions under which Molière, Madeleine, and several members of their troupe undertook a barnstorming provincial tour with the Defresne company in 1646 are not known to us, but we do have information on the general conditions of professional theater in France at this period. Travel was hard and often dangerous, and the director had to find space and audiences as they proceeded. Popular favor was high, however, and the demand for dramatic entertainment had reached a high peak all over the land by the time Molière left Paris. A government ruling of 1641 had given official recognition and legitimacy to such enterprises, and acting no longer had so much of its traditional church-imposed stigma. Some social respectability smoothed the way, but handsome princely patronage was its great lubricant, and generally it was unstinting. The problem of the ambitious company headed by Molière was to tap the sources of patronage and guarantee themselves a secure living. The search for a patron led them first to the southern provinces of Guyenne and Languedoc, for provincial nobility was more accessible and surely as mad about theater as the Parisian.

Interest in the professional theater had grown rapidly from limited beginnings in the court of Henri II, whose queen, Catherine de Medici, imported Italian comedians in the 1550s. Amateur theater had long existed, with an ancient tradition of religious mystery and miracle plays, schoolboys' Latin dramas, and students' satires. Marketplace farces and jugglers were common in the Middle Ages. By the 1620s a vigorous society in a France ruled by an elite of actual or titular powers encouraged all types of theater. The physical resources of Paris for both amateur and professional troupes became strained as both competed for theater space, but this did not discourage a phenomenal growth of theatrical writing and production.[2]

Under the reign of Henri IV, from 1589 to 1610, France enjoyed increased domestic harmony and unity after decades of civil tumult, and the concept of consolidation of power under a central government was brilliantly exploited by Cardinal Richelieu, prime minister of Louis XIII. As the monarchy assumed command of all aspects of the state and its culture, Richelieu promptly assessed the value of the public theater as a shaper of thought and tastes. Command of this medium of mass communication was both good politics and a sincere effort to encourage the fine arts. By natural inclination and official patronage, this society gave hearty support to authors like Alexandre Hardy, Tristan L'Hermite, Théophile de Viau, Rotrou, and the Corneille brothers. Most of their works were of heroic and moral cast, but the popularity of such plays is shown by the fact that there is extant an extraordinary number of them. To be preserved for so long, there had to be numerous productions and copies of the plays, and we possess 414 plays from the period 1589 to 1634.

This busy world of theatrical activity was the one Molière sought to enter but only after serving a long, practical apprenticeship with his touring company. After finding patronage among the nobility in the southern provinces, Molière was obliged to move northward as his fortunes changed. Records of the city of Nantes in Brittany show him requesting permission of the city commissioners to perform in 1648. We know he was asked by the cities of Agen and Toulouse to come, and he traveled around Provence for a while until a brief stay in Lyons in 1652. There a formative experience awaited him. Lyons, rich in its cultural associations with neighboring Italy, was familiar with the lively theater called commedia dell'arte, and the public expected comedy to be clever in its miming, witty in speech, and carried on sheer physical momentum. Although Molière had been introduced to

Italian comedy in his youth in Paris, he was now directly challenged to create theater in this mode.

The Italian Comedy

The commedia dell'arte depended upon strong conventions and virtuosity in improvisation to carry off a production based only on a sketch scenario. Heavy gestures, set comic routines, and witty invention were the stock in trade of the Italian comedians who regularly assumed stock roles familiar to the audience. The sad clown of the Pierrot type or the mercurial rascal Harlequin had a fixed costume and personality, so their playing fell into set patterns. With a great store of ready-made material, these actors could take a simple plot and elaborate upon it as the comedy developed, introducing topical jokes, capitalizing upon slips of the tongue, or simply resorting to mock beatings with a stick or bladder. The rapid pace of the performance was one of the keys to its success, sweeping the audience along by sheer comic energy. Often vulgar and cobbled together out of material going back to Roman comedy, the commedia still showed Molière the value of comic timing and strong physical movement. The balletlike arrangements of a number of his later works have their origins in the Italian style. To these elements the playwright added a factor of which he was becoming the master, carefully composed speeches in verse keyed to the motivating ideas of his play. Molière thus profited from and elaborated upon the Italian comedy, combining its kinetic character with his own comic poetic genius.

Several years were spent next enjoying the patronage of a member of the house of Bourbon, the Prince de Conti, who resided in Languedoc as protector of the royal estates in southern France. When the prince viewed himself as a bon vivant, money was plentiful for the players, but a turn toward puritanical piety caused him to regard theater as sinful and to withdraw his support. This event fortunately did not occur until after he had underwritten the production of Molière's first great comedy, which gave promise of the things to come. In 1656 *Le Dépit amoureux* (The lovers' quarrel) was presented at Béziers. The comedy will be analyzed later, but it suffices to say that the play showed how much the author was profiting from the lessons of the commedia and its vigorous style. Already he could write clever verbal exchanges that preserved the verve and pace of the Italian style of comedy. A critic comments that this play and its quarrel scene bring to mind "a younger, more intense Marivaux," comparing its tone with that of the plays of the eighteenth-century master of scenes of young love.[3] The lovers speak of their determination to leave each other, yet every protestation of indifference reinforces their knowledge that separation is unbearable.

The company followed a roundabout itinerary to Paris via Orange, Avignon, and Rouen; this last city, the home in Normandy of the Corneille brothers, was an important base of operations for a strike at the capital's theater. Nothing short of royal patronage and acclaim would satisfy the young impresario, and by 1658 his way had been so well prepared that it did not seem beyond his grasp. A brilliant reputation in the provinces had caused some stir in Paris. Numerous trips to the capital by Molière resulted in his successful wooing of the favor of the brother of Louis XIV, and under the protection of such a mighty patron the troupe, confident through its experience in the provinces, planned to capture the major audience of courtiers and Parisians.

The Court and Its Comedians

The imposing formality of the court of Louis XIV should not prevent our seeing that much of the elaborate setting and ritual had a richly theatrical quality and that much of the dramatic presentation of royal splendor must have been conceived as spectacle for its own sake. The king loved theater in all forms. In a fascinating study of the function of game playing in culture, Johan Huizinga tells us how important a function costumed spectacle has in impressing the public with the majesty of ruler, church, or laws.[4] As a king thoroughly imbued with a sense of his divine right to rule, Louis could not have taken himself more seriously, yet he clearly knew the value of theatrical display of his unique importance. Art gave visual reality to grand concepts. We think at once of the great stage sets formed by the palace and grounds of Versailles, stretching on for miles as space planned for regal action. The ruler's sense of theater at this period is exemplified by his propensity for participating in court ballets and for appearing in special costumes at public fêtes. In 1662 Louis staged a vast display of costumed splendor and knightly prowess, a *carrousel* to celebrate the birth of the Dauphin. In genteel imitation of medieval knights the king and his nobles paraded, galloped, and tilted at rings and Turk's heads, but the primary purpose of the show was to create awe and delight by the massing of gorgeously dressed riders and soldiers in skillful evolutions on the field, which came to be called in Paris Place du Carrousel. There were troops of "Roman" cavalry led by Louis in gold and red, "Persians," "Indians," and even fanciful "American savages," each group led by a great nobleman. The scene was remarkable, yet wholly characteristic of this age of prosperity, kingly power, and sumptuous dramatization. It was the equivalent, in secular form, of a huge church drama of earlier centuries, at once a naïve game and a grave rite of display and glory. It explains well the eager acceptance accorded by the court to a man like Molière, whose trade it was to create superior theater.

An age avid for entertainment fell between 1643, when the child Louis XIV ascended the throne of France, and the early 1660s, when he began to assert his personal control of the government. Not devoid of the turmoil of the wars called the Fronde, when the nobility tried to regain power taken over by the king, the period was characterized by a typically regency atmosphere of emphasis upon elegant and refined pleasure, and the regent queen, Anne of Austria, set the pace. Under her patronage, and that of other members of the royal house and the government, the theater flourished. The Italian-born Cardinal Mazarin had become first minister after the death of Richelieu, and his more subtle means of governing were matched by his personal manner and tastes. The grandiose and rather monolithic style of the works of his predecessor was replaced by a refined taste in lovely town palaces and in volumes for the library that was to bear his name. The Petit-Bourbon palace was the location of the cardinal's theater, and naturally the Italian comedians were the favored performers. The Italian opera had been introduced as well as musical spectacles with elaborate mechanical scenic effects of Italian origin.

In the future Molière would be involved in the production of royal entertainments of this type, for which the taste became great. Music, pageants, pastorals, tragicomedies, tragedies, farces, and commedia dell'arte were all available to a public composed of the nobility and also of the upper middle class of Paris, that educated and rising bourgeoisie that rivaled the court in taste and discrimination in the arts. The Hôtel de Bourgogne troupe of the actor Montfleury continued unchallenged as the leading exponents of bombastic tragicomedy, while Scaramouche of the Italians set the pace in comic theater. Molière's players stepped upon the scene in the capital with a performance for the court of a little farce entitled *Le Docteur amoureux* (The doctor in love), winning for themselves permission to appear at the Petit-Bourbon when the Italian troupe was not performing.

The esteem already attached to the name of Molière and to his company was rather great because royalty had lent them patronage, and there was wide interest in the new players among the courtiers. Montfleury and his actors were concerned with possible rivals. The old section of the Louvre was the scene of the testing and proving of Molière, since it really was a crucial trial for the actors intent upon success. Professional skills were to be displayed before the harshest of judges. A performance for the king called for some lofty offering in the tragic mode, a drama suited both to the occasion and to the style of the players. Molière decided to give Corneille's *Nicomède,* a type of play in which he had had long experience since the Illustre Théâtre. Heroic rather than truly tragic, the drama had speeches and characters less inflated than most of the tragedies he could have selected. Montfleury was convinced that no other troupe could equal his in the declamation of poetic lines, but Molière really had no thought to try, being concerned with giving a bill that would display the talents of his people and hit the right note for such an audience. *Nicomède* was a mediocre success, but the master showman rose to the occasion as he requested permission in a gracious speech for his company to put on a small farce that had achieved some popularity in the provinces. The broad style of *Le Docteur amoureux,* a one-act farce, was calculated to appeal to a youthful monarch and his gay court. The text of this farce has disappeared, but it apparently pleased the king sufficiently for him to reward the troupe with the privilege of playing at the theater of the Petit-Bourbon.

To perform in the Petit-Bourbon on the off-days (Monday, Wednesday, Thursday, and Saturday) when the Italian comedians were not there meant accepting the times least favorable for a good audience. On these days court functions tended to reduce the size of the house. Sunday afternoon was a favorite time for theatergoing, and the church had to protest as the time of the curtain raising crept forward toward the hours of holy services. Molière welcomed the chance to play in a major theater, however poor the days, for he knew that a foothold was all he needed to be on his way up to front rank in Parisian theater. The presentation of *Les Précieuses ridicules* (The folly of affectation) in 1659 was to confirm his status as leading comedian, but before examining this small masterpiece we must look briefly at some earlier works that show his artistic development.

Chapter Two
From Farce to Social Satire
La Jalousie du barbouillé and *Le Médecin volant*

The plays created by Molière during his years of apprenticeship are available to us only after some literary peregrinations, because at first they existed only as unpublished scripts from which the troupe played. Molière entered the ranks of published authors with the printing of *Les Précieuses ridicules,* his Parisian success of 1659, and this publication was really an act of self-defense. Literary pirates copied hit plays from notes made during performances, and these inaccurate versions promptly appeared in bookshops. Also, unfriendly critics were prone to misrepresent an author's words to injure him professionally and personally, so Molière was obliged to see that correct copies of his plays were available. The early farces were first printed sometime after 1659, and their existence on the periphery of the greater works of Molière kept them from being included with his complete writings until the nineteenth century, when scholars unearthed and authenticated them. They are of considerable value, however, in that they permit us to observe Molière's early construction of the solid framework of his plays, the farce.[1]

La Jalousie du barbouillé (The clown's jealousy) pleased audiences in the provinces and then in the capital, having seven revivals from 1660 to 1664. The influence of the Italian style of comedy is evident, as is Molière's inheritance from old French farces. Indeed, the name of the title character, the *barbouillé,* or clown with painted face, establishes a relationship with the popular clown type of entertainer who played in fairs and marketplaces throughout the Middle Ages. The floured face and bumbling antics of the clown are familiar and expected, nor does Molière fail to follow the tradition. Married to an unfaithful and flirtatious young wife, the clown is destined to suffer comic disasters, marital and physical, since he is by definition ineffectual. Coupled with this stock character is another one familiar to the audiences of the age, the pedantic learned doctor whose charlatanry only complicates the troubles of the clown who seeks his aid. Putting these figures together and adding some routines of coarse physical humor, Molière invented little but rather employed an existing store of material. Predictably,

9

the clown is deceived by his wife Angélique, is locked out of his own house, and resorts to violence against the doctor whose learned advice has only confused matters. This is scarcely elevated comedy, but in creating it Molière attached himself with a sure instinct to one of the taproots of comic theater, and from this he drew sustenance during all of his career in the theater. The psychological themes of sex and control over others are at the base of this farce, and they will never be lost from sight even in Molière's most highly developed creations.

Farces of the type of *La Jalousie du barbouillé* have an impetus and a movement that derive from the basic themes and also from the style in which they are conceived and played. A brisk pattern of gestures and stage actions depended upon the virtuosity of the actors in the Italian comedies, but Molière took care to write such a pattern into his plays. The speeches composed by the playwright govern the physical business to be carried out by the actors, nor does the action depend upon stage directions, as is the common practice in modern theater. Molière's innovation was to develop a total integration of word and gesture, embodying the latter unmistakably in the sense of the speeches. But this was to come later with the growth of his skill, and we find in *La Jalousie* that Molière resorts to instructing the clown to drag the doctor from the stage by a cord around his foot.

The best example of the integration of speech and action is in the role of the doctor, whose orientation is highly verbal. His great verbosity, which is carefully rendered in amusing parodies of philosophical arguments, produces none of the results it is intended for. The plight of the clown is not aided by words, but by actions, and the learned words become a frustrating obstacle for him. This situation is what causes the clown to take physical action against the doctor. False logic and Latinisms that pose as knowledge lead not to clarity but to further confusion and finally to violence. Molière has thus carried his clown farce from its simple original lines to a satire of verbose pedantry. The follies of those who take high-sounding words and literary clichés for guiding principles in life will be one of the dominant features of his comedies. The literary orientation of *La Jalousie du barbouillé* is the element in its composition that points toward the future development of Molière's theater. Farce, retaining all of its basic drives, can be the foundation for comedies of great literary sophistication. This is hinted at by the treatment Molière gives to the traditional material of his early play about a clown's marital troubles.

In *Le Médecin volant* (The flying doctor), another farce created before 1659, Molière again drew from the storehouse of popular theater, copying the Italian *Medico volante,* a standard routine of commedia. *Le Médecin volant* shows a number of features that will enter into the scheme of comedy being developed by Molière, notably the broad satire of medicine which will appear in plays such as *Dom Juan* and *Le Malade imaginaire* (The imaginary invalid). He also employs a plot framework that will become a fixture in his later plays. This involves a witty rascal of a servant who plots successfully to aid his master to win a bride despite the opposition of an old father. The servant is named Sganarelle, again a borrowing from the Italian commedia and its stock characters, and the name will be used many times by Molière for similar figures. The tricky fellow poses as his own twin brother, who is a doctor, in order to deceive the old man jealously guarding his daughter. The deception involves rapid changes of costume and personality that Sganarelle effects by "flying" into a house and out again a moment later. The comic routine will be used in its entirety in Molière's last comedy, *Le Malade imaginaire*.

It is important that we see these early works as part of the whole context of Molière's theater because they present elements that are solid and permanent parts of his creation and because they usher us into a theatrical world that has a structure built of accumulated and reused pieces. Recognition of the familiar figures of the pedant or Sganarelle not only enables us to see what the playwright has done to expand the characters but also gives us a large frame of reference against which the author can elaborate new material. The theater of Molière becomes distinct and self-contained in this way, assimilating its borrowings and giving them an unmistakable stamp. For reader and audience, each experience in the Molièresque world is progressively richer and more enjoyable because familiar items appear, then are altered in brilliant innovations. The most typical parts of this theater are its stock figures and their farce routines. The genius of Molière takes these elements, preserves their strength, and invents ways to make them express a deep satirical view of man and his society.

L'Étourdi

In 1653 Molière wrote *L'Étourdi, ou le contretemps* (The scatterbrain, or the mishap), which is of interest for our study of his developing skills. Like the two farces just discussed, it has a traditional framework of comic confusions and deceptions, but it also possesses an important enlargement of the role of the trickster and an expansion of literary parody. Its use of verse in place of prose shows Molière's increasing concern with verbal and formal aspects of theater instead of the raw physical comedy of simple farce.

The antecedents for the play are Italian, and in this case the playwright transposed quite directly from *L'Inavvertito* by Beltramo making the old

material over largely by the composition in French verse.[2] The central character, the witty servant who aids his addle-brained master to win his bride, is
Mascarille and not the title figure of the *étourdi*. The role of the valet indeed
is the driving force of the play in Molière's version, and this character will
have a long life throughout all of his theatrical creation. The name, which
suggests a small mask, typifies the character as a sort of Harlequin, who always wore a half or full mask in old French farces. Harlequin in turn suggests
a volatile and agile type, dressed in a multicolored costume and flourishing a
stick to prod the other figures into action. This indeed is the style in which
Mascarille functions. He has an Italian counterpart called Scappino, nor will
Molière fail to adapt this figure, calling him Scapin and creating for him similar roles in his plays; *Les Fourberies de Scapin* (Scapin's tricks) was written in
1671. As Mascarille, Molière personally undertook the role of master of revels on stage just as he did in writing the plays. We shall have to return to
Molière as an actor to observe him playing roles that frequently are those of a
Sganarelle, a Mascarille, or a Scapin.

L'*Étourdi, ou le contretemps* carries on its series of confusions and errors for
five acts, linking them together with a slight plot bearing heavily on
Mascarille's schemes to set right the circumstances that his master's blunders
persist in complicating. A sample of the action from the first act and a brief
look at the plot will suffice to show the tone of the comedy. Lélie, the *étourdi*
master of Mascarille, is in love with Célie, a Gypsy girl bound in slavery to an
old man named Trufaldin. Lélie is hindered by his father's opposition to such
a bride for his son, nor does he have the money to buy Célie's freedom. Meanwhile, his father has arranged for him to marry another more suitable bride.
Mascarille must try to get the money, dupe Trufaldin and Lélie's father, placate Hippolyte (the girl selected for Lélie by his father), and arrange for her
marriage with another man whom she loves. The witty valet promptly manages to get an interview between Lélie and Célie, telling Trufaldin he is con-
sulting her as a fortuneteller. The stupid Lélie blurts out that this is not true,
to the annoyance of Mascarille. His next ruse nearly separates an old man
from his purse of gold, only to have Lélie blunder in and pick up the purse
from the ground to return it to the man. The third error of Lélie occurs as he
prevents Célie from being sold by Trufaldin to the father of Hippolyte, a device contrived by Mascarille on the pretext of getting Célie out of the way so
Lélie will marry Hippolyte. This sort of action is continued through the five
acts, dependent on the fertile inventiveness of the valet, who sees his good
work undone at all turns by Lélie. At the end an old Gypsy woman reveals
that Célie was stolen from Trufaldin, who is truly her father; Trufaldin gives

the hand of his daughter to Lélie, ending the comedy through this contrived device.

Mascarille plays the dominant role throughout this mad scramble of plotting and blunders. He is the author of the action, just as in fact Molière was the literary creator of the play and the actor-director shaping the staged production. *L'Étourdi* is a vehicle for Mascarille, whose role calls for a virtuoso performance of great energy. The character functions above all through words rather than through physical actions, and this sets him off from his predecessors of the Italian commedia and old French farce. He continually devises little scenes in which he has the others assume roles unknowingly or at his direction as accomplices. In effect, he is a theatrical director building illusions. He takes various parts himself, playing a woman and then a Swiss who speaks with a German accent, and he makes the other characters play along with his inventions.

Critics have noted that the Italian play by Beltramo has elements of parody of lofty drama, and Molière certainly parodies the formal language of tragedy, especially in Mascarille's speeches.[3] The comic effect of heroic words in burlesque circumstances will be a favorite device of Molière. We also gain a heightened impression of the ebullience and enormous self-esteem of Mascarille as he expounds on his own worth in the classical form of alexandrine verse, the twelve-syllable rhymed couplets of French tragedy. He exclaims while contriving a low trick: "Honor, Mascarille, is a fine thing. Do not pause in your noble works." He views himself as a rogue of heroic proportions, and he longs to have his portrait painted, complete with laurel wreath on his brow, inscribed in Latin, "Vivat Mascarillus, fourbum imperator!" (Long live Mascarille, emperor of the rogues!).

The lines of action throughout *L'Étourdi* are a comic version of a hero's struggle with a fate that thwarts him. Mascarille suspects that Lélie is possessed by a demon who enjoys defying him, and thus it is suggested that some superior force is at work against the hero. Even at the end, when Lélie has won his bride, the valet wonders whether the "devil" in his master will destroy his happiness.

Perhaps the unifying quality of all these aspects of the play is the conscious theatricality, the constant awareness on the part of players and audience that it is all "true and pure comedy" as Mascarille describes it. No pretense at creating an illusion of reality is made, but instead an atmosphere of gay frenzy and endless possibility of fun exists. The satire in *L'Étourdi* is directed against heroic tragicomedy, being wholly literary and not social.

Le Dépit Amoureux

During its tour in Languedoc Molière's company presented a play entitled *Le Dépit amoureux* (The lovers' quarrel) in the town of Béziers in 1654. Drawing upon Italian sources once more, Molière so changed his material as to make it very much his own. This comedy is of interest particularly as an example of development of a thematic idea. The author's inexperience shows, in that his theme is good but spread too thin.

Rather than copy the commedia dell'arte style of buffoonery, Molière here turned to Italian comedy of the Renaissance of a more intellectual type, *L'Interesse* by Secchi, written in 1581. The version of 1654 is thus not a vehicle for the antics of a Mascarille, although a character of this name has a role. The part is slight, nor did Molière play it as he did the role of Mascarille in *L'Étourdi*. The play by Secchi had a thematic unity on the subject of financial gain and self-interest, but this is replaced in *Le Dépit amoureux* by a theme of confusions and contradictions between feelings and words, fact and fancy, reality and appearances. This comedy is in verse, as are most of the plays composed by Molière from this date on.

The five acts that are in the total version originally presented by the playwright are too labored for modern tastes, and the play is cut to one act now at the Comédie-Française. This version retains the scenes of the lovers' quarrel.

The Italian play deals with a situation in which a girl is raised as a boy so her father can win a bet that he will have a son. The girl is fully aware of her true sex, for she has fallen in love, married, and is with child. The crude comedy that deals with efforts to conceal pregnancy is completely eliminated by Molière as unsuitable for the tastes of his audience. He retains the scheme of the secret marriage and then complicates the confusions of several sets of lovers. Eraste loves Lucile, daughter of Albert, and he is jealous of a rival, Valère, who seems very confident of having Lucile's love. Valère's attitude is due to the fact that he is secretly wed to a young woman whom he sees only at night and whom he believes to be Lucile. In truth, Valère is married to her sister, Ascogne, the daughter who poses as a boy by day. This sketch of the situation serves to show the highly contrived nature of the work. Molière wanted a pretext for exploiting all manner of confusions, and his five acts are an exercise in wit and ingenuity that prevent too much hollowness.

Although the servant characters are not pivotal in the plot, Gros-René and Marinette, respectively valet of Eraste and maid of Lucile, are essential to the comedy because they give a wonderfully comic counterpoint or parody version of the elegant love affairs in the foreground. A fundamental idea of this comedy is set forth as these two peasant types cut through all the confusions of fine manners and verbiage that impede their betters; natural instincts lead them to happiness, while Eraste and Lucile stumble about in a maze of notions about their love. The parody produces fine comic routines, but the essence of the work is its play with shifting realities and appearances. Gros-René is used in the first act to express the theme by mocking the lofty style of Eraste and stressing physical realities in life.

The principle of this portion of the play is the contrast between the natural behavior of the servant and the stilted manners of the master who is a product of his education and his social class. Eraste accuses his valet of betraying him to his rival, and the fellow replies, "You show your ignorance of character in faces. People with faces like mine are not accused of being rogues or schemers. We are given that much credit, and I merit it because I am frank and open in everything" (1.1).[4] The French text uses the word "*rond*" or round, well-suited to his shape as "Fat-René." He goes on, "I don't know much philosophy. I trust what my eyes see," answering Eraste's words, "No matter how well one smothers a flame of passion, a bit of jealousy will occupy one's soul" (1.1). The master's ideas are clichés of thought, whereas the servant's are based on a simple trust in the senses. Eraste conducts a courtship in formal language; Gros-René says to Marinette, "I want you; do you want me?" The parody of the soulful leave-taking of lovers is as follows: Marinette says "Adieu, handsome poker of my fire." Gros-René rejoins "Adieu, dear comet, rainbow of my soul" (1.2).

Yet even the instinctive ease of this sort of love encounters difficulties the moment Gros-René becomes a bit infected by the virus of elevated manners and style. He abandons his true nature and decides that to show his worth he must ape Eraste and accuse Marinette of faithlessness: "Do you still dare speak to me, iniquitous female? You deceiving crocodile, whose thieving heart is worse than an Oriental potentate!" (1.5). He then stumbles around in a welter of confused ideas and misapplied figures of speech. The effect is purely clownish as Gros-René gives an outrageous parody of a person carried away by his emotions and eloquence. He reverts speedily to his true self, however, unlike Eraste, who remains trapped in his own verbal fancies.

Eraste and Valère conjure up their own versions of reality that are based upon romantic and literary clichés. The idea of confusion about one's real nature is presented through most of the characters, and the confusions, of course, extend to the identities of other characters. The figure of Ascogne, in reality a girl, Dorothée, is a crude and early form of a character common in Molière's comedies, the person living a false role. The motives for such behavior will become much more subtle, such as psychological or spiritual compensations, rejections, or search for identity. Errors based on physical dis-

guises will be used often in farce, but Molière will explore deceptions by imposture and hypocrisy. The character of Albert is an interesting example of
willful self-deception.

This deluded individual seeks learned advice to explain why his "son"
should be so effeminate, turning to a philosopher named Métaphraste. The
dogmatic pedant can only offer fixed concepts that further confuse the notions already bothering Albert. The basic trouble is the belief that abstract
theory is more valid than practical observation. Thus, we have a lover who
cannot follow his instincts, a father who cannot see that his child is a girl, and
a philosopher who cannot handle simple facts.

Reality and vain words are particularly in opposition in the major scene of
the quarrel between lovers. Eraste and Lucile persist in saying the opposite of
their true feelings, but they are so bound by their fixed notions that they do
not perceive this. Language becomes noncommunication. The servants carry
on a comic version of the quarrel, with their crude images of speech contrasting with the lofty expressions, but these two are simply carried away by the
occasion and have no intention of quitting each other. Lucile: "When you love
people, you treat them differently. You have better judgment of them."
Eraste: "When you love a person, you may have your heart overcome by jealousy at certain appearances; but while you love you cannot bring yourself to
give it up, and you have done this" (4.3). The servants urge master and mistress to be firm in renouncing each other, but true feelings finally prevail.
Gros-René and Marinette then behave as if a team they had been supporting
just lost a game, and they resume the quarrel for the sport. Gros-René: "The
day before yesterday I forgot your piece of cheese; take it back. I wish I could
throw back at you the soup you gave me to eat, so I wouldn't have anything
from you." Marinette: "I don't have any of your letters on me now, but I'll
burn them all." Gros-René: "And you know what I'll do with yours?" (4.4).
They soon break down in laughter at their own antics, quickly patching up
their quarrel.

The scenes of the lovers' quarrels are by no means purely verbal as constructed by Molière. The giving back of gifts is an amusing routine of physical comedy, especially as done by Gros-René and Marinette, but coordination of words and actions is more subtle. The stage business and arrangement
of movements are clearly dictated by the speeches such as those of farewell,
which indicate the characters to be moving each toward an opposite side of
the stage. A reprise of arguments calls for them to return to center stage. The
repetition by the servants of gestures after they are performed by Eraste and
Lucile is an obvious shaping of the visual aspects of the scene. Molière's skill
in farce, with its strong emphasis upon physical comedy, remains in evidence

in *Le Dépit amoureux,* while he continues to develop ways of blending it with verbal comedy. The composition of scenes of patterned movement on stage, all suggested by the speeches, is characteristic of Molière's writing. It has much of the quality of ballet choreography, yet it is achieved above all through his verses.

Le Dépit amoureux reaches an ending by the simple expedient of the revelation of the true sex of Ascogne-Dorothée. This plot has been a flimsy basis for the creation of an involved series of confusions, with common sense deserted on all sides. It served its author as an exercise in comic techniques, and it continues to amuse us by its key scenes. The difference between this play and the next one, *Les Précieuses ridicules,* is striking because of the new ability of Molière to use his stock in trade of comic routines to express some sharp social satire.

Les Précieuses ridicules

The farce on social and literary pretensions that Molière created in 1659 was truly a point of departure for him. With *Les Précieuses ridicules* (The folly of affection) he stood firmly on his experience, then took a bold step forward in the development of theater. It landed him in the front ranks of the writers of comedy, for the combination of social criticism, suggestion of reality, and farcical style produced a small masterpiece.

In order to understand this work we must concern ourselves first with the *précieux* concepts specified by the title, the currents of social thought and usage in the period, and considerable literary background. This comedy is at once commentary on literary tendencies, on manners, on human nature, and even on the theater itself. The marvel is that so much is contained within the brief prose farce, but that is a sign of craftsmanship. The skill with words that Molière possessed would have led him to give scant respect to the inflated figures of speech and pretentious shoddiness that characterized much literature called "precious."

The term *préciosité* was applied to the style of excessive refinement or exaggerated nicety in ideas and forms, a style not confined to France but symptomatic of a general tendency in European life and letters in the late Renaissance. Such "precious" or "manneristic" style existed, to be sure, among Greek and Roman poets who employed a rich and fanciful metaphorical technique. Indeed, at any period when formal elegance and refinement become objects in themselves, we may refer to its literature as "precious" and equate the failings with those that Molière was mocking. France had a considerable heritage of medieval romances of chivalry, notably those of

Chrétien de Troyes, and in the sixteenth century the poetry of the Pléiade group of writers was concerned with delicate expression of sentiments. Italy, a powerful cultural influence in this era, offered the examples of Petrarch and his sonnets and the ultrarefinement of the poet Marini. England contributed its form of *préciosité* in the euphuism of Lyly, and Spain had the equivalent in *Gongorismo,* named after the poet Góngora. The creation of a literature of these characteristics may be viewed as a manifestation of the baroque spirit of the age, although *préciosité* is merely one aspect of this cultural phenomenon, analyzed so well by a number of modern critics.[5] The particular aspect of the writings of the early seventeenth century that furnished Molière with his material for satire was a rarefied sort of simperingly romantic novel. For such literature to be popular, a class of readers had to exist.

In the 1630s royalty and nobility joined together to exercise political control of the land after many decades of civil war. Aristocracy's triumph was cultural as well as governmental, and the ten percent of the population who were nobly born lived by and for the monarchy and its power structure. This brought about certain reaffirmation of the values of the medieval feudal society of lordly privilege. Knightly heroism in romance—the literary form of this type of social order—thus enjoyed a revival, but to have contemporary validity and meaning it had to be refurbished. The leisured readers wanted to identify with gentle knights and ladies without seeming to be old-fashioned, so a new type of escape novel was invented for them, a blend of chivalrous adventures and pastoral idylls. The public, of bourgeois as well as nobility, eagerly consumed the delicate offerings of the novelists and even carried the formal playing of a game of love into the life of the salons.

The foundation upon which writers such as Honoré d'Urfé built their great series of romances was the same one on which the creators of films of love build today. The theme of irresistible passion, which leads, usually, to the union of the lovers only in death, is so fundamental that our literature, both past and present, could not exist without it. Mixed in with this idea is another that is regularly found in a highly organized and sophisticated society, the idealized image of a world of nature where all is simple and pure, a pastoral refuge from the corruption of civilization. In the *précieux* novels like *L'Astrée* by d'Urfé, composed in the first two decades of the century, thousands of pages are devoted to the amorous adventures, all highly decorous, of pseudo-shepherds and their loves. The main occupation of the characters is to debate tirelessly the niceties of correct behavior between the sexes. The modern reader finds it difficult to cut through the heavy language and conventional episodes to perceive the core of psychological truth that is really there, but for the refined public of the seventeenth century no amount of delicate argument and imagery could be excessive. The dialogue on love and sex was truly endless. As best-sellers the books were great successes, nor do we have anything comparable for concentrated cultural influence in our present society. Social custom followed literary example, just as a popular culture now forms itself on Hollywood stereotypes, but the tone was elegant and aristocratic. D'Urfé, Mlle de Scudéry and her brother, Gomberville, and La Calprenède were the shapers of an age in which an idealized dream of love smoothed the many rough spots in real life. The situation cried aloud for satire, and others besides Molière responded, yet his was the work that hit exactly the right combination of farce and veracity.

In *Les Précieuses ridicules* there is just one act of rapid movement. The play begins as two young men, La Grange and Du Croisy, rejected as inelegant suitors by the *précieuses* young women, Magdelon and Cathos, plot a trick to show the women the folly of affected snobbishness. The father of Magdelon, Gorgibus, is furious with her and her cousin Cathos for scorning the young men he favors as husbands for them. They explain that romances must take place as in the novels of the day, with delicate adventures of the heart and never a hint of vulgar marriage. The girls deplore the dull spirit of Gorgibus and feel that they really cannot be related to such a common person. At this point, there is announced the arrival of the "marquis de Mascarille," actually the valet of La Grange, sent by his master to court the girls in the style of a fashionable nobleman. Magdelon and Cathos accept Mascarille at face value, and the trio holds an animated conversation on the latest fashions in literature, language, and dress in the capital. The exaggerated parody of high style is great verbal comedy. Mascarille admits that he is a poet: "You will see, created by me, running about the best intimate spots of Paris, two hundred songs, as many sonnets, four hundred epigrams, and more than a thousand madrigals, without counting enigmas and portraits" (scene 9). The language is tortured in its refinements: "Your kindness carries a bit too far the liberality of its praises; and we are incapable, my cousin and I, of lending our serious belief to the sweetness of your flattery" (scene 9).

Visual and physical comedy is strong as well, for Mascarille wears a fantastically exaggerated version of the clothes of the dandy. He sings a song of his composition, leads the company in a dance, then invites the ladies to feel the scars of his wounds of war. He is joined by the valet of Du Croisy, the "vicomte de Jodelet," who enthusiastically joins in the action. The play comes to a rapid end when La Grange and Du Croisy enter to strip their servants of the finery and to reveal to Cathos and Magdelon the real nature of the persons whom they took to be stylish noblemen. The girls are nonplussed at the hoax, while the valets, carried away by their own acting, behave with a mock wounded dignity.

A closer look at certain parts of this play will elucidate Molière's handling of his themes. The parody of the *précieux* literary work is important because Molière dwells upon the folly of making life conform to a pattern drawn from popular novels. Magdelon explains to Gorgibus how a proper courtship should be conducted, basing her ideas on a work such as *Le Grand Cyrus* by Mlle de Scudéry:

Marriage must never take place except after other adventures. The man who is in love, in order to please, must know how to say beautiful sentiments, how to express the sweet, the tender, and the passionate, and his courtship must be according to form. First, he must see in church, or walking, or at a public ceremony the person with whom he falls in love: or else he must be led fatally to her home by a relative or a friend and come away full of dreams and melancholy. He hides for a time his passion from the object of his affections, and meanwhile pays her several visits during which there is unfailingly a discussion of a problem of the heart which gives play to the wits of those assembled. Then comes the day of declaration, which ordinarily must be made in the walk of some garden while the other people are at a slight distance; and this declaration is followed by a prompt and blushing anger which banishes the lover for a while from our presence. Then he finds ways to appease us, to accustom us gradually to the expression of his passion, and to draw from us that confession of love so reluctantly given. After that come adventures: rivals crossing the path of true love, persecution by fathers, jealousies falsely conceived, sighs, despair, kidnappings, and so on. That is how things are done in proper style, and those are the indispensable rules of gallantry. But to start right off with the conjugal union, to make love only by marriage contract, to turn the novel in reverse,—there is nothing more vulgar than this procedure, Father, and the very idea makes me sick. (scene 4)

The suitors have come in direct fashion to ask for the hands of the girls, but this style of approach has outraged the literary pattern of romance. Ignorance of the laws of love is no excuse in the eyes of Cathos and Magdelon, for they conceive of courtship as a game of great seriousness with a code transferred to real life.

Literary clichés governing behavior in life represent a theme treated by Molière in *Le Dépit amoureux,* but it emerges here in *Les Précieuses ridicules* as the basis for a powerful farce set in contemporary surroundings, a step forward in stage creation. Molière successfully merged social satire with the riotous action of the farce, entertaining his audience with broad comedy while speaking to it about the folly of manners that did violence to nature in the name of delicacy and refinement of taste. The existence at this period of a rather decayed and neurotic impulsion toward the ultra-aristocratic in art and life was correctly observed and analyzed by the author. He perceived the incongruity of these *précieux* elements in society at a time when the driving force was the thriving middle class, a group marked by realistic values. With the elements of comic theater at his command, he could express his ideas brilliantly on stage.

The complex of ideas in this comedy revolves about the theme of romantic notions in conflict with healthy social behavior. Manners at first seem to be the subject, yet we should consider just why the girls are so intent upon making novels come true in their lives. They are both consciously and unwittingly taking refuge in fancies to escape the dull reality of bourgeois marriage. The situation is funny, but the hint of insecurity in Magdelon and Cathos gives the farce a germ of psychological truth. Reminders of the physical side of love and marriage are present in the play not so much for their contribution of gross humor as for statement of the realities of love that the girls are rejecting. "I find marriage a thing completely shocking," says Cathos (scene 4). Molière is giving a love plot an ironic twist in that a traditional business of comedy is to show young lovers reaching a happy union after overcoming obstacles. Gorgibus is a stock father type intent upon marrying off his girls, but they revolt, not because his choice of husbands is strange, but because they dupe themselves into accepting a false image of happiness in love.

Cathos and Magdelon make fools of themselves over their suitors' valets, Mascarille and Jodelet, who come to call disguised as fashionable noblemen. Their obvious fakery is taken for real value by the girls who are eager to accept a semblance of romance and social success. Curiously, the same motives are driving the valets, even though their pretense is deliberate. They enjoy being accepted for what their clothes proclaim them to be and consistently reject their true identities. Jodelet, a clown of fixed personality who always wore a white makeup associated with his stage name, is patently a buffoon, but the title of "vicomte" suffices for the girls and for him. He dresses and acts the part, for "clothes make the man." The burlesque assuming of a new identity can be destroyed effectively by the stripping away of the fine clothes and fake title; the case of Cathos and Magdelon is rather more serious because they suffer real pain upon being required to return to their true selves. Mascarille and Jodelet are subjected to a beating which puts them rapidly back into the status of lackeys, but the girls must be given a psychological shock treatment. "Farewell, our finery," says Jodelet. "There are our titles cast down" echoes Mascarille, as his clothes drop off (scene 15). The relationships between physical unmasking and psychological revelation will be a frequent part of Molière's theatrical structures. The ending of this comedy is not a simple admission of error on all sides, however, for the author indicates that Mascarille has become so infatuated with the role of marquis that he refuses to drop it with the costume. "Treating a marquis like that! That's the world for you. The slightest misfortune makes people scorn us who used to love us. Come, friend, let's try our luck elsewhere; I see that here they care only for vain appearance and have no regard for naked worth" (scene 16). The image of the words and its literal enactment are neatly worked out as he marches off in his underclothes.

The play thus ends with the stripped pair stalking off and the girls lamenting the "cruel play" or unwitting farce in which they have been made to act. Gorgibus rages against the precious literature that has misled his girls into supplanting reality by fantasies; "pernicious amusements of idle minds, novels, verses, songs, sonnets, and 'sonnettes' may all go to the devil!" (scene 17).

Literary and theatrical forms have doubly deluded the would-be *précieuses* because they induced the original false notions and then disabused them harshly by a dramatization of the desired romantic encounter. The chief thematic elements have been suggested in our brief account of the comedy, but we may look now at the active structural parts that have a vital function in carrying the play along and giving us a sense of what the themes amount to. The unity we feel in the work comes not only from its brevity but from its steady repetition of scenes based on actions of rejection and acceptance.

Thus, the suitors set the pattern of seeking acceptance and being rejected, a scheme of activity that will have several variations dependent upon the characters involved and their ideas. Cathos and Magdelon, of course, wish to be accepted by Parisian society and to be ushered into a world of fancy. The narrative of the courtship which was quoted is concerned with rejection and acceptance of a lover. Old Gorgibus finds himself rejected by La Grange and Du Croisy, so he in turn ends up by thrusting away the girls and their silly notions. The entry of Mascarille is made possible by his use of conventional signs that show him to be worthy of acceptance, and he can then introduce Jodelet. The four characters, girls and valets, take to each other eagerly because their dreams of high life are accepted and made real for them by this little "closed society" of *précieux*. Once on stage, Mascarille is received willingly by the young women, but his quarrel about money with the chair porters permits another sort of variation on the central structure; the "marquis" who haughtily refuses to pay the porters is made to accept the "reasonable" argument of a lifted stick. Jodelet has to follow Mascarille's lead and engage in a fast dance despite his recent illness. Mascarille urges the girls to praise his literary skill, and they are persuaded to feel his scars of war. The hint of bawdiness comes in here, suggesting that the young women who reject "the idea of marriage" are so carried away that they may give physical consent. Mascarille and Jodelet are at the peak of acceptance, but the masters arrive and drive them away after forcing them to drop their fine disguises. The "*précieuses ridicules*" must then reject the image that they had created of themselves. Similarity and analogy of structure exist in the actions on stage, and when they are strung together at a rapid pace the effect is one of great impact.

The use of themes with psychological validity and strength may explain some of the worth of this comedy, but its theatrical structure is probably what makes us feel that it is a wholly satisfying and meaningful experience. Never forgetting how farcical the style of acting and the costumes are, we still receive a certain illusion of reality. Stylized or totally controlled theater (from the standpoint of technique) achieves a remarkable impression of life by its skillful manipulation of the elements that have been discussed. This is really an epoch-making play in the history of Western theater, quite a feat for a small farce.

That the play was such a success at the time of its creation, when the audience hardly was aware of the real innovation, indicates a response on a primary level to its surface features. But, more than this, the public could not have delighted so much in the farce unless its enactment of literary and dramatic posing in contemporary life had seemed natural and true. The audience had a clear recognition of the theatrical aspects of social behavior. The established norms were seen to be a part of a game or a play in which the individual had an assigned role, yet when a person allowed the role-playing to usurp his whole existence then he would be regarded as "ridiculous" or "extravagant." Molière had at his disposal a background of mores that were self-conscious, formal, and truly theatrical in orientation. Thus, the opportunities to deal in comedy with the relationship between stage and real life were tremendous. Partaking of this general scheme are his plays that show social posing, such at *Le Misanthrope* and *Le Bourgeois gentilhomme,* those that employ communication over the footlights between actor and audience, *L'Avare,* *L'Impromptu de Versailles,* and *Les Fâcheux,* and plays that place figures from real life into staged versions of their experience. Louis XIV thus appears mirrored in his amatory exploits by the character of Jupiter in *Amphitryon.*

Theater that is self-consciously stagy is most successful in a society possessing the same sort of nature. A flourishing tendency toward self-dramatization, coupled with a convention of acceptance of a code of refined behavior based on literary examples, made Molière's contemporary world an ideal one for his comic interpretation of life. To say that his comedies sought to correct the ways of society is an error; while showing human follies he sought to mirror man and not to chastise him. The universality of the human behavior he shows makes his plays meaningful in any age, but in our present society the impact of his comedies becomes especially great. Transposing the details of *Les Précieuses ridicules* into those of the modern world, we see the eternal "folly of affectation." The essential modernity of the satire Molière created in this comedy of 1659 is a mark of his genius. A small farce on contemporary *préciosité* becomes satire that applies to any sophisticated society. As a critic has said, it is really a "triumph of theater."[6]

Chapter Three

The Growth of Molière's Art

Sganarelle, ou le cocu imaginaire

After the auspicious creation of *Les Précieuses ridicules,* Molière continued
to add to his stock of material and techniques. Within the confines of
Sganarelle, ou le cocu imaginaire (Sganarelle, or the imaginary cuckold), his
one-act farce of 1660, the author worked a neat exercise in themes and structures such as have been observed.

The fact that the play has but the single act seems to aid the author to concentrate on a central idea and plan, for this farce does not suffer from the labored length of an *Étourdi.* The subtitle suggests the theme of the comedy
but it does not express all aspects of it. The imaginings of Sganarelle about
his wife's fidelity form only a part of the imaginings of all the characters
about one another. The cuckoldry could be replaced by infidelity as a thematic word, but even better would be a statement that the action of the comedy is "misconception about one's love situation." The term is clumsy and too
broad, but it applies when we observe that the characters are married or in
love and that they then disrupt their happiness by fancying faults in a partner.
False appearances are allowed to cause quarrels and obstacles.

The scheme of a "comedy of errors" about love is so conventional in comic
theater that one would think that it could lead to banality, yet the art has such
resources of variety within strict convention that the playwright can produce
an original effect using an old framework. Theatricality is strongly aided by
adherence to tradition, and thus we find that the setting chosen by Molière is
a "public square" in Paris, a conventional form of the original outdoor setting
of popular comedy. The abstract quality of a public square with its possibilities for chance encounters is exactly what is needed as background for a series
of misunderstandings. The theatrical usefulness of the generalized setting is
regularly exploited by the tragic playwrights of the age; the audience focuses
on the state of mind induced by the play rather than on its relation to a specific place.

The practice of repeated use of the same names for characters (Sganarelle
appears in *Le Médecin volant, L'École des maris,* and others) is also based on

25

the theatrical principle of generalized frame of reference. In repeating character names and types, Molière is following the practice of old French and Italian farce, enabling the audience to identify stock characters at once. More
important, the conventional names are a signal that the comedy is to be understood as part of the traditional world of farce. This building upon a large
and familiar foundation of theatrical convention is especially characteristic of
Molière's farces. *Sganarelle* is an excellent example of this.

The plot runs as follows. Célie happens to faint as Sganarelle chances by, so
he carries her to his house, a bit of stage set on one side with wide-open door
and window. The action is always public and visible. His efforts to revive the
girl are seen by his wife, who immediately assumes he is being unfaithful.
Sganarelle is led to the same conclusion about his wife, who has found a portrait of Lélie dropped by Célie and who admires the face of the young man.
Sganarelle thinks she has a miniature of her lover, so he accuses her of infidelity. With the unified improbability of events in comedy of this sort, Lélie enters after a long trip and sees Sganarelle, portrait in hand, and asks him how
he got it. When Sganarelle explains that he received it from his wife, Lélie
must conclude that Célie has married the old fellow, and he faints from the
shock. The previous routine is repeated with Sganarelle's wife caring for the
young man, observed by Sganarelle and Célie. Confusion prevails on all
sides, so Célie angrily consents to wed Valère, her father's choice of husband.
A confrontation of the lovers produces only a quarrel, and in the background
hovers the figure of Sganarelle, armed and steeling himself to vengeance on
his wife's lover. Since the maid is the one who understands the nature of the
confusion, she gets each to explain his or her ideas, and a way clear of the impasse seems open. In a final contrived bit of denouement we learn that Valère
has been married secretly so all can end on a proper note of happy union.

In this farce every character stumbles about beset by wrong notions about
himself and others. Célie's father, Gorgibus, for example, proceeds to equate
personal worth and financial status, saying about his choice of son-in-law,
"Whatever he may be like, with that sum of money I say he must be a cultivated gentleman" (scene 1). In similar fashion, external signs will be accepted
as inner reality by all the characters, each one having a psychologically valid
reason for such behavior. The young lovers are victims of their sensitive feelings, Gorgibus a victim of misplaced values, and Sganarelle and his wife are
subject to errors induced by circumstantial evidence. The only exception to
the general rule of fuzzy thinking is the instinctively direct statement by a
simple maid about real happiness in love. As is usual in Molière's comedies,
the "natural" and humble types utter truth when unencumbered by intellectual pretensions. Says the old servant: "Believe me, ma'am, there is nothing

like having a husband next to you in the night even if it is only to say 'God bless you' when you sneeze" (scene 2).

The title character stands out among the figures in this mix-up, for he is truly most uncertain as to just what his nature or stance must be. The old friend of the audience, Sganarelle the clown is heroically befuddled in trying to assume a pose and behavior appropriate to a man far above his station. He is called a "bourgeois of Paris" in the list of characters, and heavily middle class he is in his cautious concern for his physical safety while threatening Lélie. He has absorbed enough novels and dramas to know that the cuckolded husband is obliged to avenge his honor although he fears to act and really cares nothing about his wife or his name. The clown is victim of literary stereotypes and he submits to his delusion of grandeur as the outraged husband. The author is on well-trod theatrical ground, not only in his own previous plays but also in a long tradition of burlesque boasting scenes dating back to Roman theater, probably, and featuring a braggart soldier, the "miles gloriosus." Corneille used a Matamore (Spanish "Moor-slayer") in his *Illusion comique* of 1636, exemplifying the wide utility of this stock type and the extent to which the audience would recognize the routine. The literary clichés are brought forth in great number by Sganarelle: "My courage is on its high horses, and if I meet him there will be bloodshed. I have sworn his death . . . (*Sword drawn, he approaches Lélie*) Right in the heart . . ." Lélie inquires why he is armed, and Sganarelle replies, "It's an outfit I put on for the rain" (scene 21).

The mixture of lofty words and unheroic behavior is found not only in Sganarelle but also in Gros-René, the valet of Lélie. We recognize this figure and are gratified to hear him utter his expected confusions on the physical and the ideal. He urges his master to eat heartily to cure him of heartbreak: "Stuff yourself against the blows which fortune can deal you, and to shut out grief surround your heart with twenty glasses of wine" (scene 7). Sganarelle is a bit above Gros-René in his propensity for self-delusion by lofty ideas and words. The base and the elevated are so at war within his simple being that he, even as a clown, projects some of the tension of a figure full of doubts as to his nature and identity. In a farce like this he can be rescued, but, in the later comedies of Molière, rejoining reality will be impossible for the leading characters who have given themselves entirely over to the pursuit of a fixed fancy or preconception. *Sganarelle* is an excellent piece of self-training for the playwright who will present such a theme by means of traditional theatrical structures.

Dom Garcie de Navarre

The most unfortunate victim in Molière's attempt at heroic tragicomedy was the author himself because he, more than any of the characters in the play, was the dupe of misconceptions. The writer who spoofed those who were deluded into following hollow conventions set forth by literature was himself misled in this way. It was a lesson quickly learned and never forgotten after *Dom Garcie de Navarre.*

Early in 1661 Molière's theater offered to the public a comedy of "heroic" type based on successful examples like Corneille's *Le Cid.* With a medieval Spanish setting, it presents a hero who so holds to a "point of honor" that he is more ridiculous than glorious, although satire was not the author's intention. Why was Molière led to compose such a failure? He was eager to give the audience entertainment suited to popular taste, and this taste favored Corneille and the other authors who could dramatize a problem of moral and sentimental issues. While some could exploit the cultural current of *préciosité* in this fashion, we have seen that the comic playwright worked best by showing the absurd extremes produced in ordinary minds by such ideas. Habit was stronger than will in *Dom Garcie.* The time would come when Molière could write his personal treatment of love, self-love, and the social game of love in *Le Misanthrope,* and he would profit from his errors in the play of 1661 even to the extent of using lines from *Dom Garcie* for Alceste, the misanthropist.

The effect in *Dom Garcie de Navarre* is very much as if the clownish Sganarelle were being forced to play his role of jealous man seriously, and the misconceptions that are so hilarious in the farce become annoying and tedious in a play with the least pretense of illusion of serious behavior. The author was trapped by hope of success into taking an unfamiliar and unsuitable path, and any *précieux* who felt themselves mocked by *Les Précieuses ridicules* could feel a bit avenged by his mistake. But Molière would scarcely have been a man of his age and a professional in the theater if he had not responded somehow to the clamor and pressure for heroic style. The novels like *L'Astrée* may have had their peak of popularity earlier, but the concept of a code of gallantry and noble actions had been built into the thinking of a whole epoch, and a certain amount of elevated talk and behavior was accepted as normal. Without such a context of thought a play like *Le Misanthrope* would be impossible to create; the spectators must know the rules of the game and evaluate the actions of the hero accordingly. When Dom Garcie transgresses the bounds of gallantry in suspecting his lady of infidelity, he sets up first a tension in the minds of the viewers as to whether or not he is right morally although he strains the code of courtly love. When the Dom persists in accusing her of treachery, he loses the effect of dramatic tension and degenerates into a caricature of a gallant hero. Politeness is lost for no reason, and this is quite unpardonable, although what the playwright was trying to achieve was a contrast between great passion and the limits of formal courtship. The lover may doubt his own "merit," but he must not declare flatly that his lady is unfaithful because this diminishes her "merit" or good name as well as his.

Despite the description of heroic comedy assigned to the play by its author, it fails as such because it becomes a grotesque exaggeration of proper conduct in a romantic situation. The drama collapses as Doña Elvira continues to forgive the fiery Dom when he repeatedly violates the rules of gallantry. If the age and the literary norms permit, the author can take such a scheme and create a drama of fated passion, but we must observe that the traditional tale of the great love, *Tristan and Isolde* for example, has been smothered in the cotton batting of precious taste. The tale of the lover who overcomes obstacles and wins the woman destined for him has been so hedged about by conventions of delicacy that the psychological impact of themes of quest and fate disappears. It will remain for Racine to suggest some of this impact in his tragedies of passion thwarted by destiny. It seems clear that Molière sensed the distortion that his contemporaries had worked upon such fundamental themes, and he achieved some of his major triumphs by depicting people foolishly trying to elevate themselves by ideas that had already been diluted and debased. Reasons for actions, he saw, remained quite basic—love, sex, or power—but men insisted upon cloaking them with a variety of lofty or personally convenient motives. Dom Garcie remains hung up midway between his truly heroic milieu of ancient Spain and the world of 1661; he belongs wholly to neither period.

The play gave Molière practice in structuring a series of mistakes about identity, characters in disguise, torn letters, false news, and the whole string of routines leading to errors. The plot of Dom Garcie and Doña Elvira is doubled by a subplot of frustrated love, and in the end the couples are united in a proper comic denouement. A glance back through his plays shows how standardized the materials became. One of the truly instructive things to be drawn from study of the first works of Molière is a knowledge that they are all amalgams of very much the same sort of stuff. Criticism has long tried to sort out the elements of drama and to classify comedies as those of manners, character, or plot, yet which characteristic dominates in these works of Molière? All the parts seem to be distributed about equally and to reinforce their total comic and theatrical effect, nor will this principle disappear in the later comedies. The sense of organic unity is strong, and when it produces an effect of vitality and pertinence to reality it makes powerful theater. As the playwright continues to experiment with ways to use and comment in the theater on actual life, he will cling to the standard parts of his structure, harking back constantly to farce and commedia for their theatricality and applying their lessons inventively in new dramatic situations. Clowns never leave his stage, even when the import of the play appears grave because they and their routines have a vital impact that is not simply humorous. It was the misfortune of Molière to treat Dom Garcie as something other than a buffoon.

The style of the author had been well established by 1661, and his task was one of finding how much he could say with it. His contemporary audience was intent upon listening and reacting to his utterances on stage, and this is evident from the effect that a controversial play would have on court, city, and church. He was a professional man of the theater whose personal experience was immersed in the flood tide of French culture of the 1660s. It is perhaps due to the essential drive and vigor of this age that his comedies capture the vital spark that keeps them always young.

L'École des maris

If *Dom Garcie de Navarre* was a disappointment and failed to set up links between audience and author, *L'École des maris* (The school for husbands) more than made up for the failure. The new comedy of June 1661 was a firm assertion of technical skill and of the powers of theatricality. It contains many familiar parts compounded, however, with such a sureness of touch that it marks a distinct advance; we are reminded of *Les Précieuses ridicules,* yet we see that the one-act play was but a foretaste of the full-scale work.

The promises of great successes to come in the theater is an interesting mirroring of the temper of the society in this year when the youthful Louis XIV assumed personal control of the government. The king took a Spanish princess as his wife and looked forward confidently to the birth of a dauphin and to winning for this new heir new territories and glories. The spirit of the king and that of Molière corresponded happily, nor was direct royal patronage of the comedian slow in coming. Royal triumphs of arms, diplomacy, and culture were celebrated and complemented by lavish entertainments, and Molière was to move into the front ranks of purveyors of theater to Louis.

The scale of the royal spending on display may be judged by the public celebration of the birth of the Dauphin, who appeared on schedule in 1662. Molière had enjoyed official sponsorship and funds under the king's brother, but the rather chancy benefits to be derived from this truly ambiguous person could not compare with regal favors. The playwright flattered the king by referring to the "magnificence" being prepared for the Great Carrousel in honor of the new prince, thus giving a topical flavor to his play (1.3). All indications were given by Louis of the intention to foster lavish entertainments, and Molière warmed to the prospects of assisting in such productions. Royal commissions and favor indeed were in store for him.

The attention of all the public, monarch and commoners alike, was caught by *L'École des maris*. A summary of the basic action will permit some analysis of its qualities. Molière wrote a comedy highly unified in its source of action, the warped ideas of one character about the proper education of women. We find two brothers, Sganarelle and Ariste, who have adopted two orphan girls, Isabelle and Léonor, with the idea of rearing them to be ideal wives. True to traditional type, Sganarelle is crude, loud, and wrongheaded, living up to the expectations of the audience familiar with him from earlier plays. He is tyrannical in keeping Isabelle locked up and in ignorance of the world, while his brother, older in years but younger in spirit, treats Léonor with liberal confidence and encourages her to engage in social life. The result of these two systems of education is that Léonor happily consents to wed Ariste, while Isabelle uses every means to avoid marriage with Sganarelle and seeks out a young man, Valère. Isabelle visits Valère and tells Sganarelle that Léonor was guilty of this indiscretion. The duped Sganarelle triumphs over Ariste and unwittingly collaborates in signing a marriage contract between Isabelle and Valère.

This comedy is built first of all upon set routines suggestive of commedia dell'arte, and we thus see the heroine suffering herself to be embraced by her old guardian and simultaneously extending her hand to her lover. Or she dupes the man into believing that she is holding a conversation with her sister, returning to a tried-and-true farce routine of *Le Médecin volant*. Comedy hardly seems to make progress in this manner, but the routines from farce are integrated as meaningful parts into the whole of a play. The thematic idea is one of antithesis or duality. On a simple level, a character pretends one thing and does another, or else words and deeds contradict each other. A constantly doubled framework is employed as Molière deals with a pair of brothers and a pair of sisters; one couple will serve to show one aspect of a situation while a parallel is seen in the other duo. The scheme is carried through the imagery, the metaphors, episodes, routines, and entire scenes, with a resulting total effect that is hardly subtle but extremely strong theatrically. Bilateral symmetry is characteristic of the human organism, and a mirroring of life and its situations is as vital as it is stagy, so that the author cannot fail to communicate or stimulate with a pattern of the sort.

Duality then results in unity, just as broad comic style produces serious import. We are not trying to be paradoxical for the sake of wit, but wish to stress the fact that farce can make excellent serious and poetic theater. We must not underestimate a play's possibilities for aesthetic achievement merely because it is in the comic mode; the use of this mode is a conventional sign that the writer has fixed his boundaries or playing area. Rather than extend the action or implications toward man's spiritual existence as a creature connected somehow to supernatural forces, comedy delimits its scope to man as a social being, finite and temporal. Man moves in a physical world, bumping psyches with other people but not making any cosmic moves as a result. The physical world continues its customary rotation. But the play can still be poetic.

Combined with the material derived from farce, *L'École des maris* creates a strong poetic impression, and much of this effect is due to the masterful expression of its lines in verse. The serious intent of the author is communicated by his use of poetry, a sign that he is aiming above simple farce. We recall that *L'Étourdi* was composed in verse, an early exercise in the technique. By 1661, Molière possessed the experience of creating such sharp satire as *Les Précieuses ridicules* and the ability to express it in polished alexandrine lines, the twelve-syllable rhymed couplets standard in the theater of his day.

L'École des maris, then, asks to be considered as something above and beyond crude comic routines. An examination of the play shows depth of ideas and structural skill. The audience of 1661 would have welcomed Sganarelle as an old friend, nor could they have had any doubts about his being deceived by an Isabelle. Nevertheless, as the play progresses, we come to see that this Sganarelle is not entirely the buffoon who bore the same name in *Le Cocu imaginaire,* for, despite his being a victim of fixed notions, he is decidedly intelligent and informed in other ways. His retorts have real wit, nor can we dismiss his condemnation of outlandish fashions in dress and behavior. The Molièresque blending of illusion of reality with clowning is becoming marked in the creation of such a character, and figures like Arnolphe of *L'École des femmes* (*The School for Wives*) are foreshadowed (see chapter 4).

The play begins with a debate on social individualism versus accommodation to custom, Ariste maintaining that the usage of a society is to be observed, the position to be defended by Philinte in *Le Misanthrope.* The resolute disregard for custom and fashion by Sganarelle is shown not only by his speeches but also by his outmoded clothing and manners. He declares that he will follow his "fantasy" in such matters and holds his brother to be a fop in his dotage who apes youthful behavior. We know that by the rules of the comic mode such boorish ideas are doomed to be defeated by the force of social organization, which permits no harmful eccentricity to disrupt it. Yet, the whole truth and complete wisdom are not to be found clearly on one side or the other in this debate. The contrasts of reason and folly occur within the individual characters, not only on the two sides of an argument. Is an old man who thinks of youth and beauty more of a fool than a younger person who dwells upon keeping his belly warm and having comfortable shoes? Their quarrel then turns to the matter of the rearing of the girls whom they intend to wed, and the expression of theme through plot incidents gets under way.

Sganarelle will be present throughout the three acts of the play, keeping strict watch upon Isabelle, whereas Ariste will disappear from the scene until the denouement. Léonor will be off at a ball or other social activity, turned loose in the "school of the world" to shape her character and to lead her subtly to appreciate the worth of her wise Ariste. Physical presence and absence are part of the scheme of contrasting elements in the comedy, for they set up the equation of "guard:loss of possession: :freedom:gain of possession." Not only is Sganarelle always on the spot to guard his treasure, but he is also most insistent upon expressing his convictions on the matter. He is a highly vocal character whose propensity for talk undoes him as much as anything else.

Ariste's speeches in the second scene of the play are cut off rapidly as Sganarelle delivers himself of his opinions on the care of the wards. Ariste: "Youth wants . . ." Sgan.: "Youth is foolish, and old age sometimes is too." And, Ariste: "It seems to me . . ." Sgan.: "It seems to me, and I say it out loud, that this has to be said . . . (etc.)" (1.2). The character of the compulsive talker is soon established in our minds and we see that he speaks about guarding Isabelle much more than he really accomplishes it. The verbal drive of Sganarelle is an essential factor in the forward movement of the play because his inability to guard his tongue makes the action possible. The silence of Ariste is contrastingly eloquent and efficacious. In the final act there is a reprise of the pattern of Sganarelle's monopolizing of talk when he takes charge of things orally and forces his brother to say nothing but to observe the results of his folly. The scheme reaches its destined climax at that point, of course, for the incessant talking by Sganarelle will have delivered Isabelle to Valère, as Sganarelle discovers through his commands to her to appear.

The whole question of the social position and rights of women was a lively one at the period, so we should not think that the subject of Molière's play was hackneyed for his contemporaries. Ariste says: "Their sex likes to enjoy a bit of liberty. We control them badly with so much austerity, and distrusting precautions, locks, and grills do not produce virtue in wives or daughters. Honor must hold them to duty, not the severity that we show toward them" (1.2). He proposes to win the love of Léonor, not marry her by constraint, preserving perfectly as a gallant sexagenarian the lessons of his youth as set

forth in popular romantic works like *L'Astrée*. The seriousness of the matter
is a bit belied by its seemingly frivolous tone in the early novels, yet we must
remember that a sort of social revolution was taking place. The notion that
love can flourish only in an atmosphere of liberty with freedom to err as well
as to make the right choices is at once part of a formal code of behavior based
on literary example and a real change in the mores and psychology of an age.
Ariste and Valère win their ladies through "merit" and "esteem," if we use the
terms of the game of love, while Sganarelle has no idea how to adapt himself
to the current rules. His direct approach toward love and marriage, to try to
retain control over what he desires passionately, is unsuccessful not merely because it is unpolished but because he tries to present his transgressions against
the code of love as a better code of morals. The dragon guarding his treasure
hardly establishes an example of public morality, however, and certainly not
in a society that has set up an ideal of liberty within certain bounds. Ariste
may be held to be a bit ridiculous as an overaged suitor, but now as much so
as Sganarelle, "the ridiculous anti-précieux." Still, it is interesting to note that
the arguments of the "reasonable" Ariste are derived paradoxically from the
codified fancies of romance.

    The pattern of dualities and contrasts is thus heavily drawn. In the behav-
ior of Sganarelle we see once again the case of the jealous man like Dom
Garcie or the Sganarelle of *Le Cocu imaginaire*, but his failure in love is
played off against the surprising success of an old man. The jealous guardian
will appear shortly in *L'École des Femmes*, and the suspicious suitor will be
seen in the character of Alceste, the misanthropist. All of these figures who
demand certainty about their women are doomed to be deceived, partly because they go against the code of romance, but also because they are fools
enough to expect certainty in a matter that must always be shifting and supple. Knowledge and deception, fixity and change, control and liberty—these
antithetical elements are at the core of many major works of Molière. As the
playwright concerns himself more and more with manifestations of force,
control, and power in his later comedies, the serious implications will be inescapably clear. From the silly fixed notions of a clown to the grave errors of a
Dom Juan or a Tartuffe, Molière retains a constant preoccupation with rigidity in minds that have power, fancied or real, over other people.

    Given the tyranny of a watchdog suitor, husband, or guardian, the woman
in the comedy has no recourse other than deception, and it is really her duty to
herself. Thus Isabelle cleverly eludes Sganarelle's guard by analyzing his
weaknesses and exploiting them. In the most highly developed play on such a
theme, *Le Misanthrope*, the coquette watched over by the jealous suitor will
use the same tactics, although this comedy will show us a woman falling into

the same trap of rigidity of thought when she abuses the principle of liberty. In a study of Molière's *précieux* aspects F. Baumal demonstrates the extent to which the playwright worked with such ideas in his ballets and court plays and in *Le Misanthrope*,[1] but I am sure that we may go much further and say that all of his treatments of love are predicated on the complex of essentially precious thought generally held to be valid by the people of the mid-seventeenth century. This thought had been formulated in the early novels and given the cachet of aristocratic acceptance in the salons. It is a fertile field for a comic writer to work.

L'École des maris also demonstrates the developing sureness of touch in technical matters. For example, when Sganarelle goes as unwitting messenger to tell Valère just what Isabelle said, a scheme of complete repetition of words with increasingly comic effect is exploited. This has been called by J. D. Hubert an interplay between the obvious and the hidden because to us and Valère the meanings are obvious while Sganarelle sees only the surface.[2] Actually, this is a pattern of dramatic irony in comic mode since everyone but the character can perceive that he is working his own downfall. With a strong movement toward his fated end, like a tragic hero carried along, Sganarelle puts all of his efforts into doing exactly the wrong things. The cumulative effect of the many errors is wonderfully comic, and the audience wonders how long the absurd performance can go on. The whole business has a carefully contrived inevitability, since this has been announced by the conversations of the first act which dwell upon the fact that the woman restricted is the one who will find her freedom. Valère rages against the "dragon" who guards his beloved, and the use of the term tells us that this comedy has a frame of reference of fairy tale or legend in which the dragon is bound to be defeated. All that the hero needs is to know the fatal weakness of the guardian, and Isabelle, true to the form of legend, can supply him with the magic words to conquer the dragon.

In the second act Isabelle says that she will use "the clever stratagem of innocent love" (2.1), and the legend pattern is continued, the innocence of the lovers overcoming the forces of evil. The contrast of innocence and clever scheming might seem out of tune, but this is wholly logical in the context of the literary patterns of "love conquers all." The stratagem is to have Sganarelle be love's messenger, and this permits an elaborate comic routine to develop as the guardian thinks he is driving away Valère while really aiding him. Sganarelle is delighted to have everything out in the open, having made Valère "give up all pretense" of not pursuing Isabelle (2.2). He gloats over the apparent "confusion" of the young man. The plot incidents are as follows: Isabelle tells Sganarelle that she has received a note from a bold suitor and

that he must return it unopened for her. The communications with the lover
are established and become increasingly effective. Things reach a point where
Sganarelle feels that he can put in a good word for the young man who he
fancies is being rejected harshly. A mad extreme of delusion has him pleading
for his rival. When the trio is together, Isabelle expresses her love openly to
Valère, but Sganarelle thinks the words are meant for him. As he embraces
her, she gives her hand meaningfully to the other man. In his exuberance
Sganarelle decides to marry Isabelle the next day, and he embraces Valère to
console him for his loss. "I am her other self," he exclaims, uttering the perfect
speech to sum up the situation of his putting himself in the place of the girl
and wooing as intermediary with Valère (2.9).

The final act of the three is fittingly staged at night to augment and confirm our impression that Sganarelle is truly benighted. The confusions and
deceptions are now carried to burlesque extremes in which Sganarelle is completely cooperative. He thinks that Isabelle has Léonor with her and that
Léonor is the girl who goes to the tryst with Valère, while Isabelle walks by
him to her lover's house. The outrageous scheme involves Isabelle who pretends to be Léonor pretending to be Isabelle to get Valère to marry Léonor in
the guise of Isabelle. The principle is that the more outlandish the scheme is,
the better it succeeds with Sganarelle. The guardian is delighted to be able to
show Ariste how badly Léonor has turned out, so he drags him onto the scene
to see that Léonor has an assignation with a lover. He also summons officials
to draw up a marriage contract so that Léonor's honor may be saved; he plans
to demand a marriage by Valère after he catches the lovers together. When his
scheme apparently succeeds and the young man agrees to wed the young lady
in his house, Sganarelle cheerfully signs the contract and thus gives away
Isabelle. The girl emerges into the light of the torches from the dim interior of
the house, and her guardian is sadly enlightened. This is her first appearance
outside of her prison in Sganarelle's home, but when she does come out it is in
complete freedom. The dual theme of liberty and restraint is physically embodied, carrying out the prediction made at the beginning of the play.

We have commented upon Sganarelle's assumption of control in this scene
as he insists that his brother remain silent to "see the truth" (3.5). His deflation is equal to his determined self-assertion when Isabelle appears;
Sganarelle has declared that he will be "enlightened," but the sudden knowledge is crushing. The ending is free of any deus ex machina because it has its
own self-contained logic and inevitability, rather a rarity in Molière's theater.
There is so often an extraordinary bit of news that permits the play to achieve
a satisfactory ending at the expense of realism that we become used to a contrived final scene in Molière. The theatrical effect is really just as good for his

sort of comedies when he uses this technique, but the ending of *L'École des maris* has the additional excellence of being wholly in keeping with the preceding parts of the play.

To terminate the work, the author shows all characters present and acquainted with the downfall of Sganarelle. None of them loses the chance to comment on the "fate" of the jealous man, and this device reminds us that the "fate" is truly one that he has wrought for himself. It is a case of poetic "justice," another term used, triumphing over the unjust treatment that Isabelle complained about: "The unjust harshness with which he treats me will make everyone excuse me" (2.1). Molière does not neglect the occasion to stress the theme of justice by having Sganarelle bring a lawyer on stage to arrange the marriage of Léonor, only to find that Isabelle has legally escaped him. With a hint of biblical reference to woman as the instrument of the devil, Sganarelle curses the sex: "The best of them are full of malice. It is a sex created to damn everyone" (3.9). Since Isabelle has considered him to be a devil, it is logical that he should call her this. Then the character who has been most assiduous in guarding women gives up the whole business and renounces "this deceptive sex." Léonor's servant has a curtain speech over the footlights in which she calls Sganarelle an example of a "were-wolf" husband who has been corrected in the "school." The dragon has inevitably been defeated by the plans suggested by true love to the imprisoned maiden; the plot ends on a perfect note of legend.

The "school" that Sganarelle has unwittingly attended is not so much one of woman's wiles but rather one of the theater as a source of manners. Léonor has been free to attend the theater and she has not been corrupted, despite the predictions of the old-fashioned moralist Sganarelle. The intellectual, social, and cultural value of theater is heavily stressed by Molière, who was acting as much from enlightened self-interest as from principle. This comedy, then, stands as one of his plays that are a triumph of theater, not alone because of the inclusion of obvious propaganda for the theater, but also because purely theatrical means are employed in the plot to bring about the ending. The disguises and illusions practiced upon Sganarelle are very stagy and contrived, showing that a literal mind can be duped by a bit of acting. This character is fixed in his ideas of opposition to précieux or gallant behavior, and he errs by going to absurd extremes in this direction, whereas we observed an earlier Sganarelle caught in the folly of imitating a pose of gallant jealousy. The delusions of the central figure in *L'École des maris* are quite self-generated, and this principle will be developed in the great characters of Molière.

A number of the aspects of the author's growing stagecraft have been examined, and the intellectual attractions of this play have been stressed possibly to the neglect of its qualities as a staged production. The physical staging of the comedy in 1661 had some facets that are equally vital for our understanding of what Molière was achieving as a theatrical innovator. He and the other major writers for the stage were moving into a new era of drama in which a certain illusion of reality was created within the still-existent conventions of the art. The effect was noted in *Les Précieuses ridicules*. Conventional plot and verse preserved an impression of heightening, or contrivance, which is proper to theater, but the technical facilities available for the staging of a play included a number of things that would lead the dramatists to work more and more in terms of realism. For one thing, proper theaters had only recently become fairly numerous; the drama had come in out of the weather but a few years before. For a play like *L'École des maris* the necessities of production may seem few and simple for us, yet these arrangements of lighting and scenery were for the first time reaching a point of technical practicality. It is essential to remember how much theater had long been played in the street, the *place publique* that is the setting for our play, and that the tennis courts of Paris had housed troupes for lack of better halls. A roof overhead was a great step forward, permitting playing in all weathers and stage effects of darkening and artificial lighting. The torchlit scene at the end of *L'École* is a small but important technical triumph. Italy and her scenic artists set the pace for such growth of theatrical craftsmanship, yet it was to be the French authors and actors who would develop a theater of illusion, using the means given to them by the Italians.

Molière's stage apparatus in the Petit-Bourbon is not known to us in great detail, but a historian of the epoch has described the things in use at the Hôtel de Bourgogne from 1633 to 1686, so we may assume from this record that the comedies had flats and backdrop.[3] In *L'École* the painted cloth showed a public square and the houses on each side were made of flats and provided with windows. The effect sounds quite ordinary, but the theater had only recently started to work in terms of unity of setting as opposed to the multiplicity of simultaneous sets that showed, all together on the stage, houses, rooms, towers, ships, or any location needed for a scene. In place of such naïveté harking back to medieval theater the plays of the 1660s focused the action in a reasonable sphere. This itself became a convention but the way had been cleared for a much more sophisticated concentration of psychological interest. Molière was on hand to create comic theater that could profit from precisely this state of technical development, a happy period when realism of setting or pure spectacle for its own sake had not taken over staging, but when enough suggestion of illusion could be effected to give an obviously farcical work new depth and significance. *L'École des maris* realizes the new possibilities of a growing art.

Les Fâcheux

From Parisian theater and its beginnings of one sort of modern staging we move to the ground of a magnificent château and see how the craftsmen of the age produced an open-air spectacle. The series of sketches that Molière combined into *Les Fâcheux* (The bores) proved beyond critical or royal doubt that he was a real master of his art. Fouquet, finance minister to Louis XIV, called upon Molière and other professionals to create a great entertainment for the occasion of a royal visit to the minister's estate. History reminds us of the ironic outcome of Louis's inspection of the château of Vaux; the patent enormity of Fouquet's appropriation of public funds for his own purposes led to his removal and disgrace. Even as Louis was viewing the massive display of wealth with a dubious eye, he was being fêted in a regal way, and *Les Fâcheux* was the high point of the festivities.

The play was created in two weeks after Fouquet requested it of the successful author of *L'École des maris,* and at Vaux on the evening of 17 August 1661, *Les Fâcheux* emerged amidst fountains, music, and fireworks. This comedy was the result of collaboration between Molière, the poet Pélisson (who wrote the prologue), and musicians, dancers, and technicians who designed and built the landscapes and sets. The speed of production may astonish us, but a corps of royal entertainers had long existed to create spectacles of the type upon demand, and the royal taste for court ballets and fêtes in costume reflected a tradition of at least a century. Drawing upon Italian example in stagecraft, princely courts on the Continent and in England had used spectacles and "masques" as entertainment and as a political instrument to impress both visitors and retainers. When the spectacles were performed outdoors, various scenic illusions were possible by the use of sets and machines, and, when the productions moved into proper theaters, the possibilities of contrived illusion were increased. A theater of sheer technical illusion and spectacle was to emerge and win the favor of the king and public in the late seventeenth century, and Molière was able to adjust his works to profit from such a taste in theater without losing the dramatic poetry and action that gave real life to his plays. *Les Fâcheux* is important as an example of the playwright's exploiting and adapting the aspects of spectacle that aided his purposes. It is his first *comédie-ballet,* his own invention.

Not only did Molière work in close cooperation with his technical and professional colleagues, but he also found that the king was interested in having a hand in the planning of the play. His Majesty suggested a type of "bore" to be included in the comic roster, and this direct command from Louis to Molière marked the start of a fruitful relationship between patron and artist that was to continue until the death of the latter. Molière astutely observed what sort of entertainment pleased the king, who tended to accept ideas presented in marvelous spectacle rather than in realistic drama. The successful author had to command the resources of both sorts of play to enjoy patronage while creating what he himself wanted.

When "a Naiad," or water nymph, came forward from the fountains and greenery at Vaux, her verses invoked the other nymphs and satyrs to materialize miraculously and to perform for the real miracle of nature, "the world's greatest king" (prologue). Molière explains the scheme for such a beginning in his *Avertissement,* which describes his prior appearance in street clothes before the curtain.[4] He is apologetic about not having his troupe with him for a performance for the king, but nature seems to spring to his aid as a giant shell opens to reveal a Venus-like Madeline Béjart, the naiad. The fountains play, the mythical figures appear, and the performance is brilliantly started. Flattery of the royal guest, natural and stage settings, music, dance, and spectacle all merge in a masterful bit of theatrical effect. We may note parenthetically the existence of the curtain, which is to be "raised," showing that the play was presented in a framed space covered by an arch. Even though this is a fête in the open air, the comedy is conceived as taking place in a limited area set off from the audience by formal boundaries. The nymph speaks directly to the spectators, drawing them into the performance first, as is appropriate for a royal entry or festival, but then the comedy commences within the confines of a curtained stage and the audience must be apart and no longer participating. The initial business of direct dealing with audience heightens the shift to pure stage performance. This is Molière's theatricality in action. We notice that he thinks in terms of the closed stage.

With nymphs and satyrs supposedly taking the roles, the play begins, and a gentleman, Eraste, appears to complain about his being a victim of a fate in which he is constantly bothered by bores when he is intent upon seeing his beloved Orphise. The stress on theater continues because the setting of the first study of a bore is a performance of a comedy that is interrupted by a noisy spectator. Eraste describes a type of nobleman who seats himself on stage during a show, talks constantly, and makes himself the chief spectacle. Molière could hardly have resisted the chance to get some digs in at this very real sort of disrupter of performances. Eraste, the central or organizing character, next suffers from the unwelcome attentions of a figure called Lysandre, who insists that he take part in a ballet that has delighted him. Theater and dance become obstacles to the lover who glimpses his lady on the arm of another man but is unable to break free to go to her. Frustrated by such bores in his efforts to see Orphise, Eraste finally will find himself in a position to save the life of the guardian of the girl. The annoying delays thus put him into an advantageous situation, and he wins his love's hand. The plot line is the merest thread to string scenes upon, and the author's playing with the idea of Eraste as the figure called upon to take many roles is what interests us. He has to suffer the ministrations of an inept valet, to cope with being maneuvered into a duel, and then he is shunted about like a ball caught in the middle of a croquet game, done in ballet.

Entertainment furnishes another type of "bore" when Eraste is cornered in the second act by a card player intent upon telling him the details of a game. A *précieux* then insists upon having his opinion in a matter of gallantry, and an ardent hunter recounts his experiences at great length. (The huntsman was the king's contribution to the scheme.) An entr'acte ballet again thrusts Eraste aside physically, just as the characters have done verbally, and act 3 introduces a pedant who asks him to aid his campaign to correct spelling in public signs. Another "bore" solicits his support for a mad plan to turn the whole coast into ports. Amusements, hobbies, and preoccupations are seen to be the causes of the behavior of the *fâcheux*. The *comédie-ballet* is, in its way, as keen a commentary on the power of diversion as Pascal's discussion of this psychological truth.[5] The play ends with a series of rapid actions involving a plot to do away with Eraste and his sudden reversal of fortune. Orphise enters with a torch to illuminate the scene and clarify the situation. The betrothal is agreed upon, violins are summoned to celebrate the occasion, and a musical finale seems to be prepared. In a last surge of action the *fâcheux* intervene as a wild troupe of masked dancers enters, taking over the stage from the violinists. "What? Always these annoying people! Hey, guards! Get these scoundrels out of here" (3.6). A ballet group of Swiss guards chases away the maskers so that the stage may be used for the dance planned, a delicate pastoral ballet. The final repetition of the *fâcheux* theme is done in a clever theatrical manner, with one ballet turn replacing another. The ultimate effect is one of the universality and the power of the theatrical and imaginative, manifest in the importunate enthusiasms of the bores and in the absorption of all action into dance. Theater is triumphant throughout *Les Fâcheux*.

It is possible to see a strong organizing idea running through this comedy, no matter how disorganized it may appear to be in its string of episodes. We may sum it up in the one word "diversion," which implies both the amusements that preoccupy the *fâcheux* and Eraste's being diverted from the course he wants to follow. The entire play, then, is a series of variations and analogies on the theme of "diversion," the hastily concocted comic ballet displaying a great unity of theme and structure. Molière showed a real mastery of his craft in using dance, music, and spectacle to convey an impression of unified dramatic action. The incorporation of a bit of triumphant royal-entry pageantry into the proceedings was a skillful frosting of the cake.

Les Fâcheux is noteworthy as a comedy that skillfully integrates theme, music, and dance into a coherent theatrical whole, but it is of interest also as an early statement by Molière of certain principles of human behavior perceived by the playwright to be proper to the social creature and thus an important basis for structuring comedy. The persistent human predilection for social masking and role playing is by its nature theatrical and allied to play activity.[6] We have just observed in Les Fâcheux the bores who divert themselves in play and who divert the hero from his desired progress. The use of play and games is quite elementary in this comedy. Later plays will exploit the concepts more subtly.

Eraste is forced to run an obstacle course, much like a moving piece trying to reach a goal in a board game. The garden setting, with Orphise disappearing behind bushes, strongly suggests a garden maze or labyrinth in which a player is diverted and baffled. This comedy thus remains at a fairly simple level of physical games, but in later plays the obstacles are psychological and social. These obstacles will be offered by maskers, individuals who assume a social identity and who seek to have it recognized and honored by others. Le Misanthrope is of greatest interest in this respect.

In Les Fâcheux let us note that a highly competitive game is being played by Eraste, who must extricate himself from the bores. A game implies the existence of rules by which to play, to be sure, but Eraste's adversaries do not think in these terms. They are absorbed in their own concerns and their efforts to absorb other people. Eraste is governed by the rules of polite society that do not countenance rudeness. Conventions of behavior oblige him to give a semblance of courteous attention while striving to free himself to pursue his goal. Society thus creates the form of the game, the comedy being a concentrated model of human behavior of the sort. The strength of Les Fâcheux is in this sense truly deeper than is at first apparent because the playwright has contrived a formalized series of social contacts based on real mores. The play is an early and rapidly created piece that yet displays Molière's sure instinct for focus upon fundamental human behavior in social contacts. Its lessons will be put to good use in great works to follow.

Chapter Four
Personal and Professional Controversy
L'École des femmes

Critics frequently depict an author projecting himself and his experiences into his writings, and an apparent opportunity to observe Molière placing his own marital situation on the stage is afforded by comedies like *L'École des maris* and *L'École des femmes* (*The School for Wives*). This makes for an interesting interpretation of the "school" plays and leads to other possibilities of seeing Molière himself in characters like Alceste, the misanthropist in love with a flirt.[1] The theory is that real life is transferred piecemeal into art, and one is tempted to apply it when the fact is that the playwright married a younger woman of independent spirit. Before we make any attempt at deciding about the merits of such a critical approach, let us look at the story of his marriage and the nature of his comedy of 1662.

In the spring of 1661 Molière had shown his intention of taking a wife by requesting two shares of the troupe's profits. In February 1662 he wed Armande Béjart, variously identified as the sister or daughter of Madeleine. Coincidental with the time of his evident engagement was the production of *L'École des maris,* with its treatment of the shaping of the character of a bride-to-be. The similar *L'École des femmes* came to the stage first in December 1662, and thus the apparent parallels of real experience and comic plays suggest to the biographer that life and art be equated with each other. It is evident that the author was interested in the relations between the sexes, but one must observe that this was the standard subject matter of comedy and one very much present in his early works as well as those of the period of his marriage. The whole matter of Molière as lover and as author treating love cannot be resolved very simply, we suspect.

His amatory career, such as we know it, ranged from his early liaison with Madeleine Béjart, through intimacy with Mlle de Brie, another actress of his theater, to romances with various ladies of the stage. A frank sensuality and a pleasure in feminine companionship are indicated by all biographies of the

man, and it is suggested by writers such as Fernandez[2] that the entangling
passions may not have furnished any relaxation to a man whose life was harried by professional wrangles with prima donnas. For whatever reasons,
Molière took as his bride Armande, who had grown up with the troupe and
who was affectionately called Mlle Menou, "Miss Puss." She was considera-
bly his junior, that much is sure, but her true identity is obscure.

Calumny against the successful author, which was seldom absent, held her
to be the illegitimate child of Madeleine and conjured up the nasty picture of
Molière marrying his own daughter. The aristocratic lover of Madeleine, the
Count of Modène, may have sired the child, who was christened in 1643 and
ascribed to Madeleine's mother. The general impression of irregularity of
morals is probably justified, and Molière may well have had his fears of being
deceived by his youthful wife, but may we conclude that he composed
L'École des femmes as a treatise to shape the mind of Armande? The creative
process has convolutions that cannot be traced, and art often is the model for
life and not its imitation. The subject of the young bride and the old man was
on his mind, that much can be said, but the true business at hand is to see
how he handled the subject as theater.

In *L'École des femmes* the familiar routine of the jealous guardian and his
efforts to watch over his young ward is brought forth once again. Rather than
work with a dual structure like that in *L'École de maris,* Molière focuses
tightly upon a central character who needs little antithesis from outside to
illuminate his situation. The figure of Sganarelle is replaced by Arnolphe, a
character who marks a great advance in the author's skill in portrayal of
human nature. In the one character are elements from the jealous Dom
Garcie, the frustrated Eraste, and the duped Sganarelle. The plot gives every
evidence of being the standard sort in which innocent love finds a way to out-
wit the watchman, so we must look carefully at the treatment of themes and
structures to see how inventive the play is.

Professor Hubert shows how much tragedy enters into the composition
of this comedy,[3] for Arnolphe may be construed to suffer in a genuine way
as fate denies him his love. The innate seriousness of such a treatment of
human weaknesses need not necessarily lead us to say the work is tragic in
mode but rather to observe the nature of comedy. Even the broadest of
farces have a basis in real human folly, which is not always laughable, but
the low mode and the nontranscendent scope of the works clearly define
them. A play based on a character like Arnolphe, who strives to triumph
over the natural and social worlds of his temporal existence, has a certain
grandeur, but the error and sure downfall are wholly his own and affect no
body of people. Sensitive souls in the audience are at liberty to identify with

figures of the sort, just as Rousseau felt akin to the "misanthrope," but such interpretations of comic characters ignore the nature of comedy as relentless for the man who violates the order of society. The battle of the nonconformist is not seen as heroic but as absurd. His actions do not change the world; it isolates him in his folly. As a parody of tragic drama and style, this play gains greatly in meaning and strength, to be sure, and this must be kept in mind. Arnolphe and his fellow sufferers in Molière take themselves seriously as tragic figures, but this is a resource of comedy being exploited by the playwright. Arnolphe has his delusions of tragic grandeur that are not really different from those of Sganarelle, "*cocu.*"

The ingenuity of this comedy lies also in its pretending to be dramatic as well as tragic; that is, it seems to make claims upon the audience to involve it emotionally in a clash of human interests on stage. There is an evident scheme of emotional tensions just as there is a heavy suggestion of a struggle between man and destiny. Molière's use of alexandrine-verse form goes beyond the simple experiments in parodying heroic style that we observed in his early works. The poetry is easy, supple, yet somehow elevated in tone, conveying the seriousness of Arnolphe, and from his speeches a feeling of drama emerges. Yet he is truly a comic figure. He tells his friend that he will not be duped by any woman because he has chosen a girl of complete innocence: "To marry a stupid girl is to avoid deception. In all charity, I admit the wisdom of your ideas, but a clever wife is a bad omen, and I know what it has cost certain men who have chosen theirs with too much talent" (1.1). The dramatic issue of whether or not he has any right to impose ignorance on another person is very real, but the focus will be upon his becoming a spectacle like the Parisian husbands he mocks. Towering jealousy and rage are not comic in an Othello, for an example of a dramatic embodiment of the ideas, but Arnolphe's mingled love and suspicion become only more comic as he emulates a really noble character. At the end of the first act Molière shows us Arnolphe's concern with elevating himself above his former social status by using the title of Monsieur de la Souche. The name suggests that he is to be the "stock" of a great family tree, but also that he has the density of a "tree trunk." His attempts at self-glorification are neatly summed up here. When he later turns to expressing a great self-pity in dramatic style, we will hardly be disposed to take his plight to heart.

The stock situation of the old man eager to wed a young wife comes to its foregone conclusion as the innocent Agnès manages to go off with young Horace. The cramped spirit of an Arnolphe can hardly enter into the natural scheme of union of lovers preached as gospel by traditional comedy. The social organism will not permit abuse of its plan of marriage by an interfer-

ing and selfish individual, so Arnolphe must be defeated. The strict tradi-
tionalism of Molière in these matters need not be dwelt upon, but it is well
to avoid seeking a different "message." What drama there is in the play lies
in the inevitable conflict of an egoist with a conformist social world. The
other people observing his extravagant actions function as an audience and
see him as a "spectacle," the word that Arnolphe had applied to the deceived husbands of Paris, so we are reminded to evaluate the play as a theatrical version of life and not as life transferred to the stage. Arnolphe literally
makes a spectacle of himself.

Confusion in analysis may arise because, although the play is highly theatrical and comic in themes and structure, its intellectual content is equally appropriate for serious treatment in other modes. Indeed, warped motives of
sex and control over others would seem to call for a different literary approach, yet it is not hard to see that they underlie Molière's comic material,
giving reality and vigor to a plot like that of *L'École des femmes.* To extract
these ideas, however, and to impute them to Molière as his life's concerns, is
as unwarranted as to say that such deep thoughts dictate that they should be
expressed in tragic drama.

We have noted that a traditional sort of comic situation is to be played by a
character drawn with greater depth than the early Molière types. Beyond the
fundamentals of sexual and power motives, it is necessary to find a unifying
principle of action in the comedy, and this principle is expressed by one of
Arnolphe's favorite words, *sureness.* "Against this incident [being duped] I
have taken sure measures" (1.1), he declares in a typical speech. On the level
of plot, this "sureness," or certainty, is that of the husband undeceived by his
wife; thematically, the idea of certainty touches upon the character's sure
knowledge of just who he is and his confidence that he can order everything
to suit his ends. It is essentially a theme of egoism and power. The adopting of
a noble title shows Arnolphe's wish to fix his identity, as does his wish to be
known as a man whose wife is faithful. The question arises, is he aware of trying to achieve a new identity or of trying to reject an old one? The situation
was burlesqued in *Les Précieuses,* but it is much subtler here. If there were
tragedy, the hero would be eager to learn the truth about himself, bad as it
might be, but the comic hero avoids it strenuously and persists in building illusions about himself. Certainty in illusion and delusion characterizes him.

Arnolphe has waited for twenty years while bringing up Agnès, in the
hope that he can marry her in confidence and start a new life. His plans will
backfire, and he will be brought face to face with his folly and be obliged to
acknowledge his real self. Concomitant with "sureness" is the idea of
"knowledge," which is regularly played off against the stupidity of Agnès,

the blunders of Horace, and the doltish behavior of the servants. Arnolphe knows all about the plots of Horace to get Agnès away from her guardian, but such knowledge will be his ultimate undoing. He is quite intelligent throughout the episodes of the play, in which Horace, not knowing that he is Monsieur de la Souche, gives away all his schemes to the wrong person. The young man is more of a stock clown than Arnolphe, for his stupidity in confiding in Arnolphe is suggestive of the confident actions of Sganarelle in *L'École des maris* that set up the escape of Isabelle. The sure information possessed by the guardian is still fated to fail to prevent the union of Horace and Agnès, and Molière stresses the triumph of clumsiness and ignorance that are destined to conquer when led by love. "He is everywhere punished by the things that he thought created the sureness of his precautions" (in *La Critique de L'École des femmes,* scene 6) says a spokesman for the author analyzing the downfall of Arnolphe; for knowledge to seek sureness by the use of ignorance is an error. The passage in which the servants shut him out of his house and buffet him is a graphic demonstration of the idea in the second scene of the comedy.

The confidence he has in his system of control is seen in his words: "Heroines of the times, Mesdames the Learned Ladies, sighers of tender and lovely sentiments, I defy all of your verses, your novels, your letters, billets doux, and your knowledge to match in value that honest and modest ignorance" (1.3). The sources of corrupting romantic notions are those against which Gorgibus inveighed in *Les Précieuses.* The role of self-will in the figure of Arnolphe may be noted as well, for he has said that he wants "to follow his way in regard to a wife, as in all things" (1.1). Self-assurance like this will be confounded by the dull minds with which he has deliberately surrounded himself, and these supposed safeguards of his chosen identity and social position unfailingly betray him.

The fact that he truly loves Agnès commits him deeply to dependence on her, but he seems to be ignorant of the law of love, seventeenth-century code, that there can be no sure possession or knowledge in matters of the heart. In analogy with *L'École des maris,* the character who seeks certainty is doomed to lose, but in the later play the utter naïveté of Agnès shows the working of the law even more clearly. Sganarelle lost only a bride and a bit of self-esteem, but Arnolphe is stripped of all confidence in himself and his identity. Molière thus creates a psychological profundity at which the earlier comedy only hinted. The process of dissolution of the confident man begins at the end of act 1 when Horace confides that he is in love with the ward of Monsieur de la Souche. A fated true love is sure to defeat a jealous possessor, and Arnolphe says: "I tremble at the misfortune which could happen to me, and one often

seeks more than one hopes to find" (1.4). Even a little knowledge is a dangerous thing, he realizes.

In act 2 the impression of sure control is quite destroyed when he gives way
to a mad rage at the servants' carelessness. A hint of uncertainty about Agnès
overwhelms him physically: "I'm suffocating . . . dripping with sweat; let's
have some air" (2.2). Horace has had a rendezvous with the girl, and
Arnolphe questions her about how he "cured" her wounded heart. "Oh, vex-
ing examination of a fatal mystery, in which the examiner alone suffers!"
(2.5) is both a fine dramatic-sounding line and a statement of theme. When
he explains that caresses outside of marriage are sinful, Agnès delightedly assents to marry, believing Horace is to be the bridegroom. Misunderstandings
of the sort stress the idea of contrasting knowledge and ignorance. Arnolphe
resumes his rage when she tells him her thought, and the act ends on the note
of angry uncertainty with which it began.

Act 3 shows Arnolphe's increasing efforts to make his position secure as
he lectures Agnès on wifely duty and gives her a book of moralizing maxims to read. The problem seen by this character who seeks certain control is
that part of his being will go into the keeping of his wife. "Think that in
making you part of me, Agnès, it is my honor that I turn over to you" (3.2).
The ego wants certainty, yet love and desire cause him to relinquish it. As
the girl reads the maxims on marriage she gains knowledge of how to conduct a love affair, and this will start the shift of control to her and Horace,
stupid as they may be. The resulting split in the character of Arnolphe will
become increasingly great as he ponders his role as a Pygmalion molding a
Galatea who may escape him. The artist who shapes a life "like a piece of
wax in my hands" (3.3) cannot expect to retain a grasp on it. There is heavy
foreshadowing of the ending: "as soon as her whim has decided the fate of
our honor, we have to submit" (3.3). When Horace enters and tells
Arnolphe how Agnès threw him a note on a stone, ostensibly cast to drive
him away, Arnolphe knows that his fears are realized. He has to muster a
forced laugh at "Monsieur de la Souche" and thus signal the start of the
mockery of himself. In soliloquy his thoughts show a depth of feeling for
the girl: "It hurts to lose what one loves. . . . I cannot do without her" (3.5).
The concept of love as a teacher is applied to him, and his lesson is one of
humility, the opposite of sureness of power.

Faced with possibility of failure, Arnolphe fidgets and fumes: "I think I'll
die if things turn out badly" (4.1). A lawyer arrives and discusses the matter
of sharing property in marriage, but Arnolphe's thoughts are wholly on the
danger of sharing Agnès with Horace. This illuminating counterpoint of
ideas is pure Molière. The increasing fears are shown as the servants are rallied

to defend the honor of the master, but making them responsible for his honor is disastrous folly. Arnolphe, who wanted to feel himself a "wise philosopher" (4.7), sinks to smashing vases in his anger, nor will he feel any better when Horace comes to reveal his plan for reaching Agnès's room. Sure control gives way to certain helplessness: "the stars . . . insist upon filling me with despair" (4.7) is his fatalistic complaint. A friend named Chrysalde brings some good and reasonable advice, saying that love and marriage are games of chance, but we know that chance is the one thing that Arnolphe wants to eliminate.

The unity and logical development of the play have carried it through four acts without any evidence of straining for plot incidents or continuity. A comedy in verse in five acts is usually held to be the epitome of the classical comic work, and Molière is not only conforming to this rather arbitrary ideal, but really creating its form. The *grande comédie* that was suggested by *L'École des maris* takes shape under his hand in *L'École des femmes*. Act 5 will keep the focus sharply on Arnolphe despite a rather contrived ending that brings the lovers together, a sort of denouement to which the playwright regularly resorts without robbing the play of any force. Horace is found by the servants who think that their blows have killed him, when in truth he has clumsily fallen from his ladder. Agnès has promised to flee with Horace, and he proposes to put her in the hands of a "sure" friend, Monsieur de la Souche. Arnolphe now believes that fate is on his side and he agrees that the girl is to be brought to him for hiding in the dark, "to play safe" (5.2). Even when she is delivered into his clutches, he cannot hold her because her true innocence figuratively illuminates the dark scene of possession and leads him to pardon her. Arnolphe thinks that such goodness will succeed where force failed, so her offers Agnès her freedom. "How far passion can make me go!" (5.4) he exclaims, realizing the change that has taken place in him. Her choice of Horace enrages him, and he threatens to throw her into a convent, "a sure place" (5.5). The comedy comes to a swift end when Horace's father arrives (the one extraneous element), intent upon having his son complete a prearranged marriage with an unspecified girl. Arnolphe feels that mastery has been returned to him, and he assents to the plan, gloating over Horace. The ground is cut from beneath him, however, as Agnès is revealed to be the intended bride, and he can only exit in silence. Chrysalde sums up the theme by saying that the only sure way to avoid being duped is never to marry. The thematic patterns are well marked throughout this comedy, as control of love gives way before a destined union, and as knowledge produces no victory. In the "school for wives" love has been a sure guide for Agnès and a harsh disciplinarian for Arnolphe. He has been forced to accept his true identity.

Although this play presents the failure of a confident man, it scarcely represents the situation of the playwright whose rich sense of success was to carry him through much invective hurled by the critics of his comedy.

La Critique de l'École des femmes, L'Impromptu de Versailles

L'École des femmes was not merely a theatrical innovation, it was a bombshell. Molière had pushed farther along the way of revolution in comic theater by creating high comedy from farcical elements, and in choosing the subject matter for serious treatment in comic guise he had managed to hit upon the very things most likely to incite religious, philosophical, and social controversy. Under a thin cover of dramatic and literary criticism, those opposing his ideas (or the thoughts imputed to him) attacked his comedy with the purpose of discrediting the liberal current they perceived in it. The opposition had a very good reason for taking alarm because the ideas that could be read into L'École des femmes were precisely those set forth by Rabelais, Montaigne, and other free-thinking writers. The pattern of independent reasoning and the following of a course suggested by nature was not welcome to the forces intent upon establishing a religio-political authoritarian regime in the 1660s. A direct confrontation of the principles of liberty and conformity seemed to be the unintended result of a venture in comic theater. However informed Molière may have been about the reason for the animus of the attacks on his play, he wisely elected to keep argument within the boundaries of theater, his province and strong point, replying to dramatic criticism by more drama. Polemic as they may be, La Critique de l'École des femmes and L'Impromptu de Versailles (The impromptu at Versailles) are still plays with theatrical qualities, and Molière logically uses his most effective means of expression to set forth his position. The introductions that he wrote for his works are really much less helpful for an understanding of his aims and principles than the plays themselves. The playwright is at his best as a critic when he is speaking through his practiced and controlled medium, the stage.

Every sort of charge was aimed at Molière, from lampooning real people to daring to mention matters of faith in a comedy. The discomfort felt by his opponents undoubtedly came less from real-life Arnolphes' self-recognition than from a keen awareness of the vast powers of satire at the command of the author. There was no telling where the lash might strike next, so the obvious course was to get rid of it. Genuine satire is a rare commodity and one destined to produce violent reactions in a certain group, whether they are the direct target or not. When Molière satirized the selfish abuse of personal power under a pose of pious morality (Arnolphe turns threats of hellfire for Agnès to his own advantage), he stirred up the wrath of the politically powerful who leaned upon church teachings in asserting their rule. "Monsieur de la Souche" is clearly a nobleman, and, despite the fact that he exerts control only over his ward and his servants, his behavior is symptomatic of his class. The perversion of power to cater to lusts and the cloaking of this behavior beneath sanctimoniousness were the sore points at which the comedy jabbed. The outraged shrieks showed that it had struck home.

The clever author had mustered on his side the elements of city and court that would be termed mundane or worldly. The intellectuals, witty socialites, and aristocratic hedonists were with him, and, far from alienating the salon habitués, who might have been piqued from *Les Précieuses ridicules,* he won their support by his eloquent demonstrations of the evils of suppressing women. The rights and liberties of women were staunchly championed by the "school" plays, but, more than this, they gave expression to a belief in healthy liberation of mind and body. In speaking of such ideas, Molière at once demonstrated their presence and vigor, and he communicated with an audience that was basically animated by a spirit of vitality and creativeness. The greatness of the French classical age could hardly have existed without a concentration of physical and mental vigor in a relatively limited number of people. Molière's public was a closed society in its numbers and obedience to convention, but it was a lively, developing society artistically and intellectually. The youthful monarch was part of this group which lived life as an art with great enthusiasm, and his immediate sympathy for Molière illuminates this side of his nature. When a stage was needed by the author, from which to comment on the criticism of *L'École des femmes,* Louis offered the facilities for an "impromptu" at Versailles.

The playwright had first replied to his critics by constructing his own "critique" in play form. In June 1663 *La Critique* was given in Paris, setting a discussion of the merits of *L'École des femmes* into a fictional but typical salon of the city where representative social types from high circles gathered. The salon of Uranie is peopled by the author's defenders and detractors, and the latter show their true colors as they argue about the play. The hostess observes that the gathering constitutes a "small comedy" that she proposes to record and dispatch to Molière. The framework is flimsy but adequately theatrical. The friends of the playwright counter the agitated criticisms leveled by snobs, prudes, and pedants, as Molière limits his fire to hit the petty types who can be handled by ridicule. More serious meaning remains between the lines, and only principles of theater come in for any direct discussion. The moral and religious issues are scrupulously ignored, even though they are highly pertinent. Everyone knew, for example, that the bit about Agnès's inquiring whether babies came from the ear was satire of a religious painting showing Mary and an angel in the Annunciation, yet prudence forbade any mention of such matters. His constant and effective stance is that of a playwright whose duty it is to please his public by showing human folly wherever it occurs. The psychological realism of his "schools" is thus defended most intelligently by a psychologically realistic sketch of a salon conversation. The "critique" deflates the opponents and demonstrates the excellence of the satire that he claims the right to practice.

Uranie and her cousin Elise receive a visit from Climène, a *Précieuse* of exaggerated sort who declares herself to be sickened by the filth of *L'École.* Uranie replies that "a woman's honor is not in affectations" (scene 3) and that the play gave no offense to her sensibilities. A foppish marquis and a reasonable gentleman argue about theater, the former displaying pretentious absurdities in his taste. Honest and wholesome reactions to fun with sex and marriage in a comedy are played off against the opinions of the "extravagants." Molière himself played the fop who declared, "I find it detestable, by Jove! Detestable to the utmost, what one terms detestable!" (scene 5). The play must be bad for "all you have to do is see the common people burst into laughter" (scene 5) to judge it. Dorante says that the people judge in the right way, "which is to take it at face value without blind prejudice, affected superiority, or ridiculous delicacy" (scene 5). The author asks for an intelligent reception by an open-minded audience.

Dorante then gives several witty character sketches like those that will be heard in *Le Misanthrope,* depicting the egotist who wants to be flattered by a request for an opinion, and the prudish bluestocking lady. Uranie supports him: "All the ridiculous things in the theater should not bother people . . . satires like these hit at social customs and only hit people by reflection" (scene 6). Lysidas, a playwright, complains that comedies have no business touching upon things proper to tragedy, but Dorante points out that it is harder to write comedies like Molière's. "When you try to depict real men, you must do it according to nature. . . . In serious plays it is sufficient to say sensible things in good style; but this is not enough in comedies, for you have to be funny. Making honest people laugh is a strange business" (scene 6).

Molière makes a politic move in praising the taste of the court, "the great test of comedies" (scene 6), as opposed to the pedantic judgment of a Lysidas, who cites the rules for composition according to Aristotle and Horace. Such slavery to ancient precedent is exactly the wrong way to go about creating or criticizing theater. The closed minds of pedants rejected innovation, but the court circles welcomed it in art. Above all, the author stresses that he does not mind attacks so long as he gets a full house. The practical man of the theater gets in his word, but the essential message of the "critique" play was that an artist, fully aware of the possibilities for creation within his grasp, was not to be thwarted by pressures from any quarter. This attitude would carry him through a long fight over his *Tartuffe*, in which the support of Louis XIV was moral if not always tangible. Royal favor was most essential for the innovating writer, and this was fostered in *L'Impromptu de Versailles*.

Before the august patron at Versailles there was simulated a rehearsal of a comedy to be presented to the king, and this scheme permitted a discussion of principles of drama while Molière gave an example of theatrical skill. This may be termed self-conscious theater and can be found in the works of writers from Corneille and Shakespeare to Pirandello and Anouilh.[4] The plan of the "play-within-the play" permits exploration of the nature of drama even as a play is being given, and, in some ways, *L'Impromptu* is as intense an expression of the writer's position as we possess. The polemic intent is clear but the focus is on theater, and the presence of the author-director playing a stage version of himself suggests that we may believe what he utters about stage theory and practice. The troupe's leader coaches his actors in an atmosphere of carefully contrived informality, for the curtain has seemingly risen surreptitiously and revealed the company in the throes of trying to devise a comedy without time for good preparation. The players are playing themselves attempting to be good players; the situation is delightfully stagy. The glimpse behind the curtain would appear to destroy stage illusion, but Molière is actually creating a new version of it. As a device for getting an audience to suspend disbelief, it is excellent.

The cast of the characters who are supposed to be in the court entertainment reads like a who's who of the Molièresque world of satire. The troupe's leader is to play a "ridiculous marquis," while others play a poet, a bore, an affected marquise, a prude, a wit, and a coquette. Quite unprepared in their lines, they emerge as La Grange, Du Croisy, Mademoiselle de Brie, and the rest of the company of the fall of 1663. The director exclaims "What strange beasts these actors are to lead!" (scene 1) to give us immediately some sense of his problems. Everyone has an idea for a comedy, but the best one comes from Armande, who proposes the comedy about actors "which you talked about long ago" (scene 1). The temptation to parody rival actors is hardly resistible, so Molière gives a few samples, but the main effort is to create a play featuring the types from *La Critique*. Each character is coached by the director in the manner of playing that he wants to be simple and natural, not inflated in the style of a pompous tragic actor like a Monfleury. The realities of

theatrical production are brought home to us vividly as we see Molière pla-
cating his two leading ladies when they do not like their parts.

In scene 3 of the one-act piece there begins the "play-within-the-play"
proper, really a continuation of the discussion in the salon of Uranie of *La
Critique*. The idea is repeated that the author aims to "depict manners without wanting to touch people," but the main stress is on the theatrical and illusory quality of his art. "All his characters are airy phantoms whom he dresses
up according to his whim to delight the spectators. . . . As the business of
comedy is to represent in general all the faults of man, and principally our
contemporaries, it is impossible for Molière not to hit some individual." The
director steps in to show an actor how to read a line and gives a long speech on
the hypocritical types available for satire. We seem to be hearing already a
speech by Alceste, the misanthropist. Some bitterness is understandable in
the author who was personally attacked by a rival named Boursault in a satirical sketch, so he does not lose a chance for some vengeance.

He struck boldly at his professional and powerful enemies, confident that
the king and the court would support him. He proposed his troupe as chief
purveyors of entertainment for the royal court, and, in the final scene of
L'Impromptu, thanks the king for his kindness in giving a reprieve to the un-
rehearsed troupe this time. There is a strong sense of promise of great delights
to come from this group of players who have just given a demonstration of
virtuosity calling to mind the Italian improvised style. The combined artless-
ness and craft of the production is an excellent example of the theatricality of
a Molière play conceived, perhaps, just as propaganda.

Le Mariage forcé, La Princesse d'Élide

Although it may not have been literally true at all times, the personal taste
and will of Louis XIV were the final arbiters in art as well as in government,
according to the principle of personal rule. Molière did well in seeking the
royal stamp of approval, a factor for success that usually outweighed all others. At the king's command the troupe of Monsieur, the king's brother, performed a farce at the Louvre in January 1664 and *Le Mariage forcé* (The
forced marriage) had the good fortune to be applauded by Louis.

This comedy has aspects reminiscent of the early farces, but it is more of an
experiment in comedy-ballet that profits from the lessons learned in *Les
Fâcheux*. Again the dramatist worked in collaboration with Lully, the court
composer, and the royal ballet master, integrating musical and dance routines
into the body of the play. The king's taste already showed a preference for
musical spectacles, which would be stressed increasingly as the years passed,

and Lully was eager to please the monarch and promote his operas as the court entertainment par excellence. Rivalry with Molière and his comedies would come into the open later, but now mutual assistance was the rule. The comedian and the musician produced a comic ballet that catered to the king's wishes both as spectator and as participant.

The concept of the royal personage as an actor must not be construed as unusual or limited to the Sun King because an elaborately costumed king is the focus of attention whether he is in a ceremony or just in the audience of a play. We observed how Molière utilized this phenomenon in *Les Fâcheux,* but this is just characteristic of a formal royal appearance. When the king plays a role created for him in a fête, however, he deliberately uses theatrical means per se to dramatize himself. A king making an entry into a city under arches and amidst choirs and allegorical figures (a common practice of the Renaissance carried into the seventeenth century) was the chief actor although ostensibly the chief audience. The self-dramatization possible was appealing and useful to Louis, who delighted in taking ballet roles in Molière's entertainments as well as in riding in a Grand Carrousel tournament. In *Le Mariage forcé* the monarch played a Gypsy in a ballet entr'acte, and by his participation he gave complete critical approval.

The central idea, or action, of this comedy is described in the book for the ballet, possibly written by Molière: "As there is nothing in the world as common as marriage, and as it is the thing that men make the biggest fools of themselves over, it is not strange that it should be the subject of most comedies, as well as of ballets, which are mimed comedies. And that is how we got the idea for this masquerade comedy." No claim is made for originality but, rather, for identification with the main current of comic theater. Within the traditional framework, Molière will work his usual unifying magic as once again the familiar Sganarelle emerges from behind the curtains. He is the duped suitor, as expected, yet preserves some of the astuteness of his namesake in *L'École des maris.* Knowledge of a sort is his, for he is a good businessman, but the customary ignorance in matters of love and marriage will be his downfall; the idea of coming to unhappy knowledge despite one's wishes is thematic. We might want to call it a manifestation of fatality that the older man should fall in love with a young girl, although it is more properly termed standard comic fare. Sganarelle moves out of his dull backwater of existence and is swept along helplessly in a swift flow of youthful motion. The penalty for getting out of place in the social system is inevitable in comedy, and we know that Sganarelle will wind up battered and exhausted by a sort of life from which he had properly retired. The title of "The Forced Marriage" contains the thematic idea of energetic activity running away with a man unable to stand the pace, and the fact that the work is conceived as a *comédie-ballet* shows that it is primarily a kinetic structure, that is, movement for its own sake is highlighted by the vigorous dances that whirl around Sganarelle.

The central figure blunders into an engagement beyond his physical means and into dances that mime the same idea. All the while he seeks to know the truth about himself or at least he claims to want this, inquiring of learned scholars whether he is suited to wed a young girl. He wishes only to be encouraged in his folly, of course, and an Aristotelian and a Skeptic deliver themselves of some zany philosophy in this behalf. A witty friend jokingly applauds the scheme of marriage with Dorimène, saying that he "will go masked to honor it better" (scene 1), indicating that in his opinion the whole idea is a grotesque masquerade. While Sganarelle contemplates the joys of marriage, Dorimène tells him flatly that she expects her liberty, both personal and financial. This worries the fellow, who consults the philosophers only to be given a vexingly long spiel of nonsense. The verbal flow, which he cannot stop, parallels the physical flow in which he finds himself floundering. Gypsy fortunetellers only increase his doubts and confusions so that he tells the father of the girl that he is withdrawing from the match. Dorimène's brute of a brother has no intention of letting a rich man escape their control, and poor Sganarelle is obliged to go through with the wedding.

Ballet thus served as a means of expressing the basic idea of the comedy, for the harried Sganarelle was driven about by one dancing group after another. After the second scene he drops into a troubled sleep and sees thoughts of Worry, Jealousy, and Suspicion become allegorical figures in a dance. Clownish figures rise to mock him. In the second ballet routine Louis and noblemen of the court played the Gypsies, and they were followed by a magician and his demons who hounded Sganarelle. Finally, in a fitting climax, he must be led through an exhausting dance to be learned for his marriage celebration. The physically spent figure is spun through Spanish dances, a bizarre charivari, and must then witness his wife in a ballet with four vigorous young lovers. The impression is that of a living tide of energy sweeping the old bridegroom along, and the performance ends on a note of pure movement, license, and revelry. This effect is truly a remarkable reproduction of the most ancient sort of comic performance, the dance in which the Greek satyrs cavorted to celebrate sheer physical vitality.

The young king's taste for sumptuous revels was catered to in unprecedented scale in early May 1664 when some 640 courtiers, entertainers, and artisans participated at Versailles in a week of pageantry called "the Pleasures of the Enchanted Isle."[5] In this lavish "rite of spring" a theme borrowed from the romances of chivalry by Ariosto gave the king a chance to play the role of Roger, a knightly hero. In an open-air setting, spectacles, jousting plays, ballets, and feasts followed each other to the accompaniment of music and the splash of fountains. Scenes of groomed natural beauty joined with elaborate stage sets and machines to frame the events. Roger was supposed to dwell in the palace of an enchantress, ran the scenario, to be held prisoner until a ring symbolizing true love freed him in a manner familiar to readers of legends and fairy tales. The plot was standard in *précieux* novels, but it clearly signified to the court that the liaison of the king with Mlle de La Vallière was being fêted. The monarch was thoughtful enough to indicate that it was supposed to honor his queen, but no one took any stock in this excuse.

The costumes were pseudo-Greek, as was the setting of Molière's "gallant" play for the occasion; the sources were Italian; but the style of the whole show can only be called "Louis XIV" in its elegant heterogeneity. The alexandrine verses, the early baroque music by Lully, the architecture and landscaping of Versailles, and the brilliant gathering of courtiers as spectators and actors, all combined to impress by sheer scope and attention to refined detail. All this was to glorify the world's most powerful mortal. Glorious appearance and illusion were equally as important as great deeds in this world because magnificence was as effective and militant as raw might. The royal playwright had a vital role in this business.

On the first day, after the Seasons had paraded in, mounted on horse, elephant, camel, and bear, Molière, as Pan, delivered a poetic compliment to the queen. The tone of fantasy is well worth noting because on such an occasion of festive ceremony the guiding principle is freedom from harsh realities. In a play written for such a celebration all must seem possible to the mind of the spectator as to the mind of the character. Carnival license is given artistic form, with some hints of crude humor in clown acts but with decorous play prevailing. Thus the noblemen arrayed themselves in armor and tilted at rings and dummies, allowing themselves a certain freedom from their ordinary lives. The idea is thematic for a fête and is preserved in *La Princesse d'Élide,* which features a royal assemblage of the same sort.

The "gallant" comedy was given on the second day of the celebration, and it was billed as such, with note of the "music and ballet entrées" that augmented it. At first glance one might assume that the principles of *Les Fâcheux* would be visible in another entertainment for royalty, but the style of the earlier play and its mention of the king were appropriate for a royal visit or entry, whereas *La Princesse* has an atmosphere of fête established by the preceding events. The week-long activities in which Louis was the main actor were to continue and give him the chance to get a fanciful, if symbolic, role. Molière's job was to preserve the proper tone of infinite fanciful possibilities, which were suggested in the fête by technical devices such as floats with ice palaces and fountains. He saw fit to place himself in a clown's role as a sleepy huntsman who is roused for a royal hunt; then he became a buffoon named Moron, a sort of jester at a Greek court. Moron gives a comic version of the *précieux* gallantries of his master, but the main focus in *La Princesse* is upon a stage projection to the principles of elegant romance. All the precious conventions come to life in the love story of the prince and princess who are led to admit at last their enslavement by a love that they tried to deny. The wonders of love's enchantments are its subject.

The *préciosité* of Molière's play was pointed out by a scholar some years ago, but modern studies of this cultural current have shown how closely the work adheres to form drawn from novels.[6] The "conceits" such as antithesis of love's slavery and freedom, existence in self and in the beloved, or the interplay of truth and pretense are carefully exploited in *La Princesse*. It is an error to assume, however, that the author wanted to create just another precious drama, and we should see that he is taking advantage of a ready-made set of conventions of fancy in order to produce a play that has a tone of liberation of the imagination and a dreamlike quality. When the prince, Euryale, confesses that love has made him "subject to its laws" (1.1), we know what the code of behavior is to be. In a speech directed toward Louis the prince's aged tutor says, "Tenderness of heart is a great sign that one can expect all things in a prince of your age when one sees that his soul is capable of love" (1.1). Nevertheless, Euryale languishes "with an incurable wound" (1.1), indicative of the simultaneous power of love to harm and to elevate. The standard ideas of love and the words suited to their expression are brought forth, but the play's elements of royal fête really claim our attention. A chariot race is part of a series of regal festivities held at the court of Elis, and the hunt, the dances, and the songs also echo the activities at Versailles. Thus, Molière has reinforced the "Pleasures of the Enchanted Isle" by a fête-within-a-fête. The alert and sure touch of a master dramatist is evident as he adapts himself readily to the situation; *La Princesse d'Élide* capably joins together magnificence of display, festival occasion, and conventional *galanterie*. Like the whole royal celebration, it expresses both a liberation of the senses within a carefully limited field of play and an awareness of the power of passion over even a monarch. "All things" become possible provided one is "subject to its laws."

There was a duty to be done by the court dramatist, and Molière measured up to the task, although the dangers to his position as an original creator of theater were great in the service of a king who reveled in sheer spectacle. Molière's best interests were served by display of his plays in his new style, and the presentation of *Le Tartuffe* at Versailles and his long defense of it were part of a struggle to get recognition of the new art he was creating.

Chapter Five
Some Power
Structures Observed

Le Tartuffe

The shift from a comedy such as *La Princesse d'Élide* to one of quite serious content, *Le Tartuffe*, for a second featured play at the royal fête, may strike us as odd, yet the themes are not too different. Both comedies deal with illusions about love and power, and both show us figures consciously playing roles in situations created by fancy. *Le Tartuffe* treats these ideas and actions against a background of contemporary reality, however, and the result is a theatrical masterpiece.

On the sixth day of "The Pleasures of the Enchanted Isle" Molière presented three acts of *Le Tartuffe, ou l'imposteur* (*Tartuffe, or the Impostor*) with the rather unlikely seeming subject of abuse of religious zeal by a confidence man and his victim.[1] This play had been occupying the attention of the author so fully that he had managed to put into verse only the first scene of *La Princesse*, but Louis had excused this omission because of the merits of *Tartuffe*. He had heard a reading of the new work in April 1664, according to the troupe's register kept by La Grange, and must have approved its performance at the fête, an ideal setting in which Molière might win support of the courtiers as well as of the king. He would need such support in view of the inevitable opposition to the comedy by churchmen and a powerful faction of laymen who found the comedian's piety very suspect. The controversy started by *L'École des femmes* would be revived and embittered by a comedy that appeared to mock religion. To understand the violent reaction to *Tartuffe*, we must look briefly at the place of church and faith in the intellectual, cultural, and political life of the times because they had important functions beyond religious and moral guidance. Molière had aimed at human failings and had hit a great power structure.

The fact that the play treated credulity and abuse of faith was beside the point when Molière's contemporaries were all passionately involved in controversies on the nature of religion and were divided into doctrinal factions.

Each might feel that his position was parodied in *Tartuffe* in some manner, and the major Catholic lay brotherhood felt most wronged and most obliged to act to get the play banned. Fakery on the part of a lay director of conscience was no hypothetical case in this period, no matter how unlikely the matter might seem to us three hundred years later, for such figures existed in an era that took its religious forms seriously. We must recall that France had just barely emerged from a time of general slaughter in the name of piety.

Imperfectly and precariously united in a political sense, despite the imposing facade of the monarchy, the French were deeply split in matters of faith after long years of war between Catholics and Protestants. The amnesty and tolerance extended to the Huguenots in the first part of the seventeenth century was jeopardized by the warfare of the "Frondes" when religious groups sided with the various noblemen struggling for power. The increasing pressure upon all segments of society to conform and to serve a central government being built by Cardinal Richelieu and developed by Louis XIV found little room for independent thinking on the part of anyone, but the main danger to national unity was believed to lie in heresy. Religion and politics were inextricably bound together. The official policy of tolerance set forth in the Edict of Nantes under Henri IV became more and more disregarded, as Protestants were persecuted, suppressed, and exiled, until Louis XIV finally abandoned any pretense at allowing religious liberty and revoked the edict in 1685.

In addition to this great split there was vigorous dissension within the Catholic Church over principles and forms of worship. The puritanical sect of Jansenists opposed what they held to be moral laxity in Jesuit practices, and this controversy had been given a lively public airing in the witty *Provincial Letters* (1656–57) by Blaise Pascal. The literate world of court and city in 1664 was eager to approve or decry further discussion of religious issues, but the comic stage was not considered as appropriate a rostrum as the letters. Molière was in a delicate area both as to subject and form. The French Catholic church was further subjected to quarrels over the role of mysticism in faith, upheld by "Quietism," and over the degree of independence that the Gallican church should enjoy from Rome. Agnostic, free-thinking ideas were very much present, although carefully screened for fear of the real possibility of execution for heresy.

The church was fully supported by the state, and vice versa, so that a clever man like Richelieu could pursue interlocking careers in the church hierarchy and government. One path to temporal power was ecclesiastical, not only over the spirits of men but in the political and social sense. Seldom has there been a period when all aspects of a culture were so ruthlessly centralized and that yet produced true beauty of artistic creation and true progress in intellectual matters. The happy chance of the existence of men of genius like Molière, Corneille, and Racine may explain some of this phenomenon, but the combined forces of church and state must be credited with providing magnificent patronage and great sympathy for creativity that did not offer direct threat to the total structure. To say that Molière had any direct intention of speaking out against the structure of the world in which he was just beginning to function fully is to misunderstand his situation. The theatrical creator needed material circumstances that would give him full rein; to criticize government or the church united with it would destroy all that he worked to build. But when a subject involving human delusions based on perversion of faith occurred to him, he may well have felt that the lesson of false piety was for the public good. The artist had a serious role as instructor of the people, this age believed, and Molière's experiments in theater had led him to an awareness of how much comedy could say that was useful as well as amusing.

There were plentiful examples of moral tales about false piety, and actual cases of crimes hidden behind such a front. The author quite possibly had in mind a case of a layman, Charpy de Sainte-Croix, who took advantage of the faith of his patron to seduce the man's wife. The basic scheme of the "deceiver deceived" that was common in farce could be developed from such a situation, the dramatist perceived, if the seducer were duped and caught by justice. Themes of knowledge and blind ignorance, reality and appearances, love and its distortions—all suggested themselves to the comic playwright. The material for *Tartuffe* was artistically and dramatically excellent, popularly appealing, and psychologically fascinating, so there is small wonder that Molière threw himself into the project of bringing it to the stage. The subject was controversial in 1664, and it is no less interesting and stimulating at present because we cannot see or read the work without sensing the truth of its presentation of the effects of belief, love, lust, and power on the human creature.

The peculiar mixture of religion and temporal power that existed in Molière's time at once furnished him this material and the means by which his enemies would get his play prohibited. Even before the Versailles performance, the opposition was bringing pressure to bear upon Louis to keep the comedy from the public, and, failing in this, they redoubled their efforts to suppress it. The archbishop of Paris warned the king of the "bad effects" of *Tartuffe,* and the queen mother expressed her dismay. With such voices raised against the comedy, it suffered legal sanctions against its being presented, although private readings of the work were given by Molière as part of his campaign to get it before the public. La Grange, the troupe's recorder, says that the comedy was performed in September 1664, and a five-act version was presented in November of the following year, but it was not until 1669 that the present form of the play in five acts was offered on stage and in published version. In order to accomplish this in the face of hard opposition Molière fought long and skillfully, seeking powerful ears into which to read his play and suggest his arguments. The ultimate triumph he sought was not over religious groups per se but rather over pressure groups that calumniated him as an artist and as a man. Professional success and personal reputation were at stake. An attempt to present *Tartuffe* in 1667 caused the Palais-Royal theater to be closed, and, because Louis was off for eighteen months of military operations, the playwright could not make a direct appeal to his sympathetic patron. When the king returned and rescinded the closing of the theater, all Paris lined up for tickets to the controversial comedy, pouring a large sum into the troupe's treasury for forty-five city performances and five private ones. The author had accomplished a certain self-justification, and the director had fulfilled his obligation to his players to get a hit on the boards. In preserving his *Tartuffe* from oblivion, Molière gave the world a work that showed a new direction in comedy.

The material that he dealt with was not all original, it must be said, for Italian and Spanish sources suggest themselves. The standard editions of the play indicate these.[2] What he added was the remarkable psychological validity of the forces in the play projected through original theatrical techniques blending the old and the new. The title character of Tartuffe apparently takes his name from the Italian for truffle, and a certain sense of deception is in the verb *truffer* according to H. G. Hall.[3] This critic observes that the sound of the name must have been important to Molière because he called the character "Panulphe" in the abortive 1667 attempt to give the play. It was good box office, at any rate, for one name to suggest the other. In analyzing the play, we find that it uses and expands situations and characters familiar to us from the earlier comedies and that it stands as a logical development in depth and skill. The complexity of the motives and the behavior of Tartuffe and his patron Orgon moves far beyond that of Arnolphe of *L'École des femmes,* the most significantly ambiguous of the author's figures. The basically clownish quality of a situation of "deceiver deceived" is not absent from *Tartuffe,* but it is a framework for an examination of very complicated motives and their effects.

French theater had had "false" types since medieval farce, but Molière was the first author to conceive of a character like Orgon, the self-deceiving dupe whose motives are really ugly, or Tartuffe, the wily masker who chooses to drop his mask to satisfy his lust. These are not wholly humorous characters, it is evident, yet they function in the way that farce figures do, that is, as dramatic caricatures. *Tartuffe* thus remains in comic or low mode even as its meanings become serious or grim. The vehicle for such characters is largely a familiar plot with tyrannical father opposing the marriage of his daughter to the man she loves. The routine of the eavesdropper under the table is hardly proper to elevated drama, and an outspoken servant girl adds earthy wit as she aids her mistress to wed her love. A lovers' quarrel in the second act seems to have been added as a filler, or it at least is transplanted from *Le Dépit amoureux* to lighten the tone of the play. The resultant total impression is one of the surprising blending of seemingly disparate elements such as physical humor, psychological realism, and conventional form and diction. Boileau, the leading critic of the day, was sympathetic to the author yet disturbed by the odd combination of crude farce and elevated social satire. This style was not to be found in any standard text on drama such as Aristotle's *Poetics*. The very nonconformity, of course, was the reason for Molière's progress in theatrical invention, and the same phenomenon can be observed in his colleagues in tragedy. Imitation of ancient examples was a principle honored in theory but flouted in practice. So long as the playwright remained within comprehensible boundaries of techniques and expression, his audience was willing to applaud innovation.

Classification as to regular genre appears to be of no great aid in analysis of a play like *Tartuffe,* and it is of more help to try to perceive what thematic ideas are expressed and how. These are set forth, varied, repeated, and even inverted by means of the words and the miming of the players. We are trying to understand just how a stage illusion is created that does not mirror actual life but uses obviously exaggerated and stagy elements to suggest patterns of human behavior. Tartuffe is thus not just a stage imitation of a religious hypocrite of 1664 but instead is a stage caricature of certain traits that are more clear to us as we learn a bit about religion in that period. Tartuffe's primary meaning is as a self-contained dramatic persona with absurdly contrasting characteristics, an ascetic who is fat and lustful. The same remarks apply to the other characters and to the parts of the plot that seem to reflect faithfully contemporary life because realistic elements immediately take on a stylized effect. By the use of exaggerated, theatrical effects the playwright imparts to us a knowledge that he is dealing with general matters of belief, trust, and love.

The idea of belief is paramount in *Tartuffe* and expressed through many parts of the play, although not as religious belief because the stress in the central figure is upon his belief in himself and in his power over others. Similarly, in Orgon belief is not in the religious faith but in a perverted system of dogma that will make him triumph over his family while gaining salvation. Orgon and his mother, Mme Pernelle, want to believe in Tartuffe because he nourishes their pet notion and desires, while the rest of the characters protest against belief that has degenerated into credulity. The facts of Tartuffe's hypocrisy are evident, but Orgon feeds his mind on fantasy and establishes his own faith in which all doubters are infidels and damned. He treats his family like an inquisitor and declares that for his belief he would see them perish like heretics. The ruling figure who pursues an existence in a world of illusion to which he tries to bend all reality is characteristic of Molière's major comedies.

The thematic ideas turning about the axis of belief become more complicated as we observe that the psychology of the situation is that of the "confidence game," the idea that one may reap great rewards (here it is salvation) for belief and an outlay of cash. Belief must be expressed to the confidence man by some tangible means, so that the dupe establishes himself as purely credulous when he gives something for nothing. Tartuffe and his victim need each other in a sort of symbiosis of cupidity. The concomitant faking of belief by the agent is imposture and hypocrisy, and thus the subtitle of "the imposter" for which we might substitute "the confidence man." The word *confidence* is most useful to suggest the basic action of the comedy in which Tartuffe is confided in by Orgon, who in turn feels confident. Trust is misplaced and abused until it becomes distrust and then disbelief. But before such a denouement of shattering of confidence on both sides there must be established an impression of confident belief in Tartuffe and Orgon. Each proceeds with utter trust in his own judgment and control of his life, all the while unknowingly committing part of this control to the other as a system of mutual confidence is created. The play turns upon the relationships between these two figures, and thus we may call it a play of nexus, a drama of a causal link of belief and confidence.

The use of the words "confidence game" also reminds us of the playwright's perception of the game playing that goes on in human contacts and how it may serve as the structure for a comedy. We recall how *Les Fâcheux* was built on this basis. In the case of Tartuffe we see a masker and poseur of great skill acting out a role designed to dupe others and to give him power over them. The title figure is a supple and strong player in the sparring for advantage that goes on within the family, able to accept small losses while concentrating upon the ultimate goal of control of a fortune. The play shows us the skirmishes of a group of people tightly bound to each other, all disguising true feelings and intentions beneath the exteriors conventionally required for their roles. As the struggle within Orgon's home becomes more intense, the occasional slight dropping of a mask shows us the seriousness of the game being played. The sexual advances by Tartuffe toward his host's wife are a remarkable example. Elmire rapidly makes adjustments in her mask with Tartuffe to play for advantage, suggesting that an affair would not be impossible. The competitive game for the confidence of Orgon is being played in dead earnest beneath the masking that the audience finds so amusing. The tension of a "no win" situation emerges despite the farcical apparatus of placing Orgon under the table to overhear the courting of Elmire by Tartuffe. The power struggle is only intensified.

Tartuffe is not only the consummate masker but also a competitor who does his best to manipulate the other players. Moreover, he is a gambler who engages in a great game of chance because the outcome of his pursuit of power and fortune ultimately lies in factors beyond his control. He gambles upon the unending credulity of Orgon and his own ability to stay ahead of the law. But for the ending, when the king's justice descends upon him like fate, he would emerge the victor in the game. The last scene is not merely a deus ex machina but a reminder that the most adept players in the game for power are subject to chance or destiny. Translating these observations to the mode of tragedy is not difficult, and the somber cast of *Tartuffe* becomes more understandable. A tragic hero gambles for the highest stakes and loses. Tartuffe is a sort of grotesque caricature of this hero who plays within the social world of comedy, operating as a confidence man. It will be helpful to keep in mind this remarkable character as we come to what Molière makes of the Don Juan figure in his version of the legend, his next play.

A confidence game involves play with belief and also with a special type of love, that between the gullible victim and the deceiver, Orgon and Tartuffe. The peculiar nature of love in Orgon makes Arnolphe (*L'École des femmes*) seem simple in comparison because the former combines a love of God, love of Tartuffe, and love of self in such a way as to suggest that he is acting in fear and hatred. What he chooses to call Christian love leads him to punish his family and himself, and all this is done through the agency of Tartuffe. Molière depicts a sturdy bourgeois who becomes infatuated with religious mysticism and its promise of sure salvation for his soul, but this conflicts with demands for love in his temporal life by his wife and children. The selfish side of his nature finds an excuse for denying affection and material support to them and for giving these to Tartuffe in the name of God. Tartuffe is evidently the object of his warm feelings because he is a means of indulging tastes that suggest the sadistic, even masochistic. Religion is a ready-made justification for his behavior, and Tartuffe is a living embodiment of the principles according to which he acts. Self-love by Orgon is termed love of God and is directed toward the divinity through a surrogate. The scheme is heavily drawn by the author who shows us Orgon loading gifts and favors upon the sort of alter ego who is his means of evading aspects of life that he wants to deny. If the situation were one of a middle-aged man abandoning wife and family for a young mistress, it would be quite common and comprehensible, with obvious motives of denial of age and search for lost youth. But when the love is fixed upon a Tartuffe with an avowed object of escape from the material world of flesh into a realm of mysticism, then the love expressed in this play has some murky depths.[4]

The other member of the central linked pair is equally interesting. Tartuffe in some ways parallels Orgon, for as Orgon is the "would-be mystic," Tartuffe is the "would-be seducer." The use of spiritual love to deny the flesh by Orgon is balanced by a hardly concealed eagerness in Tartuffe for the pleasures of the flesh with Orgon's wife. The confidence man intends to seduce Elmire, his patron's wife, and his sensual proclivities are seen in his crude eyeing of the bosom of the maid as he rebukes her for immodesty. He plans prudently to combine pleasure and profit by marrying Orgon's daughter for her beauty and her large dowry. The real similarity of the two main characters is their great self-love, however, for Tartuffe is oblivious to the bad impression he makes on all the feminine characters, being supremely confident in his egotism. (We cannot include the deluded Mme Pernelle because she has a function of echoing her son. The old woman is well beyond attracting Tartuffe, and the role was taken by a man.) He is shown as plump, gluttonous, and lecherous, hardly a dashing figure to play the Don Juan part that he envisions for himself. The seed of his destruction is in this sensuality that will cause him to drop his mask of puritanism. The spiritual love relationship with Orgon is thus Tartuffe's way to physical triumphs in sex and in control over the lives and fortunes of others. In the idea of power over others Tartuffe and Orgon join hands and work with similar aims, each one cherishing the other because he offers a means to rule. Their feelings are like those of conspirators cooperating yet planning selfish ends.

Normal and healthy forms of love abound in the comedy to reinforce our impression of the peculiarities of the central characters. The daughter, Mariane, and her suitor pursue the typical romance of comedy and are betrothed at the end, but the picture of family love of mother, sister, and brother for one another and for Orgon is set against the ugly distortions. Such a family situation is treated with a depth of feeling and realism not found before in French theater, and this alone would make the play noteworthy. The middle-class interior has a certain warmth and natural quality despite the obvious conventions observed; the wifely concern and impetuous loyalty of the son emerge despite the alexandrines of their speeches. The reactions of the family to the real threat of destruction naturally create some dramatic interest and tension, even though we know that a proper comic ending will come.

Indeed, we must not forget that comedy traditionally affirms such an ending of love's triumph as part of its values. This genre has as a regular tenet the social goodness and health of mankind, and this is a value that cannot brook distortions and perversions of love, sex, and procreation for alien purposes like those of Tartuffe and Orgon. Selfishness, hatred, and lust that seek to find ways to command are the great enemies in comedy's world, and Molière moves from merely hinting at them, as he did in early plays, to presenting them boldly. It turned out that the most glaring case of the enemy in action was to be found in the social manifestations of religious faith, or rather the use of the externals of piety to exert political and personal power. The play dwells upon the warping of the principle of love, both Christian and socio-comic, in a household that is a microcosm of society. With no intention of ir-reverence, we might say that the informing idea or action of the comedy is "to love thy neighbor" and how not to. The strength of this play becomes evident, as does the size of the wrath of ecclesiastical circles in 1664.

The opening scene emphasizes the rupture within what should be a loving family group as Elmire and the son and daughter, Damis and Mariane, accompanied by Orgon's reasonable brother, Cléante, argue about Tartuffe with Mme Pernelle. The old mother-in-law is on her way out, according to the speeches. Elmire: "You are walking so fast that I can hardly follow you" (1.1). Stage directions are contained within the lines themselves, but the first impression is one of great naturalness. A very contrived arrangement of speeches ensues promptly, however, to remind us of the nature of this sort of play. Each character remonstrates ineffectually in turn with Mme Pernelle who cuts each one off with a withering comment, limiting them to one syllable of speech less at each exchange. The battle lines are clearly drawn as Damis mentions "your Monsieur Tartuffe" to his grandmother and gets the reply, "He is a worthy man to whom you must listen, and I can't bear to hear a fool like you criticize him" (1.1). The young man sets forth a theme by complaining that Tartuffe usurps tyrannical power in the family, and the rest of the scene illuminates the character of this figure. By the time Tartuffe makes his entrance in the third act he is so well known to us by reputation that the appearance is an exciting moment. According to the maid, Dorine, he "controls everything" and has made himself "master in the house" (1.1). "Hypocrisy" is her sharp analysis of his game, nor does she fail to see that he is coveting Elmire: "I believe he's jealous of Madame" (1.1).

A variation on the discussion of personal integrity and its counterfeit is in-

troduced as Mme Pernelle criticizes what she thinks is shameless social freedom in Elmire. Cléante defends her right to visit friends and to move in polite
circles despite any gossip about her. Dorine then describes a prying and slan-
derous couple who find fault with everyone to cover their own indiscretions.
The thematic idea of hypocrisy and good faith in matters of love and sex is
thus brought out early in the comedy in the discussion of a wife's fidelity and
its appearances in the eyes of others. The scene in which Tartuffe makes his
proposition to Elmire is being prepared. The foreshadowing of things to
come is neatly accomplished also by a suggestion that physical violence accompanies an assertion of power. Mme Pernelle slaps her servant and rudely
shakes off the family, and this farcical version of violence will be followed by
scenes of rage on the part of Orgon. Damis is like his father in his impetuous
anger. It is to be remembered that the most violent acts are done in the name
of persuading people to piety and that Tartuffe will eventually offer a genuine physical threat to everyone. The containment of the threat masked under
humble pose is the core of the dramatic plot, and this idea of containing
Tartuffe was graphically indicated in early productions of the play in which
the police officer is recorded as limiting the movements of Tartuffe in the last
scene by means of a staff.[5] The stick can turn violence upon him.

An exposition scene of the customary sort occurs as Dorine explains to
Cléante her master's infatuation with his protégé, and we are thus prepared
for Orgon's behavior in scene 4. Elmire and the young people flee at the news
of his return, indicating the fragmenting of the family. The maid relates
Orgon's mad actions: "He calls him brother and loves him in his soul a hundred times more than his mother, son, daughter, or wife. He is his sole confi-
dant and director of his actions. He dotes on him, embraces him, and could
not have, I believe, more tenderness for a woman he loves" (1.2). She sums
up by calling him crazy, and this exaggeration tends to create an impression
of a clownish oaf, a true aspect of the character. Dorine also speaks of
Tartuffe's hypocrisy about women, to lead toward the later scenes.

Scene 4 features a famous example of Molière's effective repetition of a
line with increasingly comic results. Orgon's concern for Tartuffe is con-
trasted with his indifference toward Elmire and the illness she suffered in his
absence, for his only inquiry is "And Tartuffe?" and his only comment "The
poor man!" Dorine depicts the saintly man in heavily sarcastic terms that are
lost on Orgon, who then tries to explain to Cléante the merits of Tartuffe.
"He is a man who,—well, a man,—a man, then" (1.5). The inarticulate
wonder at such a creature is grotesque and revealing of the unreasonable state
of his mind, but this takes on a serious complexion as he states, "I would see
brother, children, mother, and wife die and care no more than that" (1.5), ac-

companying the speech with a disdainful gesture. The words actually para-
phrase Scripture, which then is debased by the snapping of thumbnail on
teeth. The author's prudent regard for criticism by church and lay groups
caused him to include a long argument by Cléante about the need for distin-
guishing real and false piety, a speech that is obvious polemic and not essential to the play, but this is the only place in which adjustment to criticism is
permitted to intrude. By the end of the first act Orgon has been established
not only as a deluded tyrant but as a hypocrite, for he can gloss over a breach
of faith in the matter of not giving Mariane to Valère as was pledged. He
speaks vaguely of "doing Heaven's will" (1.5).

The second act continues the presentation of Orgon's distortion of love as
he insists that Mariane be willing and indeed eager to marry Tartuffe. Parental love seems to lose all meaning here, as it does in the later scene when he
disinherits his son. The announcement of the marriage plans is made only
after Orgon suspiciously looks for eavesdroppers, an action that serves two
dramatic purposes, that of stressing an atmosphere of lack of trust despite all
the talk of faith, that of building toward the eavesdropping scenes to come.
Spying and suspicion are the results of warped beliefs and affections, so these
are important concepts that are acted on in various ways. Orgon is overheard
by Dorine, in spite of his precautions, and she stands behind him and mimes
her horror at his conversation with Mariane. The essence of this talk is that he
expects his daughter not only to appear to love Tartuffe but also to make such
"imposture" real. A violently forced semblance of pious love and belief is
what he requires of himself, of Tartuffe, and now of his family.

With deceit and falsehood the keynotes, the blunt and truthful words of
Dorine are an essential contrast. She tries mocking disbelief, cajolery, and
then sharp argument against her master, pointing to the lack of social status
and wealth of Tartuffe and declaring that such a marriage would force
Mariane to be an unfaithful wife. Such ideas are unavailing against the determination of Orgon, and his description of the joys of marriage with Tartuffe
foreshadows the tone of Tartuffe's speeches, which will mix sensuality and
piety: "He is most favored by Heaven, and it is a wealth second to none. This
marriage will fulfill your desires and will be sugared with sweetness and
pleasure. You will live together in a faithful ardor like two children, like two
turtledoves" (2.2). A bit of clowning on Dorine's part ensues as she talks "to
herself" when forbidden to speak. Her enraged master finally takes a swing at
her, demonstrating that reasonable communication has become impossible
and that violence is his recourse.

Mariane despairingly thinks of suicide while Dorine encourages her to
fight, enumerating the horrors of life in the country as the wife of Tartuffe.

Yet, the girl's notions of proper behavior for a fiancée are limited to precious conventions, no matter how great her wish to escape Tartuffe, and she rejects unmaidenly forwardness. Dorine warns against faintness of heart, saying that this will lead to getting her "Tartuffified" (2.3), her own coined term. Valère enters and the young couple perform a neatly balanced lovers' quarrel in which they manage to work themselves up to a point of parting, only to be brought together by Dorine, who then must urge them to break up the love scene. The carefully organized scene has suggested the formality of dance to many critics, and it indeed shows the great use of stylized elements in the midst of this play with its grave implications. The scene is not introduced as an attractive set piece to enliven the comedy, however, for it emphasizes the extent to which love has been disrupted and thus forms a variation on a basic theme.

Act 3 brings Tartuffe on stage at last, and his hypocrisy is entirely equal to what we have been led to expect. References in his first speech to his hair shirt and his scourge contrast with the self-indulgence that Dorine has described. The action moves rapidly toward his first declaration of love for Elmire, the famous speeches blending gallantry and religious zeal in a way both laughable and revolting. Elmire counters by dealing with him frankly in an attempt to talk him out of marrying Mariane, and this conversation is overheard by Damis. The saintly faker fondles Elmire as he elects to unmask his desires, expressing them with pious words. The perversion of love that he terms "heavenly" to sheer sensuality is of great thematic significance, especially so at this midpoint in the play, its crux and turning point. Once Tartuffe openly reveals his inner self, the means of his defeat are in the hands of Elmire and the family. Good faith and true love are called upon for maximum effort to counter the character who speaks thus: "Ah, for being a devout man I am no less a man, and when one sees your heavenly attractions, one's heart surrenders and does not reason" (3.3). We think of the unreasoning love of Orgon for his holy friend and perceive how Molière constantly works over his themes.

The words of Tartuffe are in part a parody of casuistry that finds ways to excuse moral turpitude by idea juggling. He says that Elmire can trust him, further distorting this concept. When Damis bursts out of hiding he is convinced that the evidence will rid them of Tartuffe, but Orgon shrugs off the report in his complete confidence. The accused Tartuffe is so sure of his power by now that he humbly confesses to his imperfections: "Yes, brother, I am an evil, guilty, wretched sinner filled with iniquity, the greatest rascal ever" (3.6). He can express the literal truth and not be believed by Orgon, the great test of his certain control. The father is so angered at the accusation by Damis that he cuts him off from his inheritance and gives it to Tartuffe. This is capped by Orgon's insistence that Tartuffe frequent Elmire to stop any gossip. We wonder whether the perversion of values can proceed any further, for Orgon seems bound to be the voluntary cuckold as well as the tyrant. A neat reprise of characteristic utterances ends act 3: Tartuffe says, "The will of Heaven be done in all things!" and Orgon, "The poor man!" (3.7).

If this point were the original ending of the three-act version presented by Molière at Versailles, it would certainly form a coherent whole. There has taken place exposition, development, and climax of action based upon a well-defined complex of themes. We do not know whether this was the form of the first *Tartuffe,* and scholars are divided in their opinions on the matter. Some think that the three-act version was intended to constitute a finished play, while others believe that Molière was just sounding out his public and patron with what he had prepared by May 1664. A recent theory propounded by John Cairncross holds that acts 2 and 5 were the late additions, judging by internal evidence.[6] Our present concern, however, is with the existing form and its theatrical excellence, and we may simply note that Molière undoubtedly worked over his comedy to a point where some uneven spots are visible. The slick finish of *Le Misanthrope* is lacking, but this in no sense impairs its effectiveness and strength as theater. The parts all function forcefully to illuminate each other and to focus light upon the central ideas.

Act 4 opens with an almost formal debate between Tartuffe and Cléante, the "reasoner" in the comedy. Recapitulation is thus given, and it is shown again that reason is useless against entrenched smugness and hypocrisy. A sense of desperate acceleration is created by the announcement that Mariane is to wed Tartuffe in the evening, and the efforts to prevent this must be swift and clever. Elmire realizes that Tartuffe must be induced to unmask before Orgon, so she urges her husband to test his faith in Tartuffe and listen to his words to her. Orgon gets beneath the table over which Tartuffe continues to try to seduce Elmire, and this farcical arrangement gives physical embodiment to levels of meaning in the talk. The hidden and the evident constitute a clever pattern in actions and words. Elmire coughs to alert Orgon to the meanings of Tartuffe as she leads him on: "But how can I consent to what you want without offending Heaven, of which you are always speaking?" Tartuffe: "If it is only Heaven which is the obstacle to my desires, doing away with that is a small matter for me, and that should not restrain your heart" (4.5). When he says, "Scandalizing people is what gives offense, and sinning is not sinning if done in silence" (4.5), Elmire pretends to give in and tells him to be sure they are alone. Tartuffe goes to look out the door, then returns, arms extended to embrace her only to find before him his erstwhile "love" in the person of Orgon. The lifting of the veil from the mind of Orgon comes too late, however, for the power of Tartuffe is now legally established over the property of the household. He is literally the master and can afford to drop his pious pose, giving another variation on the theme of the hidden and the revealed. He does not abandon his vocabulary, we note, as he warns that he has what he needs "to confound and punish imposture, to avenge offended Heaven, and to cause repentance in those who talk of making me leave" (4.7). The situation of Orgon has become that of "impostor" as owner of his own home, and he realizes that Tartuffe controls his destiny because he has given him a chest containing some damaging evidence against him. In summation, misdirected trust and love have revealed at last that matters have become so distorted that Orgon has ruined himself and his family. The unwilling coming to harsh knowledge has been observed as a basis of other comedies.

The sudden introduction of a new plot element creates suspense in the final act and permits the defeat of Tartuffe by royal justice at the end, but the main thing to be treated is Orgon's rescue from his unhealthy love and beliefs, and this must be done through a reunion of the family that was broken. The plot is to be resolved, the comic entertainment is to be maintained, and the thematic parts are to be summarized, so Molière deliberately simulates dramatic tension at the start of the act. An impression of danger and urgency is given by Orgon's worry over the papers in the chest, for he explains that they were held for a friend in political trouble. His blanket recriminations against all "holy men" are amusing, nevertheless. Damis arrives, intent upon punishing Tartuffe, but his uncle stops him by saying that they live under a prince who sees justice done. The comic tone is resumed in a scene in which Orgon tries to persuade his mother of Tartuffe's guilt and samples the frustrations of his family. Revelation of truth by actions is another idea repeated here as Mme Pernelle sees the legal officer arrive to order them out of the house that belongs to Tartuffe. Monsieur Loyal is thus the agent of justice that is unjust, the representation of disloyalty and bad faith, as his name ironically suggests. He speaks exactly like a Tartuffe with elaborate politeness and sanctimoniousness.

It now seems that distorted principles will triumph for Tartuffe even though love and trust have returned to the family group, to which Valère brings his added bit of good faith by warning Orgon that his arrest is imminent. Orgon may be saved from his own spiritual folly, but his material situation appears desperate. The villain of the piece returns with an officer to assert his power, and this arrangement is less important for the working out of the plot than for a reprise of the themes of false belief and overconfidence. Trust in his own abilities to control all has led Tartuffe to go to justice and denounce Orgon as a traitor, but the confidence man turns out to be the victim of his own schemes because the law recognizes him as a wanted criminal. A dramatic arrest of Tartuffe shows us the deceiver as the ultimate dupe of himself, and the comedy can end upon a proper note of betrothal of Mariane and Valère.

The denouement is heavily contrived yet so completely appropriate for the purposes of the play that we accept it without worrying about its lack of precise preparation. Thematically and structurally, the final act repeats the idea of the family threatened, and the threat turns out to be its own undoing, just as Tartuffe worked his own downfall in the eyes of Orgon. The perversion of principles of the title character goes full circle and brings evil to him. False love has been unmasked as hatred, misdirected faith has led to punishment and not salvation, and blind confidence has produced disaster. The family unit has been regrouped, as a paternalistic royal power extends its protecting hand to one of society's menaced parts, and the comedy can thus finish with a stress upon a higher and greater structure of power that it is the playwright's duty and pleasure to uphold. Cléante holds back his brother who wants to take revenge upon Tartuffe:

> Stop, brother, do not descend to such indignity. Let the wretch go to his evil fate, and do not be part of the remorse which is overpowering him. Rather wish that his heart may return to virtue and mend its ways while he comes to hate his vice. May the great Prince temper his justice while you go on your knees to give thanks for such generous treatment.

ORGON: Yes, that is right. Let us go to his feet with joy to praise his goodness which his heart extends to us. Then, having performed some of this duty, we shall have to provide for the needs of another duty and for Valère crown with marriage the devotion of a noble and sincere lover. (5.7)

Within the sheltering limits of a healthy social convention and organization, sincere love is rewarded and the distorted form is condemned.

This analysis has been rather long, not in an attempt to be exhaustive in pointing out themes and their expressions but to show how thoroughly the author controlled a unified theatrical work. Other ideas will occur to the reader of *Tartuffe,* but all will be found woven into an integral theatrical pattern. It may be observed how the comedy fuses together into a new type of creation elements from the traditional farce, conventionalized playing, and a grave moral problem. Molière managed to offer a study of the abuse of power in the name of religion, a matter seemingly requiring a tragic dramatic treatment, in standard comic entertainment. He mixed psychological realism, a certain illusion of contemporary reality, and familiar comic routines and techniques. In a word, he was inventive. Unfortunately, all of his public was not ready to welcome theatrical invention that overstepped its bounds of subject matter. Molière not only had a fight on his hands but also a lack of a new hit for his troupe, so he endeavored to remedy both situations with typical creative industry and wrote a new play. In his *Dom Juan* we suspect that he intended to preserve some of the achievements of *Tartuffe* while seeming to move toward theater of spectacle in which latent ideas are less likely to offend. He may have figured to appear to deal in fantasy while holding his ground on the principles of comic theater enunciated by *Tartuffe*.

Dom Juan

The misfortune of Molière in 1664 was to have on his hands an artistic triumph that he could not get on stage. His troupe had the opportunity to offer in June the first tragedy of a young author who showed much promise, Jean Racine, but what Molière really wanted was some vehicle to embody the new concepts of comedy that he had evolved. He turned to what seemed to be a certain box-office success, the Don Juan material, because it gave him a chance to work with the ideas and techniques that had led him to compose *Tartuffe*. The resulting comedy, *Dom Juan, ou le festin de pierre* (Don Juan, or the stone banquet) came to the stage in early 1665, bearing characteristics that in part require little explanation, like the character of the legendary seducer, but also provide some critical enigmas.

This play is the most challenging of all to interpret. We must assign it a post of importance in the development of his theater, and yet we find critical opinion undecided as to what it signifies as a work in itself.[7] Our aim will be to stress its special logic and coherence, qualities that have been observed in Molière's previous plays and that the skill of a practiced dramatist would not easily permit to escape him at this stage in his career. The possible philosophical implications of the work perhaps tend to obscure analysis of the great theatricality in the inventive joining together of some hackneyed material into an original comedy. When Molière takes traditional material and gives it a fresh orientation, he creates a play that is both about and an example of theatrical illusion, that is realistic yet fanciful in its satire, that shows a dynamic hero often inactive, and that thrives on its paradoxes. Its unity depends upon the merging of contradictory elements such as the power of a tyrant and his utter dependence upon the victims.

The fact that *Dom Juan* is written in prose testifies to its hasty composi-

76

MOLIÈRE, UPDATED EDITION

tion, as it seems that the playwright would regularly block out a play in prose and then versify. The work that was receiving most of his attention of this sort was *Le Misanthrope,* a major effort and one that he did not want to offer up half finished to a critical public. The unevenness of tone and the seemingly disordered assembling of parts of *Dom Juan* are frequently taken to be sufficient reason for condemning the whole comedy as unworthy of the master, but, when he was intent upon writing a certain hit, the incorporation of traditional scenes was obligatory. The audience would not have like a Don Juan who did not bid a moving statue to dinner or disappear in hellfire. Not long before the authors Dorimond and Villiers had each presented a seriocomic version of the Don Juan story, and these successful works must have been fresh on Molière's mind, more so than the earlier Italian and Spanish treatments of the legend. He adapted freely and rapidly, yet the looked-for success was impeded by the same groups of people who had fought against *Tartuffe*—the church and lay factions who discovered impiety in the new play as they had in the previous one and who worked to get it banned. The allegedly atheistic work delighted the public from February until Easter but then disappeared from the boards in its original form.

The struggle going on behind the scenes in high circles may be understood by the fact that Louis saw fit to name Molière's players the royal troupe in this year, while the pious *cabale* managed to have its way with the work on which the author was counting for practical success. A secret order forced withdrawal of *Dom Juan,* and cuts and alterations of lines failed to placate the opposition, who would accept in no shape a comedy that dealt with religion. In 1677, after the death of Molière, Thomas Corneille was commissioned to rewrite the comedy in acceptable form, and this was produced until 1847 at the Comédie-Française when chance discovery of the author's first version restored it belatedly to the repertory.

Those who opposed *Dom Juan* as a continuation of the offensive thinking of *Tartuffe* were indeed correct in perceiving similarities, but they were dealing only in matters of irreverence and immorality. The underlying similarity was not so much in subject matter of this sort, although it is certainly present, but more in Molière's repetition of a theme of abuse of power by an egoist intent upon shaping the world to his personal illusions. Love is again thematic, particularly the self-love and lust found in *Tartuffe*. Once more society, conventionalized yet real in the implications of such conventions, is the setting and the object of the actions of the tyrant. A higher power steps in at the end to set things right in a world of people victimized by a violent and hypocritical usurper of control. The pattern beneath a seeming patchwork of scenes is clear: Molière is experimenting with another theatrical scheme for expressing much of the same complex of themes that he had put into his *Tartuffe*.

Some of the confusion about what he was struggling to say in *Dom Juan* comes from the assumption that it was all philosophical, a declaration of the rights of the individual to be free of tyranny of any sort. But the author was meeting a professional challenge, not an ideological one, and he believed that he could amplify comedy as a means of considering powerful threats to social sanity. His problem was a matter of proving the capabilities of an art form, which had heretofore been held low in esteem, to express elevated ideas, all without abandoning its essential characteristics. Therefore, he resumed his treatment of the same sort of themes and showed that this could be done even by employing techniques of the theater of fantasy and illusion. Spectacle and stage effects thus come to serve the purposes of lofty drama with psychological realism and truth. This is the core of the paradox of *Dom Juan,* one that projects such an aura of intellectual and artistic ambiguity that criticism finds itself groping for a sure position for analysis.

The interplay between themes of illusion of power and techniques that exploit the power of illusion forms a brilliant piece of playmaking and is undoubtedly the most "modern" of Molière's works. The notion of using the antirealistic to produce effects more real than realism seems to have been understood long before Brecht. Molière's creation may be called baroque in the best sense of the word, or we may just say that his theatrical experience in this period led him to think along such lines when he was faced with a great professional problem. To descend to purely realistic drama would be an abandonment of what he knew made the most effective theater, yet to produce spectacle for its own sake would give the theater of court and city over to the devisers of Italianate opera. He made the greatest effort for compromise and survival as a practitioner of theater, but he got little chance to be judged as such. His poetic and dramatic brilliance could not shine through the charges of impiety and free-thinking. What might have been a guide for the development of a new style of theater was smothered for ideological reasons, and theater broke down into the divisions Molière foresaw, destined to reach sterile ends. *Dom Juan* had a cometlike career, a brief flash of brilliance that portended something not understood, but was destined to come again. The intellectual content is less philosophical and moral than it is theatrical, and this is a key to our understanding of the play.

The legendary material that Molière employed might have been sorted out for significant episodes suitable for unified dramatic treatment, one could complain, for *Dom Juan* seems to range over a broad area of action as well as to disregard unity of setting. The presence of the Don is often the only unifying link between scenes. What was gained through the use of a bourgeois household for the setting of *Tartuffe* seems to be abandoned for a fanciful use of rapidly changing setting in a sort of mythical Sicily. The theatrical experiment is dealing with an expanded concept of action, however, and the active, restless nature of the Don is reflected in the constant movement toward new worlds to conquer. His downfall is foreshadowed when he becomes sedentary at the end of the play, and in this was the author works with the relationships of psychological or dramatic action and physical activity.[8] Don Juan is the constant focus of the play, and Molière has made him into a noble and self-contained Tartuffe who needs no aid from an established canon of belief to rule the lives of others. Self-confidence and self-assertion are carried to the ultimate in this comic character, and it would appear possible to say that Molière at least in this case has constructed a real "comedy of character." But is the play just a series of scenes designed to paint a psychological portrait? I aim to show that it is more than that, since much of its meaning lies in its theatrical structure as expressive of its themes. Let us look briefly first at the character of the Don, some of Molière's models, and his plot.

"A great lord who is an evil man" is the servant Sganarelle's definition of his master, and he thus sums up, in the first scene, a number of important aspects of the character. Power is given to the Don by birth, wealth, and position, and this power is used for seduction, fraud, and corruption. The traditional figure of the wholesale seducer of women becomes a complex, self-seeking libertine who exploits everyone around him for his immoral ends. *Libertin* implies "free-thinker" in religion, and there is no doubt that the Don's atheism and hypocrisy are intended to continue the treatment of these themes begun in *Tartuffe*. For an author eager for certain success, it would seem odd to court disaster by touching upon the very matters that brought about the banning of the earlier work, but Molière may have felt that he had the king's ear and that the spectacle of an archsinner going in damnation would placate the pious faction. Public approval was probably what Molière wanted most, however, and the fascinating devil of a Don had very fine box-office appeal. A great rascal with sexual attractions was the surface character of Don Juan, but essentially he was useful also to the author in that he permitted an examination of a monstrous ego in action. The egoism was that of a powerful noble who abused his position for any reason, and Molière had had some experience with this sort of individual. The portrait of the Don is based on generalities, at least for the most part, but the early years of Molière's career gave him an example of such a type who used his powers first for, then against, the playwright. His patron, the Prince de Conti, became an implacable enemy, and this case lends credibility to a character whom we may think overdrawn in respect to animus and ego.

The Prince de Conti was Molière's patron in Languedoc in 1653, but this same self-indulgent *frondeur* later turned his sort of capricious exertion of hereditary power to the purposes of the Society of the Holy Sacrament, having become convinced of the sinfulness of his youth. This lay organization was the group that led the fight against Molière's plays, and thus it represented for him the height of intolerant abuse of authority. Not only as a powerful nobleman who took advantage of personal prerogatives but as a disappointed seeker of political position who found a lever for pressure in the church organization did Conti serve as an example for the author. The phenomenon of conversion to faith, faked by Don Juan, was not uncommon or improbable, and it is easy to understand the reactions of a Conti to the comedy. Ramon Fernandez comments, "We may presume without much fear of self-deception that Molière had, in the Prince de Conti, an excellent visible object lesson in the selfsame delusion of power that he was to condemn as long as he lived."[9] The unhealthy and disturbing mixture of the moral and the corrupt that we find in the Don's character is not so strange when we recall the sort of world in which the writer lived, a witness to extremes of violence, persecution, and tyranny and to the illusions of grandeur that men connected with these evils. Religious and political warfare was conducted in the name of the highest ideals, but fear lurked under the assured surface. Heretics continued to burn, courtiers dabbled in satanism in the notorious "Affair of the Poisons,"[10] and Catholics and Protestants killed each other. Extremes of thought and behavior characterized the age in which so much emphasis was placed upon reason and decorum, and it was the basic situation that the comic playwright found begging for comment and satire in his theater. The theatrical possibilities of a Don Juan type in contemporary life were irresistible, even as his potential for political and practical trouble must have been inescapably clear to Molière.

In general, *Dom Juan* is based upon the title figure who is accompanied by a constant attendant, a sort of Sancho Panza to his Quixote, as they roam about. Again the playwright uses a scheme of linking or nexus, but the interdependence of the two figures is decidedly different from that in *Tartuffe,* although important as an expression of the one of the play's themes. Sganarelle (the familiar name once more) is rather clownish, as we must expect, yet he has the sharpness of some of his predecessors and enough knowledge to give real bite to his remarks. As a stock character, Sganarelle sets basic comic tone, opening and closing the comedy and illuminating the character of the Don. At the start, he tells the servant of the Don's wife that his master is setting off on another amatory voyage of exploration, for he is incapable of satisfaction with one woman. "He marries all about him. Woman, maiden, housewife, peasant, nothing is too hot or cold for him; and if I told you the names of all he has married in various places it would be a chapter lasting till evening" (1.1). Fear of the man and his power makes of Sganarelle a willing aide in such doings, he admits. Don Juan enters in scene 2 to comment on his restless desires and his plans to kidnap a young bride from her husband; jealousy of happiness in others makes him "look forward to the pleasure of disturbing their love and breaking up his marriage by which the delicacy of my heart was offended" (1.2). We see that the character is immediately depicted as insatiable in his wish to possess all and to deny love to others. The endless search for such mastery condemns him to wander the earth and end in hell. "The anger of Heaven will strike him down one day" (1.1) has been the correct prediction by his servant.

Doña Elvira comes to plead with the Don, but she is spurned as he addresses her through Sganarelle. He cynically says that his conscience dictates that he should return her to the convent from which he stole her. In the second act he fails in his attempt at kidnapping, suffers shipwreck, and is rescued by a peasant. Pierrot is rewarded by having the nobleman try to seduce his girl Charlotte and her friend Mathurine, and success in this is prevented only by the arrival of news that the brothers of Doña Elvira are after him for vengeance. The next act shows the Don and Sganarelle disguising themselves for flight, discussing belief and credulity as they go. The hero declares that he believes "two and two are four" (3.1) while the principles of faith and reason are given a clownish defense by the valet, who falls flat physically and intellectually. They encounter a poor mendicant who begs alms, and he is vainly tempted to swear by Don Juan who then rewards him with gold "for the love of humanity" (3.2). The brother of Elvira, Don Carlos, is next rescued from robbers by the brave hero, but he does not reveal his identity while promising that the Don will meet Carlos on the field of honor. The series of episodes continues a sort of backtracking through the career of the Don, for he comes upon the tomb of the Commander, whom he had killed. He mocks the pomp of the tomb and the statue of the dead man, invites the statue to dinner, and receives a nod from the "stone guest" for the "stone banquet."

In act 4 his defiance of the supernatural is stressed, foreshadowing his finish in hellfire. The warning from heaven is disregarded as he bilks a merchant out of his money, then mocks the admonitions given by his father. Elvira finds him and arouses desire in him by her tears and simple attire, but her message is another warning of a bad end to come. The statue arrives for dinner and is accepted calmly by the Don, who agrees to go to the Commander's home for dinner the next day. In this act there is a turn of action because Don Juan has ceased his travels and retreated to his own domain where he cannot function as effectively as at large. People and specters from his past come to seek him out fatally. Professor Hubert points out this change from mobility to fixity as a turning point in the play, and it is surely significant.[11]

The last act shows Don Juan retreating into a fixed position of hypocritical piety which he assumes to dupe his father, adopting the "stylish vice" (5.2) to suit his needs also in an interview with Don Carlos. We recall Tartuffe's words as the Don claims to follow the will of heaven in refusing to fight the promised duel. Next arrives a specter of a veiled woman who changes into a "Father Time" figure, then appears as a warning to the sinner, but he is resolute in his disbelief and defiance of the supernatural. Unflinchingly, he accompanies the statue of the Commander off to hell as stage flames envelope him. Sganarelle has predicted this end for his master, yet his thoughts are not on the divine justice but on his unpaid wages: "I'm the only unfortunate one, who, after so many years of service, have no other reward than seeing the impiety of my master punished by the most frightful punishment in the world. My wages! My wages!" (5.6).

The total impact of this series of episodes has been assessed in many ways, and criticism has often found it chiefly episodic. Throughout the play it is evident that moral principles are being exploited, warped, and mocked by Don Juan, and human society seems quite vulnerable to the attack. Love, faith, honor, courage, filial piety—all are distorted or beaten on the Don's terms, nor can we say that these are just social conventions that are being punctured. The mockery of all sorts of human vanity is suggested as thematic by one critic but this may be rather insufficient as a central idea in the comedy.[12] He has also remarked that *Dom Juan* implies a wide range of social criticism and that this effect increases in the later plays of Molière when a title character truly menaces the social structure by turning its conventions against basic human dignity.[13] A Tartuffe or a Don Juan is a genuine threat, to be sure, but society in the comic genre has such a resilient vigor that it can regroup and combat the antagonist. The curtain speech by Sganarelle may represent human folly, but at the same time it suggests a quick resumption of the normal order of things when the danger is removed. We must be careful not to read into all of this any moralizing treatise, however, either deflating or inflating values. The presence of the supernatural complicates the matter, for the damnation of the evil man tends to make us place this work outside of the usual comic context of the plays.

The problem of interpretation of meaning is evidently knotty, but perhaps we may have some success if we resume our position of stating that value is to be found in the theatricality of the work as it exists in relationship to thematic elements. Satire of convention and upholding of human dignity are both important concepts related to the play, and still they seem to be less central than the theme of illusion of power as it is expressed by highly illusory and contrived dramatic techniques. The use of supernatural stage effects makes sense if we see their appropriateness to symbolize how much escapes the control of even the Don, deluded in his human limitations. Illusions of man's powers, his independence, and his ability to shape his existence and his surroundings are the thematic core of this play. For an author like Molière, aware of what could be contained within the genre that he was revolutionizing, a theme of limits of human power had great attractions because it was the matter treated by his colleagues in tragic drama. Racine was to examine the character of Nero in his *Britannicus* (1669), and the heroic dramas of Corneille constantly probed the problems of human grandeur or vice. *Dom Juan* is less a depiction of a debauched nobleman of the mid-seventeenth century than a study by original theatrical means of an abstract figure of amoral individuality reaching its outer limits. It is a free-ranging piece of imaginative theater that merges the harshly realistic with fantasy to show the success and downfall of the ego that would be wholly self-contained and self-creating.

The structural strength and coherence of the play come partly from the use of traditional material, but Molière builds his work about an originally conceived Don who transcends his predecessors, becoming the great seducer seduced finally by his own illusions. The self-centered character looms large in this theater, but nowhere does he tower as in *Dom Juan,* occupying the center of the stage in most scenes or being the topic of discussion by the other characters when not present in person. The egoist is led through a contrived series of encounters with various human types, and to implement this general scheme Molière uses typical parts from his bag of comic materials which include scenes of misunderstanding, misrepresentation, and misidentification. Disguises and deceptions are piled up in rapid order as the Don uses people for his purposes and leads them into acting out their roles in the scenes he composes for them like a master stage director. His power over others seems to be summed up in this ability—but he paradoxically cannot exert it without persons to do his bidding. The various individuals with whom he is brought into contact, in an apparently free theatrical roaming in a world at once real and fanciful, are placed there to react to Don Juan or to the image of himself that he chooses to project. The leading actor goes forth in search of a constantly changing cast of supporting players, and the term "supporting" assumes a quite literal sense because he depends upon them to uphold his personal image. Independence and dependence are not clear-cut, for much of the coherence of the play lies in the need for reactions by others to achieve full self-awareness. If this seems to impute existentialist thought to Molière, it is quite without such intention but rather results from a recognition of a basic tenet of comic writing: that social communication is sought by the individual to give some substance to his illusions about himself.[14]

The masking and the series of encounters during a journey ring a familiar note as we consider how Molière falls back upon a theatrical structure used in earlier plays, notably *Les Fâcheux.* Once more the basic elements of game playing furnish the framework for a play, and the pattern of movement in *Dom Juan,* which is often viewed as disorganized, becomes more clear in the light of the comedy ballet in which the hero makes his way to his goal through obstacles. *Dom Juan* is a brilliant and sophisticated reprise of the game structure, depicting the title figure maneuvering his way through encounters with characters who wish to have him live up to their desires or expectations. He indeed finds them to be bores. The world through which he travels has a certain quality of the game board, the figures placed in the Don's way having a contrived nature as impediments to his progress or as tests to be passed. The storm at sea or the meeting with the poor hermit seem to be such. The competitor hero must surmount all obstacles as he moves toward power over others and complete personal autonomy. Don Juan is constantly assuming masks and poses, even forcing Sganarelle to adopt disguises to aid him. He may literally assume the person of his valet or merely play a role of geniality or cooperation with another character, as occasion demands. He is consistently aggressive and the winner in each encounter until he meets up with forces on a spiritual level outside of his realm of play. Molière transforms the legendary seducer into a protean game player who can seemingly talk his way through any encounter, all the while making the supreme wager that he can control his fate in this world or any other.

The great game of chance in which Don Juan is engaged is no less than his staking of his soul upon his ability to cope with any situation he meets. His gamble continues with success right up to the end when higher powers call his bluff and send him to eternal damnation. His struggle for power is on a more profound level than that of Tartuffe, but both of these characters share abilities as skillful players in competition and masking. They lose their games for moving into areas controlled by fate or heaven. Delusions of individual power carry them beyond their limits. It is wonderfully ironic that the powerless character of the valet Sganarelle remains on the scene at the end after the downfall of his brilliant master, for Sganarelle is the play's example of the inept player. His major function seems to have been to serve as a bit player for the Don's little playlets. He is also a big loser at the end, crying for his wages for which he had staked all his faithful service to a cruel man. The constant presence of this loser throughout the play calls for some explanation. How does Sganarelle fit into the structure?

The particular person on whom Don Juan calls for a reflection of himself is Sganarelle, and this may explain the constant attendance by the valet. The image reflected by Sganarelle is hardly accurate, for we must observe that his dominant characteristic is confused loquacity, especially in his communications with his master. He is verbose, and he is occasionally sharp in his comments upon the Don to other characters, but he tends to stumble over his own tongue in talking with the central figure. Don Juan thus has at hand a ready mirror or sounding board that is nevertheless warped and faulty. We must assume that such a foil fills a need for him and for the play's expression of its ideas. Sganarelle's personal thoughts and opinions, even when correct, are treated as comical distortions by the Don, but they are constantly being summoned forth. Aside from his function as part of a relationship indicative of the psychological import of the comedy, Sganarelle is a thorough, classical clown type who is fated to utter truth and to be laughed at in his ineffectualness. Because he is such a buffoon, we perceive that the cast of characters for which Don Juan is always arranging roles has a similar "stock type" quality, and we note that Elvira is the typical "wronged woman" and the Don's father the "irate parent." The dominating figure is insistent upon having people behave on the terms he lays down for them because, although he needs the reactions of others, he claims the right to set up the desired reactions. The tyrant treats the world as his personal theater, a stage upon which the power to create illusion gives him his sense of control. The vanity of the whole procedure may be called philosophically meaningful, but I prefer to observe that Molière is making the concept of theatricality an essential part of the meaning of the play.

Sganarelle tries to convey his thoughts to Don Juan without any success, nor can the other characters such as Elvira or Don Louis, the father, meet with other than scornful rejection of their interpretations of the hero's nature and fate. Any image of himself that differs from his own is totally unacceptable. In the first act Don Juan does not even make a polite pretense of listening seriously to his wife, and this is stressed when he makes Sganarelle his spokesman. Later, when she appears suited to his aims, he designs to communicate with her. The scenes of the comedy are grouped according to the central figure's use of and communication with the various other characters, and they form part of his existence only in their willingness to accept the roles that he gives to them. Naturally, the roles of dutiful husband or son are not adopted when others try to impose them upon him, yet he hypocritically plays them in the last act when he conceives that they suit his needs.

The limitations on communication that are evident in the talk between master and servant emerge early in the play. Sganarelle is afraid to speak too boldly so he abandons part of his own self and becomes the mirror for the Don until the curtain speech restores to him his autonomy. His efforts to speak his mind are unavailing, and he even loses the privilege of eating his own dinner and ultimately of being himself. Don Juan takes Sganarelle's clothes as a disguise, leaving the poor clown in a dilemma of wondering what would happen if they were killed in the exchanged garments and were confused by the administrations of heaven and hell. The thematic idea of exterior and interior nature is neatly suggested. Sganarelle's major action on his own during the play is to dupe some peasants by his disguise as a doctor. He dispenses medical advice (idly wondering whether he might cure someone) but only because he is no longer himself in the eyes of others. When urged to speak his mind by his master, who is prepared to be amused, he becomes a silly puppet of a man, who can only fall flat on his face unless guided by a superior hand. The role of the Don as the great manipulator of people is clear in this episode.

Control is exerted by words, of course, and Don Juan appears as a master seducer through language rather than actions. As a matter of fact, verbalizing is his forte, and we seldom observe him other than in a situation of persuading, browbeating, or cajoling his dupes. The great lover is rather the great talker. "How you can run on!" exclaims the admiring Sganarelle, "You talk just like a book" (1.2). The verbal image that he erects of himself is truly much stronger than any idea that one would gain from his deeds, and we see that he is infatuated as much by his eloquence as by anything. Histrionic ability and skillful badinage are his major weapons; he resorts to fighting with his sword only in a matter of showing courage of a physical sort, the routing of the attackers of Don Carlos. This suits his self-image, however. For the most part the title figure accomplishes nothing on a heroic scale, as we have been led to expect, but instead puts on a sorry show at the start of act 2. Failure in the abduction and shipwreck are hardly made up for by the fast-talking approach to two country girls, but this cheap success seems to suffice to buoy the spirits of the Don. The stress on control by words is made apparent as the peasant Pierrot fails to make any headway with his girl because of his lack of eloquence, while the Don quickly turns her head.

The acting ability and the theatrical turn of mind of the character are seen in act 2, scene 5, in which he determines that his strategy will be the assumption of the role of his valet. The fluidity and mobility of the title figure are most evident in such an episode that shows his propensity for masking and posing, all the while retaining a fixed notion of what he really is. Poor Sganarelle is reduced to fearing that he will thus lose his soul's identity, but his master believes that all appearances and natures are ephemeral and changeable according to his will, so he changes his exterior frequently and makes other people do so. The relationship between this tendency toward fluid change and his inner fixity of purpose lies in the fact that both contribute to his illusion of power. Don Juan avers that all men are willing to accept false appearances (*grimaces*) for reality because they trust their senses, and it is his function to arrange appearances to his personal advantage. He calls upon his servant to discourse on the nature of man, remaining silent on purpose so as to watch him try to achieve a reasoned depiction of humanity as God's creation. Sganarelle fails and falls flat in demonstrating the wonders of the human machine: "My reasoning is that there is something remarkable in man, whatever you may say, which all the wise men can't explain. Isn't it wonderful that I'm here and that I have something in my head which thinks a hundred different things at once and which makes my body do what it wants? I can clap my hands, lift my arm, raise my eyes, lower my head, shake my feet, turn right, left, backward, around" (3.7). The human machines seem badly in need of direction, and that is the Don's province, the providing of *grimaces* on which they can pattern their actions.

Molière's free introduction of thematic variations continues with the enigmatic scene of the poor beggar rewarded by Don Juan. The idea behind it may be less one of contrast between this episode and the symbolic pratfall by Sganarelle in the previous scene than a sort of analogy. Don Juan recognizes in the Poor Man an example of inner strength and fixity like his own, an individual who can reject *grimaces* as false and be true to a principle. We note that religious faith is given no credit for this steadfastness, as the Don gives alms for the love of humanity. The mendicant then seems to represent an acceptable form of humanity, which for Don Juan is a creature resembling himself. The gold is given almost as a tribute to the self-image that is perceived in the Poor Man, who has refrained from trying to persuade the Don of his sinful ways. The incident is satisfactory because Don Juan does not feel that it has threatened him or what he wishes to appear to be. The scene with Don Carlos has a like function of permitting the Don to play a role that he would select for himself, the brave swordsman defending an outnumbered man. It is proper to his self-esteem to do this act to which honor could be attributed because the illusion of the nobleman's power lies partly in the threat of force, death by the sword. The egoist has thus been afforded occasions to seem generous and honorable at no cost to his real principles.

The time will come, however, when he must encounter things outside of his seemingly limitless control. After the meetings with assorted human types and situations, Don Juan meets manifestations of the supernatural, a realm outside of his thinking. The rigidity of his ideas forbids adaptation to the new or strange, so the wonderfully mobile character suffers defeat by his paradoxical inability to change beyond certain limits. The process of self-creation and aggrandizement turns out to be self-limitation, and the sterile end that is hinted at for a character like Molière's miser is clearly shown as the Don is dragged off to hell. The play is surely, as W. G. Moore comments, a classical piece in its treatment of "the limits of humanity."[15] The supernatural is far from the hero's ken and conveys the theme that the illusion of human power is truly human weakness, although it would be impossible to have a comedy if the Don were allowed to grasp this idea. The basic "action" of the play is underscored at the end because the self-creating hero is wretchedly unchangeable instead of being nobly unchanged. He has succeeded in creating above all an illusion for himself that turns out to be another vain *grimace* that deludes man. Thus, the author retains the traditional ending of a Don Juan story and makes it part of his scheme of meaning and construction. Theatrical spectacle is made to serve a high purpose of thematic expression.

As an experiment in new theater, *Dom Juan* succeeded but shakily with the contemporary audience and with posterity. The change the play suffered in rewriting and in being used for the Mozart opera kept Molière's ideas from the public for a long period, and much of the interest in his original version has been critical. Modern criticism can serve the memory of the dramatist best by seeking the merits of a comedy that has importance as theatrical innovation in the ways suggested above. Its inner cohesion as theater lies, appropriately enough, in its experimentation with themes and structures of illusion and power in their interaction.

Le Misanthrope

The removal of *Dom Juan* from the stage aggravated the personal struggle of the author with the powers arrayed against him, but the needs of the troupe, members of which shared in the profits of the productions, had to be met with yet another quickly contrived play. In 1665 Molière created his *L'Amour médecin* (Love as the doctor) to fill the gap, meanwhile continuing to prepare for the opening of *Le Misanthrope,* which would not reach the theater in Paris until June 1666. When this work at last was played, success was achieved because he managed to avoid the difficulties stirred up by the two major comedies and gave no offense to specific religious groups. If his contemporary audience did not find in this play all the rollicking fun of the farces, they were justified in feeling a bit puzzled. The experimenter in comic theater was at work again, dealing in a more subtle way with themes from *Tartuffe* and *Dom Juan*. The ground that he gained in a professional sense in the two plays is held and consolidated in the comedy of the misanthropist who has his own peculiar illusions of power. The seriousness of the work bothered the public of 1666, but this was because Molière was creating comic theater by the strict rules of neoclassical drama, a technical tour de force that affected the tone of the play. As a highly intellectual and artistic achievement *Le Misanthrope* seems to lend itself to many interpretations, and we shall focus on its qualities as theater, both as an entity and as part of the development of Molière's new style.[16]

The comedy's contradictory aspects are indicated in its original subtitle, *L'Atrabilaire amoureux* (The grouch in love) and we may well be warned that some confusing contrasts will appear in the speeches and characters. A straightforward moral message has been sought because of the apparent clash between rectitude and false behavior, but it becomes difficult to synthesize a tenable moral position out of a series of witty scenes of conflict. "The moral dilemmas arising in *Le Misanthrope* are simply insoluble," comments critic James Doolittle[17] and points to the conflicting positions of individuals' and society's conventions and institutions. Doolittle's idea that such aspects of society do run counter to and harm human dignity may be truly said to explain much of the typical Molière plot, but it keeps criticism still on moral grounds. The reminder that he gives that we cannot expect to see Molière in one sure moral stance is important because early critics usually erred in assigning him one. What is the play about, we must first inquire—especially, what relation does it have to *Tartuffe* and *Dom Juan?*

The idea of abuse of power by an individual would seem to be common to the three plays. One uses a scheme of direct threat to a social unit, the family; another is more abstract in its menace to human values. In *Le Misanthrope* a very formal, conventional world of high social circles is the field of operation of a character who tries to turn against it the noble principles that are paid lip service but flaunted by the salon habitués. Honesty and true consideration for others are paradoxically turned by Alceste, the misanthropist, into weapons that threaten the foundations of such a world. This would seem to make him a moral hero, but his purposes are more egotistical than noble since everything he does is for the creation of his personal illusion of control of others. The fact that he does not entirely grasp this himself nor openly discuss it makes of him the most complicated character yet drawn by the playwright. With such a psychological theme Molière combines satire of the precious manners of the age, a number of brilliant theatrical portraits of types, a witty exposé of the function of language as indirect or as noncommunication, and questions about the relationships between mores and morality. The resultant play is probably the world's greatest "comedy of manners."

The alexandrine verses upon which Molière expended four years of labor set the key of formal poetry and notify us that conventional theatrical illusion and style is to be the rule. But nothing else would really suit a play about such a formal society. The free sort of experimentation with theatrical techniques evident in *Dom Juan* and the rapid changing of scene are replaced by a strict observance of the unity of place and that of time as well. It is as if the author determined to show what could be done with theater dependent upon rigid conventions for its effects, extending its meanings into the area of sharp psychological and social realism. Within the neoclassical canon the poetic and the stylized are construed as creating an impression of verisimilitude, a heightening or abstraction of ordinary reality. Successful application of such principles to high comedy is the remarkable success Molière achieves here, and his example of the accomplishment of flashes of insight by means of rigorous artistic discipline makes him a worthy colleague of Racine. The two dramatists explore the farthest limits of their art form, infusing life into conventionalized drama by true poetry.

Thematically coordinated in all its parts, *Le Misanthrope* deals with love and self-love as manifest in exterior actions and interior motives. The basic scheme is a playing off of true feelings against a formal sentimental code, and this exploiting of the behavior of a society shaped by precious ideas was pointed out by F. Baumal in a study that examined this comedy alongside of *La Princesse d'Elide* and *Mélite*.[18] The salon group plays at love like a formal game, and not only in its vocabulary and expressions but also in its basic beliefs. As far as we may judge, this social world revolves upon the psychological principles of *préciosité* which were examined in our study of *Les Précieuses ridicules*. Thus each character works quite seriously at acting out a chosen role or roles that offer scope for the indulgence of a certain sort of personal illusion. The willfully illusory exterior behavior renders this society, and the comedy treating it, highly theatrical. Game playing and playacting with love are central and interacting parts of this piece of theater. Themes of falseness and sincerity are clearly being dealt with here, although we must be alert to the need for a cautious assignment of values of morality to certain characters or attitudes they represent. In a simple example, it is obvious that some social good can be served by deliberate insincerity that flatters a person harmlessly. If Alceste protests that this is immoral, then he is failing to see that the rules of the social game require suppleness of role-playing, itself a form of pretense, and that this process creates a morality of the group. The one rule of the game of love and self-love, which is understood by all except Alceste, is that the ego is permitted a certain self-indulgence but not to a point where it disrupts the opportunities of other people to enjoy the same pleasure.

The study by Roger Caillois, *Les Jeux et les hommes,*[19] analyzes the various types of games created by cultures, and his observations are helpful in perceiving what takes place in the social interaction in *Le Misanthrope.* Caillois calls the four basic sorts of games those of chance, competition, masking, and vertigo. His final term refers to physical play that creates mental or emotional states by kinetic means such as the dance. All of these categories are present within Molière's works in varying degrees, but for purposes of understanding Alceste and the other characters one must focus upon the elements of competition and masking. A highly competitive game of psychological and sexual nature is played throughout *Le Misanthrope,* with egos projecting themselves upon others with aims of power, love, and self-love. To participate in this each player creates a persona displaying a certain mask of appearance and behavior. If all players observe the rules and accept the masks of others, all are gratified. Credence is lent to the poses of other people in exchange for acceptance by them of one's own pose. Alceste is literally a spoilsport in the game, however, failing to play by the rules. The question remains as to whether this is due to ignorance, ineptitude, or intention. His sincerity and morality (or their mask) have long been an impediment to analysis of this play because critics have tried to find the playwright's views of morality and ethics embodied in the character.

The ideas implicit in such a play are stimulating from a philosophical standpoint, and we ponder Molière's view of social man, while observing how advantageous it was for him to have at hand a world that so lent itself to transposition into a play. The fact that men and women accepted as normal their natures as actors and actresses of roles with set limits and guidelines was a wonderful benefit to the dramatist. His job is to place in a given situation characters whose powers are clearly delineated, just like cards in a deck or chessmen. This is particularly true in tragedy, in which each character must represent certain capabilities and be aware of what his limits are. If he does not know at the start of the play, the audience does, and he will surely know by the end. Alceste, the misanthropist, does not play the social game successfully because he refuses to know himself and accept his true role. Everyone else seems to know his inner nature, no matter how vigorously he keeps up a false front, and the denouement of *Le Misanthrope* is only possible because all of the characters except Alceste feel that this clumsy individual is threatening the masks and poses. Paradoxically, we might observe that Alceste is the most thoroughly comic of the characters in his blindness about himself and that it is the other characters, who seem so much like comic caricatures on the surface, who give a serious tone to the play. They at least are sure they are social players.

This game of social masking with its motivations and conflicts has been studied clinically by the psychoanalyst Eric Berne, whose *Games People Play* is an account for the general reader of such phenomena.[20] His studies can aid us in seeing what is going on within the characters introduced into the salon of Célimène by Molière. Apparently the playwright, long before any invention of a science of psychology, understood what was driving an Oronte or an Arsinoé as they maneuvered for acceptance of their masks in the social world. Beneath the poses of such figures it is easy to see an aggressiveness. It is an error to dismiss these characters as merely fatuous, amusing themselves in a harmless game of "one-upmanship." The insult felt by Oronte, whose sonnet Alceste reduces to shreds, is a serious one, and it would have led to a duel in earlier times. The characters are all playing "for keeps" in the social game in which the stakes are high—prestige, power, recognition. The characters in *Le Misanthrope* are truly existential in that they depend upon the acceptance of others to give reality to their lives. Status, advantage, and success are the prizes in the games these people play.

A game, according to Berne, is basically an engagement with a self-seeking aim of winning some advantage. "Every game is basically dishonest," he notes, but if the advantage sought does no real harm to others then the game is "good."[21] One would expect the games played in comedy to be of this sort, and in most of Molière's works this is the case. In *Dom Juan, Tartuffe,* and *Le Misanthrope,* however, real harm is very much a threat, so these plays have a somber tone of inimical human relations. Molière creates a balancing act of the innocuous and the harmful in the game playing, leading to the endless controversy about the real nature of the serious comedies. Molière, of course, is reporting keenly on social behavior, much of which is what Berne has called the "games people play." The characters all joust for advantage, consciously or not, as they play their roles in the comedies. In real life the behavior that we can see about us is captured in the formalized theatrical situation by the playwright. No wonder his comedies are capable of speaking to the society of any age.

As each person strives to shine in social intercourse to impress others and especially to win love, this motive takes on all sorts of protective coloration. The ways of love are strange, Molière has shown us in *Tartuffe* and *Dom Juan,* and we are not surprised that in Alceste it assumes an aspect of intransigent misanthropy while trying to win the favor of Célimène. His love for the flirtatious young widow is genuine enough, we are led to see, for he says, "I lost my judgment when, upon seeing you, I took, to my sorrow, that poison that is killing me" (4.3). The expression of his feelings in proper precious style is interesting because it shows how even he is bound to use the means of communication accepted in his society. The same style of language just as often expresses shallow flirtation, but he takes all words literally. His self-love is wounded by her unfaithfulness to him, but it is self-love that is being cultivated most strenuously by her and by the others; the suitors are obviously fatuous egotists, and the prudish Arsinoé can no longer inspire love so she seeks to attract others by assuming an admirable pose of great virtue. Love, respect, and esteem are desired, or at least the outward forms that express them because it is recognized by all that the exterior signs are about all that one can get. The ideas are original neither to Molière nor indeed to any one author of the period, although they are summed up most eloquently and succinctly in the *Maxims* of La Rochefoucauld, a nobleman of long experience in the games of life in court and in the world at large.[22] A rather embittered cynicism characterizes his witty maxims about the dominant role of self-interest in worldly affairs, and he perceives the extent to which society functions behind façades of acceptable sorts while pursuing paths of sheer egoism.

A most fundamental and sophisticated power structure is perceived by men like Molière and La Rochefoucauld. It is based on a strict code of manners that permits individuals to erect structures of illusions for themselves. The venture must be cooperative, for each one must offer some aid or at least tolerance to the efforts of the other people engaged in the process. If some one person refuses the token acceptance of the mask of another, then the whole scheme of society is threatened, and the total group has to deal severely with the offender to make him conform or to isolate him in harmlessness. The pattern has been observed so frequently in the comedies of Molière that it needs no elaboration. Alceste is actually trying to draw undue attention to his own worth, being unsatisfied with the token esteem automatically accorded, and, even though he deals in terms of the highest virtues like honesty, he is still trying to wield personal power to gain love and control of others and is thus an enemy of the social order. The threat is covert and a bit vague, so that Alceste resembles an Orgon rather than a Tartuffe or a Don Juan. *Le Misanthrope* sets forth this complex of themes in a tightly focused classical piece of theater that shows us a series of variations in which characters discuss the interplay of exterior and interior factors. The plot is not of primary importance, and really is not strong, because ultimately Alceste departs for his wilderness as he has predicted he would do and society is left to consolidate its usual strength. This strength is resident in the seemingly illusory acceptance of poses and masks for reality, yet this theatricality or value-in-illusion quality emerges as a powerful social principle. It is as if this great comedy of manners said that "all the world's a stage" and that this is not vanity but a human strength. In *Le Misanthrope* society's triumph is shown by theater, and vice versa. This concept is probably at the heart of Molière's success in combining so much poetry with so much realism.

The way in which all this is accomplished is admirable. The comedy first introduces the title character in conversation with a friend, Philinte, whose name suggests that he is the "philanthropist" or at least the "reasoning" foil of the egoist. Alceste demands that everyone "be sincere and say only what is in the heart, like an honorable man" (1.1). His friend is a realist who points out, "But when one moves in society, one must pay back people with the customary civil compliments" (1.1). The wild lack of proportion in Alceste is stressed by his serious use of violent and grave words in speaking of Philinte's polite flattery of a man they have just seen: "You should die of pure shame . . . If I had done such a thing I would go out and hang myself in remorse" (1.1). The theme and conflict of the comedy are strongly enunciated, nor did the contemporary audience fail to call Alceste an "extravagant" or foolish eccentric, seeing that he misapplied moral rigidity. Philinte's chief claim to the title of wise reasoner lies not in his defense of social usage but rather in his perception of the theatrical nature of the game one must play. "This deep philosophical trouble is a bit too wild. I laugh at the black fits in which I picture you, and I believe I see in the two of us, brought up much alike, the two brothers who are depicted in *The School for Husbands*" (1.1). Molière seems to spoof both his own pretensions as a social critic and typify Alceste by this clever reference; he makes Alceste reply, "Good Lord! let's have out your weak comparisons" (1.1). The wants of the figure are made clear to us as he declares his opposition to "all the human race" and his intention to "flee in a wilderness any human contact" (1.1). He plans to lose a lawsuit for the virtuous martyrdom resulting, but we must observe that he wants thereby to be praised and noticed, an attitude not wholly consonant with the avowed wish to disappear. Even as he can declare in the speech just cited, "I hate all mankind," he wants to be "distinguished" and particularly by Célimène, with whom he is deeply in love. As usual, his speeches are strongly worded, and when he speaks the vocabulary of gallant love, he sounds as if he truly believes its imagery: "I confess my weakness, she has the art of pleasing; In vain I see and blame her faults, but despite this she makes me love her" (1.1). The great egoism emerges as he says he is sure of her love for him and that his noble passion will purge her vices of hypocrisy and flirtatiousness. We see that Alceste is, despite himself (or perhaps willingly?), deeply entangled in the world of formal social relationships that depend so much on conventional externals. Does he not see that he is cooperating with the system he casti-gates, in friendship, lawsuits, and love, because his distinction and power lie in being known as the Great Protestor? He would cast down social illusion, according to his speeches, but this would undermine his own role. The char-acters of Tartuffe and Don Juan are conscious illusionists, while Alceste is an unconscious one.

This is not an attempt to put the figure on the psychoanalyst's couch but rather to place him in a context of theatrical themes that are known to us from the previous major plays and are integral in the character's attitudes and behavior. A great ego partially succeeds in establishing his control of the world surrounding him, but a higher power brings about his defeat. In the case of Alceste, nothing is really desired but the true esteem and love of others, and these are accorded him in the affectionate regard of Philinte and in the tenderness of Eliante and Arsinoé for him, mentioned at the end of scene 1. The very antipathy that Alceste stirs up nourishes his illusion of being extraordinary, so he welcomes another chance to make an enemy of a fatuous nobleman who thrusts himself upon Alceste with the demand that he flatter his literary efforts. Oronte effusively greets Alceste, then insists upon having his opinion of a sonnet, but the uncompromising bluntness of the misanthropist cannot permit him even innocuous flattery. The need for honesty, or for self-inflation, leads him to criticize unmercifully the graceful little poem by Oronte in a frontal attack on the man's pet illusion about himself. The unforgivable sin of *lèse-illusion* is committed by Alceste, who then rejects the friendship of Philinte for having tried to placate Oronte. Act 1 ends with a withdrawal by Alceste, just as will each act, stressing the basic action of the play.

The movement of the title character, it has been remarked by René Jasinski,[23] consists of this tendency to leave which runs counter to his re-peated efforts to obtain a satisfactory interview with Célimène. A pattern of alternating movements thus is employed, with Alceste being pulled away from Célimène each time he sees her. Act 2 begins with a conversation be-tween the two, and Alceste tries his power tactics upon her: "Madame, do you wish me to speak frankly? I am very dissatisfied with your behavior. Against it too much bile gathers in my heart, and I feel that we shall have to make a break" (2.1). The last thing he wants is to lose her, so we must attribute de-liberate falsehood to the honest Alceste as he attempts to shock her into sub-mission. Célimène, a "merry widow" whose sustenance is the admiration of a string of suitors, wishes to keep Alceste in attendance and thus assures him of his special place in her heart. The relationship between these two figures is the key one of the comedy, of course, so the nature of this nexus of love and self-love is especially interesting. The conversation is illuminating:

CÉLIMÈNE. But you are jealous of everyone.

ALCESTE. That is because you receive everyone.

CÉL. That is what should reassure your angry soul, since my friendship is extended to all, and you would have more reason to take offense if you saw me centering it upon one person.

ALC. But I, whom you blame as too jealous, what do I have more than all the rest, if you please?

CÉL. The happiness of knowing that you are loved.

ALC. And what reason does my tortured heart have to believe it?

CÉL. I think that, having taken the trouble to tell you so, a confession of the sort should satisfy you.

ALC. But who will assure me that at the same time you were not saying the same to others?

CÉL. Indeed, for a lover, the compliment is gallant, and you are treating me nicely. Well, to remove such a worry, I take back everything I said, and nothing can mislead you but yourself. Take that!

ALC. Good Lord! Do I have to love you! Oh, if I ever get my heart back I'll bless Heaven for this rare happiness! I don't hide the fact that I am doing all I can to break this terrible attachment, but my greatest efforts have been useless so far. It is for my sins that I love you thus.

CÉL. True, your love is unequalled.

ALC. Oh, yes, in that I'll challenge the whole world. (2.1)

The ironic banter by the woman seems lost on Alceste, who is full of his own exceptional person. Célimène refuses to accept the role that he assigns to her because his possession or control would destroy her freedom. The attitudes and ideas reveal precious characteristics in Alceste, since he accepts the fatal power of love, and in Célimène, who gives the proper impression of fleeing while consenting. Her admission of love for him should be understood as the ultimate of feminine sacrifice, a gesture that Alceste most ungallantly does not honor but doubts. *Préciosité* gives us the perspective in which to see the extremes of Alceste's "extravagance." The appropriate words are used, and the basic situation of submission to love exists, yet both the characters are going through the notions only to nourish their own illusions and self-love.

The ensuing scene of fashionable salon chatter features Célimène, who shines at making verbal portraits of acquaintances. The mordant wit she displays cuts through the masks worn by those who have exaggerated manners, an air of importance, pride, or cleverness. The boring raconteur, the dull conversationalist, and the man who is frequented because he has a good cook all come under fire as she exposes the exterior feature of the personality and shows how little is behind it. *Lèse-illusion* is a parlor game permitted when the butt of the joke is not present, but Célimène is proceeding to her own downfall when her comments on Alceste, Oronte, and the foppish noblemen Acaste and Clitandre, her suitors, are brought to confront her in letters at the end of the play. She will overstep the rules of the game, just as Alceste has done. A legal officer informs him that Oronte has brought suit against him (actually appealed to noblemen's court of honor) and that he must leave.

Acaste and Clitandre start act 3 with an argument as to which one enjoys the greatest favor from Célimène, and they end up by making a wager as to who will win her bed if not her hand. The plain sexual aims of the marquis characters are evident beneath the polished gallantry they show in the salon. Their "blind" self-confidence is the keynote, and this will suffice to permit their masks to be dislodged. Arsinoé, the "prude," arrives to warn Célimène, as a dear friend, that tongues are wagging about her and her many gentlemen acquaintances. A mutual hair-pulling match is conducted on a level of polite social talk, with the evident meanings between the lines. Under the guise of cautioning about possible misinterpretations that people might make of actions, the women accuse each other of sexual license beneath proper exteriors. The elegant salon begins to resemble a dueling ground, serving as a substitute field of action because real duels were forbidden by law. The affair of honor between Oronte and Alceste would come to swordplay unless this were outlawed, it must be realized. Conflicts with no holds barred are not permitted, but these characters will come close to exceeding the limits, and in the cases of Alceste and Célimène people are wounded too much to pardon. Real harm to positions of social power cannot be allowed. Arsinoé enters into the in-fighting by inviting Alceste to see some evidence of infidelity by Célimène, and he cannot resist a chance to be certain, so off he goes at the end of the act. The error of the title character in seeking certainty in love is a familiar Molièresque theme.

The threatened power structure of the tight little society seems to cast no fear into Philinte and Eliante, the reasonable characters who offer a balance to those we have just observed in battle array. Even these two are encumbered by the forms of behavior and expression permitted in their world, for Philinte's proposal of marriage is so precious as to be almost incomprehensible. Alceste then rushes in to offer his hand to Eliante to "take vengeance" on the false Célimène, the two parallel scenes offering a sharp comment on the contrasting motives of the men. Neither true love nor selfishness sways the gentle Eliante who tries to hold aloof from the quarrels going on. Alceste confronts Célimène: "All the horrors of which a soul is capable cannot be compared with your disloyalty. Fate, demons, and angered Heaven have never produced such an evil product as you." Célimène: "There indeed are the sweet words I admire" (4.3). She reduces him to abject pleading for mercy, however, saying that the letter he thinks damning was written to a woman. His desperate wish to believe in just an illusion of her love for him is very revealing of his utter dependence on the falseness he condemned: "Stop pretending to be guilty and give me back that innocent letter. My love makes me extend my hands to you. Make an effort to appear faithful, and I shall try to believe that you are" (4.3). In his desire to win her he says that he wishes she were entirely dependent upon him, "without rank, birth, or possessions, so that the dazzling sacrifice of my heart could make it all up to you, and so that I might have the joy and the glory to see you owing everything to my love" (4.3). The aberrations of the ego hit their high point here. Act 4 ends with Alceste's being summoned away by his valet, who warns of his threatened arrest.

The final act is a careful repetition of the scenes of the preceding acts, for we first see Alceste and Philinte in conversation. Disillusioned with man's evil, Alceste is determined to make good his threat to retire to a wilderness, but his friend says that society, false as it is, must be the proving ground of virtue. The reasoning falls on deaf ears, and Alceste determines to ask his love to accompany him in his retreat. Oronte enters, repeating his function of arguing with Alceste in the correct spot in the order of events. Célimène pleads her inability to express a choice between the two men, since her feminine modesty forbids it, but the pose is no longer acceptable in her. Acaste and Clitandre then come in with Arsinoé to complete the assembling on stage of the cast. If this were a wholly conventional comedy the expected ending would now take place, with the inevitable pairing off of the proper couples. All would join hands and step forward for the curtain speech and a bow. Molière pulls the rug out from under this typical structure, however, for instead of coming to patch up quarrels, all have arrived to demand satisfaction of Célimène and her sharp tongue and pen. Acaste has some letters that contain mocking "portraits" of all present, and these are read aloud to the complete discomfiture of the author. Alceste asks her to go with him, but she cannot face abandoning society even when it rejects her: "Solitude frightens a soul of twenty" (5.4). The salon characters exit and leave her, and then she moves off, for once silent. The neat arrangement of influx and ordered exits finishes with the departure of Alceste for his wilderness, closely followed by the faithful Philinte and Eliante who say they will try to bring him back. The action is a dash off the stage with a peculiar sense of projected energy utterly foreign to a proper resolution of a drama. Indeed, nothing is at all finished or settled, nor was the contemporary audience wrong in finding the ending very odd.

The early *comédie-ballet Les Fâcheux* can be of help in understanding the unconventional structuring of *Le Misanthrope,* if one compares the plays. To be sure, the flight of the title character at the final curtain is unsettling in a comedy, but the overall structure of the play about Alceste is really analogous to that of *Les Fâcheux.* The principal character moves like a piece in a board game, blocked by obstacles while trying to move toward a goal, in both plays the woman desired. The bores in the early play are caricatures of persons engrossed in their pet diversions, whereas in *Le Misanthrope* the impediments to Alceste are all serious players of the social games we have discussed. The pattern of the plays is still very similar. We noted the rhythmic movement of Alceste in his approaches to and retreats from Célimène, repeatedly summoned away from the salon at the end of each of four acts and then leaving voluntarily at the play's end. Once reached, the goal of Célimène's love is rejected angrily by Alceste in the pyrrhic victory scene. He has succeeded in proposing to her but set such conditions that she will not be able to accept. He may have won his egocentric game, but he leaves behind the persons who played against him with their masks stripped away. Society regroups for a resumption of the normal game playing without his disruptive presence, and it is vain for later playwrights to consider writing a sequel about the return of Alceste. One cannot imagine him as a changed man because this would constitute an interpretation of *Le Misanthrope* that would oversimplify its wonderful complexities. The final note in the play is a sort of gesture toward restoration of true human values in a shattered society. Philinte and Eliante show real friendship and concern as they exit after Alceste, hoping to bring him back, while all the others go off to repair their damaged masks.

Molière created in *Le Misanthrope* what is probably the world's greatest comedy of manners. In a piece of theater that respects all the conventions of the art, he encapsulated an essential part of human social behavior. The two words "comedy" and "manners" should be kept in mind as we try to sum up the nature of this masterpiece. It is a playing out before an audience of a heightened human situation that, through formal techniques, creates the impression of a significance beyond that of ordinary experience. The comic piece

remains on the level of social man, avoiding any of the transcendent implications of tragedy. The hero, even as he makes for himself a high goal and then
rejects it, never represents the human spirit in conflict with superhuman
forces as in the tragic mode. There is no great defeat because it is clear that the
social world will continue as before with the same proportions of folly and
nobility. The games of love and power will be played out endlessly, one feels
at the end of *Le Misanthrope,* for manners such as those depicted are basic to
human commerce. In essence these manners are the actions of people as they
approach one another for purposes of love, support, domination, or other
major concern. What follows the approach, then, is the matter of the play, be
it acceptance or rejection, union or destruction. *Le Misanthrope* remains the
outstanding exposition of this principle.

The playwright works all sorts of variations on the scheme, with the patterns of approach/retreat, acceptance/rejection being played out by all the
characters in brilliantly devised interaction. The tensions created by Alceste's
ambiguous signals and by Célimène's duplicitous replies are central to the
comedy, but the roles of the other characters, while simpler, still involve send-
ing out messages by word or sign and looking for responses. Each figure employs a particular variation of his or her persona, dependent upon the person
approached and the goal of that bit of game play. It is instructive to analyze
what goes on throughout the comedy in these terms, nor is it difficult once
one stops asking what moral or ethical point Molière is making.

The greatness of this comedy may be said to lie in the author's structuring the "action" (in the Aristotelian sense of the term) about a basic human
social function, people approaching one another.[24] The action is best rendered as a verb, and so one may declare with some accuracy that the action
of *Le Misanthrope* is "to approach others." No comedy shows better the
human creature engaged in this fundamental social activity, and that is the
source of its strength.

The Three Plays Compared

A careful study of the major works of Molière in this period of his career
would bring out the relationships of *Tartuffe, Dom Juan,* and *Le Misanthrope*
in ways that we have not been able to examine.[25] Although our treatment
may be limited, the focus has been upon the thematic essence that makes for
the theatrical strength of the three plays. As a creator of illusion in theater,
Molière clearly experimented to see how his techniques could express on
stage manifestations of a great preoccupation of his age, the concept of power
as illusory. It has been shown how one particular human relationship of love

and control between two characters is the structural basis of the comedies; the Tartuffe-Orgon nexus is paralleled by that of Don Juan-Sganarelle and Alceste-Célimène. The function of this core relationship is to reflect the greater implications and ambitions of the title character, a real menace to the social order. In each comedy a higher power intervenes to suppress the ambitious figure; in *Tartuffe* the royal decision of justice is like the ending of a Corneille tragedy, *Horace,* for example; in *Dom Juan* supernatural power carries off the Don to show his human limitations; and in *Le Misanthrope* Molière returns to the basic ruling force of comedy, human society. The last is thus most truly comic in orientation, despite the impression of seriousness given by the play. The conflict between one eccentric individual and the public good is a timeless scheme for comedy adopted and used by Molière in his most successfully developed works prior to *Tartuffe,* his *L'École des maris* and *L'École des femmes. Le Misanthrope* is the most subtle and far-reaching treatment of the theme because this play depicts the comic, social principle at work in a case that avoids buffoonery and suggests that a seemingly moral hero can be the comic eccentric.

In creating his three plays the author seems to have worked in terms of variations on a theme, and these variations may be viewed schematically as forces in action in a sort of triangular diagram. Tartuffe and Orgon are linked by a line of mutual dependence and faith which creates a sense of power in each character. The third power center in the diagram is that of society-family-king, with the king speaking for this force that assimilates both Tartuffe and Orgon. This scheme is really quite simple, but things are rather more complex in the arrangement of forces in *Dom Juan.* The relationships among the Don, Sganarelle, and the world are, of course, paradoxical and confusing, but if we keep in mind the Don's use of Sganarelle and all other characters to mirror his own image, the pattern is clearer. The efforts of Sganarelle and society are bent upon making Don Juan into the man they want him to be, but the arrows of force in our diagram never reach the Don because his strong will and ability turn every effort into a reflection of what he wants to see. His inevitable resulting movement is away from others, and the end of the play shows the logical extreme of this. Sganarelle, the "captive audience" or mirror, wants to rejoin the rest of the world, and this becomes possible only when Don Juan's power over him is removed.

In *Le Misanthrope* the scheme of forces in play is at once simple but very sophisticated in its reverses. Alceste concentrates upon Célimène and rejects society; Célimène directs her attentions toward society and holds off Alceste; society's forces take Célimène to be part of them and try to exert power over Alceste to conform to usage. The resulting path of motion is circular, and that is just our impression of the action throughout much of the comedy. Note that this "action" is thematic and not simply physical. But the direction of flow of concerns is switched toward the end of the comedy when Alceste abandons his plan to win Célimène. He retreats to his refuge, ceasing to threaten society, and society's big concern is now to reject Célimène. She feels lost and agrees to marry Alceste, although not to accompany him to his wilderness, and he then makes his reversal and cuts himself off from the love of her. Thus Molière writes a triangle play (jealous lover, the beloved, and the rival) in which no member of the triangle is eliminated and in which there is no resulting solution. The chief impression is that the direction of usual concerns has been suddenly reversed (the jealous lover rejecting the girl) and that the final movement is one of mutual removal. All parts of the schematic triangle move away from one another and apparently lose contact. The irresolution of the comedy is the most daring bit of theatrical trickery that Molière undertakes.

This brief attempt at schematization is not intended to represent any definitive analysis of the depths of these plays but only to show Molière's remarkably skillful and conscious playing with theatrical structure. The challenge that he was struggling to meet was one of his profession as well as a philosophical and moral issue, we must remember, and he appears to have approached the problem of creating elevated comedy within the accepted confines of the neoclassical canon with some bold experimenting. On one hand, he knew that comedy could express truth as well as could tragedy, and on the other, he saw that serious theater was in danger of being overwhelmed by the illusionary spectacle. Taking as his central informing idea the concept of the illusory in human power, he proceeded to turn to his advantage the possibilities for stage illusion (*Dom Juan*) and then the possibilities for the suggestion of the importance of illusion in real life in a formal society (*Le Misanthrope*). The artist triumphed in all cases.

The great significance of the famous trio of comedies for our understanding of Molière's contributions to the development of theater is that each one was a brilliant answer to the key professional problem of the age. The interplay of the illusionary and the sort of reality that was then called "natural," abstract human values, was the field of action of the playwright. Molière was far from finished in his discovery of innovations, but he had adopted his basic stance as an artist by 1666. This much is clear in the three major works; he would merge the theaters of illusion and of realism to make a "new comedy" with a personal style, a theater showing the highest function of the dramatist.

Chapter Six

The Craftsman of Entertainment

*L'Amour médecin, Le Médecin malgré lui, Le Sicilien,
La Comtesse d'Escarbagnas, Monsieur de Pourceaugnac*

One obvious way in which the professional man of the theater—Molière—
could solve his problem of how to create plays both meaningful and entertaining was to develop his stock in trade, the farce, *Les Précieuses ridicules*
had shown how much could be accomplished along these lines. It paid to
keep his hand in practice, moreover, for the elements of farce were his basic
materials, and they would serve him well in the final years of his career. Naturally, farce succeeded with the public, both bourgeois and noble, and a primary duty was to please. To acquit himself as a responsible author, director,
and entertainer Molière found it most practical to forego some of the elevated
tone he achieved in *Le Misanthrope* and to exploit the farce.

We noted that *L'Amour médecin* (Love as the doctor) was created in 1665.
This prose work in three acts was performed for the king at Versailles and
then played at the Palais-Royal for the Parisian public. Molière called it a
small sketch or impromptu, composed and given within a space of five days,
and his preface in the collected works goes on to warn us to read it with a performance in mind, for the piece is not a literary creation. A *divertissement*
with farce framework, music by Lully, and dances, *L'Amour médecin* was
made to be played, and the author says, "it should be read only by those who
have eyes to discover in the reading all the theatrical performance." The advice is valid here and in general, and it is particularly applicable as we examine his comedy ballets, pastorals, and court entertainments. Spectacle, music,
dance, song, speech, and gesture merge in works like *Le Médecin malgré lui*
(*The Doctor in Spite of Himself*) of 1666, *Le Sicilien, ou l'amour peintre* (*The
Sicilian, or Love the Painter*) of 1667, and others. In the present section we
shall look at the farces, treating a number of *galant* comedies later. To see
Molière's functioning as an active man of the theater at the service of his royal
patron and his public, the chronological order of creation seems less important than an ordering of the types of plays.

The literary canonization of the great comedian has tended to cause us to forget that the bulk of his efforts went into devising entertaining routines and sketches for the troupe of His Majesty. The title of "Troupe du Roi" accorded to the company during the fight over *Le Tartuffe* brought prestige to Molière and his people, but the responsibility to be entertaining was very heavy. For our purposes of criticism and understanding of his many facets, study of the lesser works gives a true perspective of the theatrical career and achievements of the man and permits us to see how he used his techniques of comedy until the mode of expression became almost instinctive and was able to bring to life plays like *Amphitryon, Le Bourgeois gentilhomme (The Would-be Gentleman),* or *L'Avare (The Miser).* Each of these is a masterpiece in a different way, but all depend for their effect upon a practiced, professional hand.

Louis XIV honored and demanded much of his favorite comedian. A royal fête, for example, held in 1666 at the château of Saint-Germain, called for three brief pieces from the comedy troupe, *Mélicerte, La Pastorale comique,* and *Le Sicilien.* This burden came at the time when Molière was struggling to get his two banned plays back on stage, but the author still turned out his comedies on command. Royal festive occasions could be turned to profit, for *Amphitryon* was offered in 1668 in Paris and then given at Versailles, while *George Dandin* was created in the same year for a "Great Royal Divertissement" at the magnificent country palace. In 1669 and 1670 five trips to the king's various residences are recorded for the troupe; at Chambord, *Monsieur de Pourceaugnac* was given; at Saint-Germain, *Les Amants magnifiques (The magnificent lovers);* and *Le Bourgeois gentilhomme* first appeared at another entertainment at Chambord. The list includes *Psyché* and *La Comtesse d'Escarbagnas* as creations for the royal patron. From *Les Fâcheux* of 1661 until the end of his life, Molière wrote sixteen works for Louis XIV, and his total was but thirty-one. From September 1668 until May 1671 all of his efforts went into royal entertainment, and the Palais-Royal theater witnessed no works offered first to the general public. The courtiers were eager to emulate the king and patronize Molière, so his troupe frequently gave special performances in the town houses of the nobility, working in impromptu theaters with portable scenery. All of this activity constituted a burden on Molière both physically and in his creativity.

L'Amour médecin is a useful example of the sort of thing that served his various purposes. The familiar Sganarelle type of farce lead appears in a satire of medicine in which five doctors are lampooned, much to the pleasure of the contemporary audience, which assigned identifications to the doctors. The purgings and bleedings common to the day are shown as harmful to nature's true curative processes, the idea stressed in *Le Malade imaginaire.* Sganarelle is the tyrannical father preventing the marriage of his daughter Lucinde to her

Clitandre, and a witty servant, Lisette, will devise ways of getting the father to sign a marriage contract. Clitandre pretends to be a doctor who cures by words alone, and the lovers communicate beneath the nose of the watchful parent. The routine is standard Molière, but even this slight work exploits verbal ambiguities in a clever way, then leads into music and dance. The final scene dissolves into a ballet as figures of "Games," "Laughs," and "Pleasures" enter and surround the actors. Says Sganarelle, "This is a nice way to cure a person. Where are my daughter and the doctor?" Lisette: "They have gone to get married. . . . Your goose is cooked, sir, and when you thought you were playing a game it was real" (3.8). The duped character is forced to join in the dance and is whirled about physically as he was verbally and mentally.

Le Médecin malgré lui was composed for the Parisian theater in 1666 with the hope of gaining good receipts at the box office. The stock farce characters and situations bear endless repetition and profit from the audience's familiarity with them. This time Sganarelle is the husband of Martine, and their life is constant strife, as shown in the opening scene. An old tale of a woman who takes vengeance on her husband by telling others that he is a great doctor but that he will perform only when beaten is the basis of the comedy. A bit about curing a dumb girl resembles L'Amour médecin, and again a lover comes in disguise, this time as an apothecary. The play evidently is a mixture of tried-and-true parts gathered by the author from his own plays and elsewhere, but it has some individual character in that Sganarelle becomes a rather more complicated type than in other works. As a brute of a drunken husband, the character is shown to be physically abusive to his wife but outwitted by her clever tongue. The scheme of verbal and physical interplay is crude yet very forceful and theatrically effective, and, despite its blunt form in this farce, the scheme is actually fundamental to the comedies considered to be "higher" in tone, Tartuffe, for example. Le Médecin malgré lui is distinguished by its uninhibited brutality, both in Sganarelle's behavior and in the blows rained upon his back, for this farcical treatment of power and its abuse sets forth its theme with harsh directness. It is interesting to compare the refined forms of power in the elevated plays of this period with this brutality of slapstick; the subtleties of social control are paralleled by the crudities of force. Human motives remain the same whether the mode of the comedy is high or low, and the theme of love and lust appears in raw clarity as Sganarelle pursues a buxom nurse, a sort of Tartuffe-Elmire scene without refinement. Love inevitably figures in a conventional romance between two young lovers, since this is standard comedy par excellence.

The effect of brutal directness does not shock as much as it amuses and imparts a sense of sheer exuberance. Sganarelle's natural desires are so open that we accept them as just as broadly symbolic manifestation of raw humanity in action. He is sympathetic in his unalloyed brutality. The brilliant idea of Molière is that this lout of a character should be made by words to abandon his true nature and play just the opposite, a quack doctor who distorts human nature. J. D. Hubert comments that here we see "a farcical variation on the typical baroque uncertainty concerning identity.[1] It would also be a variation of the theme of the illusory power of words and their relationships with reality. Thus, Sganarelle is something "in spite of himself," a prey to some higher force, despite his physical abilities to assert his identity.

As a doctor, Sganarelle depends upon language to deceive Géronte and spirit away the girl and her lover. He introduces the young man as his apothecary and then prescribes a dose of "purgative flight" and two "drams of matrimony in pills" (3.6). At this point, the old man comments, "What impetuosity of words!" and we observe how Molière couples the physical verve of Sganarelle with a similar verbal drive. The end of the play shows him apparently accepting his forced role as a doctor, but he resumes his original character at least in his threats to his wife, who now is to undergo the anger of a doctor, which may be worse than a husband's beating. These two "doctor" plays may be seen as leading toward the final work by Molière, *Le Malade imaginaire,* but even a comedy with a different theme, *Le Sicilien,* may be said to be as important an exercise in theater as these two because of its thematic and structural coordination. Standard farce and musical comedy merge with considerable wit in this work, and its lessons will be as valuable to the author as his more typical and conventional farces on medicine.

In January 1667 *Le Sicilien, ou l'amour peintre* was offered before the king as part of a court celebration of the aesthetic dictatorship of the monarchy. Royal academies laid down rules for all the arts, and it seemed in no way paradoxical to the age that such control should be praised by a series of original ballets and joyous plays. Molière's contribution to the celebration at Saint-Germain-en-Laye consisted of *Mélicerte* and *La Pastorale comique* in December, but his chief work was *Le Sicilien,* which neatly included the various arts in its plot so as to form part of a "Ballet of the Muses." The occasional piece really rises above its origins and is able to stand alone. The plot presents a jealous guardian, the Sicilian nobleman who vainly tries to keep his ward from a pursuing lover. The latter woos Isidore under the nose of Don Pedro, first by music, then by posing as a portrait painter, and his success is celebrated by a small pastoral ballet at the end. The comedy is in prose, but its effect is like a poetic sort of comic opera because there are interludes of music and poetry in the midst of the farce plot. As an experiment in incorporating the fine and lively arts into a comedy in some logical fashion, *Le Sicilien* depends upon a central character of a French nobleman, Adraste, who has many talents—more, surely, than the average courtier who saw the play. His abilities are essentially histrionic, making the comedy a triumph of playacting as well as of music and painting. A witty valet, Hali, is of great aid in the schemes, and his use of disguises suggests that "Turkish" ceremony we shall find in *Le Bourgeois gentilhomme.* The preparation of this latter play in the mind of Molière was to be hasty, insofar as the actual composition was concerned, but the experience of using "Turquerie" and a routine in lingua franca in *Le Sicilien* was valuable. The whole production of 1667 had such theatrical unity and strength that it set a pattern not only for later plays by Molière but also for musical comedy and light opera of succeeding generations. We think at once of the *Barber of Seville* of the late eighteenth century, noting that the opening serenade and the wooing in the disguise of music master are still going strong at this period. In the career of Molière we must count this small comedy as a worthwhile step in his progress toward the stylistic fusion of farce action and spectacle. When the strong satire and psychological realism that he could command were added to such a comedy, the resulting work was an *Amphitryon* or a *Bourgeois gentilhomme.*

Two other examples of practical showmanship combining farce and court ballet are *Monsieur de Pourceaugnac* of 1669 and *La Comtesse d'Escarbagnas* of 1672. *Amphitryon, George Dandin,* and *L'Avare* precede these in 1668, but we must return to them for a fuller examination. *Monsieur de Pourceaugnac,* the name of the main character, suggests both "pig" (*pourceau*) and noble pretensions with the particle *de,* so that the immediate effect is one of caricature, crude humor, and farce. The general style of commedia dell'arte comes to the fore once again in the unrestrained vigor and physical comedy of this play. With no subtlety, it presents a gullible countryman duped in a series of outrageously implausible situations, and violent clowning takes over, even controlling the sort of ballet that contributes less grace and beauty than sheer activity on stage. Musical interludes were composed by the leading court musician, Lully, and he participated personally in these scenes, so vigorously, in fact, that it is recorded that he once smashed a harpsichord in his exuberance. The comedy apparently was on the level of a modern Jimmy Durante's piano breaking. The plot framework has an older man seeking a young wife, and medical satire is heavy, but we are struck particularly by the preparation that this play offered Molière for his great treatment of a duped bourgeois, the "would-be gentleman."

La Comtesse d'Escarbagnas postdates *Le Bourgeois gentilhomme,* but a brief look at it helps us comprehend better Molière's achievement in the latter work. In one act he created a farcical "comedy-within-a-comedy" to please the king during the "Ballet of Ballets" held to celebrate the second marriage of Monsieur, Molière's old patron. Like Pourceaugnac, the countess is a provincial character with a desire like that of the *précieuses ridicules* to cultivate the high style and manners of Paris. Her companions in Angoulême are a droll group of country types who perform a function similar to that of the "bores" in *Les Fâcheux* since they impede a vicomte intent upon courting Julie, and the countess is the greatest impediment of all because she takes the attendance by the vicomte as attention to herself. The nobleman calls her "as good a character as could be put on the stage" (scene 1), indicating her nature as an exaggerated type with great claims to refinement and knowledge. The character will be fully developed in *Les Femmes savantes (The Learned Ladies)*, but here she is a quick theatrical sketch. The play is thus shown to be self-consciously stagy, and a play-within-a-play is the appropriate scheme to be followed as the vicomte offers a staged divertissement to Julie under the guise of honoring the countess. But the title character is the biggest spectacle, attempting to display her refinement while her country manners show through. She expects her provincial friends to behave like noble gentlemen and assigns them roles to play in her little court, but these are clumsily filled by a Thibaudet who is all *précieux* and by a Harpin who is coarse and blustering. A pedantic tutor, Bobinet, completes the burlesque trio. When a little pastoral play is given before this company, Harpin noisily interrupts and is reprimanded by the countess. He retorts, referring jealously to the flirtation with the vicomte, that "the real comedy is the one you are playing" (scene 8). The play ends with the arrival of news that a quarrel of their families that had kept the vicomte from wooing Julie openly is now resolved. He turns to her as the pastoral finishes, "Our comedy is over too" (scene 9). The idea of role-playing is used without much refinement here, and we shall observe how much further it can be carried in *Le Bourgeois gentilhomme*. As a brief excursion into theatrical illusion with a standard sort of farce basis, *La Comtesse d'Escarbagnas* has its merits, although Molière's continuing experiments with ballet spectacle may be of more value to our comprehension of his development.

Mélicerte, Pastorale comique, Les Amants magnifiques, Psyché

In creating farces mixed with musical numbers and dances, Molière was functioning as an effective entertainer, essentially practicing his trade. This trade, however, called for the production of plays that turned away from the tradition of sharp and stylized farce or satire played against a generalized background, the tradition in which Molière seemed most at home. The demand by court audiences for pure pictorial spectacle (and the ballets and operas of the period were largely this) had existed since the Renaissance, but the tendency in taste was toward illusionary theater in the 1660s, and the professional man of the theater was obliged to cater to taste. Thus, Molière created court ballets that presented a challenge to the inventive creator of theatrical forms; each effort at ballet was handled in a slightly different way as Molière approached the problem of just what nature a dramatic production should have. Technical means of all sorts were at his command, for scenic designers from Italy could devise dazzling effects in pictorial perspective, exploit the green vistas of a palace garden, or make miraculous apparitions in the sky. The problem that the serious dramatist had to confront was how to use such technical devices with genuine theatrical meaning. We have seen how Molière was able to infuse new life and significance into comedy based on farce patterns, elevating the genre into a *Misanthrope* or expanding it into new dimensions in *Les Fâcheux*, but the task of merging illusionary scene and significant theater as he understood it was very hard. The uneven quality of *Dom Juan* testifies to the uneasiness resulting from a mixing of serious themes with successive illusionary stage settings. When illusion was meant to be purely spectacular and nonrealistic, the author was usually forced to abandon serious purpose. *Amphitryon* will be the great exception, but the majority of the ballet entertainments are overwhelmed by their aspects that are not congenial with Molière's best talents.

Mélicerte constitutes a workmanlike accomplishment of a chore, for the royal court wished a ballet on gallant love in precious style, and Molière composed his "heroic pastoral comedy" using a plot of double substitution of children like that of a novel by Mlle de Scudéry. Delicate problems of identity and the nature of love are presented in typical style, and this play resembles most *La Princesse d'Elide*. The little work remained unfinished, since Molière had to produce other things for the "Ballet of the Muses." As a brief introduction to the royal fête he composed the *Pastorale comique* which mocks the style of *Mélicerte* with its shepherds and idyllic setting. Created for performance by the king and his courtiers, it is a gay mixture of dances and comic routines. At the start, for example, a burlesque ceremony of the robing of a shepherd by magicians and demons takes place, and we think of the beginning of *Le Bourgeois gentilhomme* as the *riche pasteur* Lycas is praised for his beauty. Lycas was played in clownish fashion by the author, and he freely introduced magic appearances and disappearances of the dancing figures to create an atmosphere of fancy as well as of comedy. Parody of serious pastoral drama is evident as the comic hero and his companion prepare to die for hopeless love, then reconsider the whole idea.

Les Amants magnifiques is a much more fully developed sort of royal ballet produced in 1670 to celebrate the military and amatory successes of Louis. It is called a "comedy mixed with music and ballet," and its conception is attributed to the king himself in a foreword: "The King, who wishes only extraordinary things in all that he undertakes, proposed to give to his court an entertainment which would be composed of all that the theater can furnish; and, to encompass this vast idea, and to link together so many diverse things, His Majesty chose as a subject two rival princes . . . who entertain a young princess and her mother with all the gallantries which they can imagine." The scheme of the work is exactly that, a pretext for elegant ballets, but we must note the settings which are described in detail because they are really more important than the banal action. Six *intermèdes* are the core of the play, and two will serve to give the tone. Beauty of spectacle and illusionary effects are stressed above all in the following:

Fourth Interlude: The theater represents a grotto where the Princesses go to walk, and while they are there, eight statues, each one carrying two torches in his hands, do a varied dance of several figures and beautiful attitudes in which they remain at intervals.

Sixth Interlude: The theater is a great hall like an amphitheater, open with a large arcade in the background, over which is a tribune closed by a curtain, and in the distance appears an altar for sacrifice. . . .

This sixth and final interlude contains all the elements that were to take over completely in court and elevated theater after the passing of Molière; against an illusionist setting imitating ancient beauties of architecture drawn in perspective (and using an arcade to frame a distant scene), elegantly garbed figures stage a solemn spectacle of music and dance. This is the opera as it will be presented and promoted by Lully, and it marks the triumph of the Italian school of scenic design as well as the triumph of spectacle.[2] Molière handles these things capably, but they have no scope for his sort of genius. The situation of the comic dramatist forced to work at the sort of thing that wastes his professional potential is repeated once again when Molière collaborates in the production of the ballet of *Psyché*.

The ailing playwright could write only the first part of *Psyché* for a court entertainment of carnival time in 1671, and Corneille and Quinault completed the verses of the play. This is termed a tragedy-ballet and is actually an excuse to use some spectacular machines and settings to delight an audience avid for such visual thrills. The hand of the comic master is to be seen in some of the characterizations in the first act, but, aside from this, little of Molière's theatrical skill is evident. The great spectacle was first given in the Hall of Machines at the Tuileries palace and then transferred for the pleasure of the public to the hall of the Palais-Royal four months later. It was the talk of Paris, and the final scene with hundreds of divinities appearing in the sky was at once the zenith of machine effects and a sure indicator of the style of theater that was to prevail.

From *Les Fâcheux* on, Molière perceived and worked with music, ballet, and spectacle as valuable adjuncts to his comic plays rather than merely tolerating and adapting them as required parts of his entertainments. The originality and skill that he could muster to exploit these elements and cause them to illuminate the ideas of his comedies tended to be overwhelmed by the massive machine plays and court ballets like those just described, and the man's health and strength were not up to the physical effort necessary to produce the sort of court entertainments that were truly in his style. The best use that he makes of dance is to express a wild exuberance and irresistible force, sweeping along an old Sganarelle. The scheme will be used to great effect with Monsieur Jourdain, "the would-be gentleman," and even the hypochondriac Argan of *Le Malade imaginaire*. The endings that feature such a dance produce a wonderful sense of sheer vitality, joy, and lift, as the raw energy first communicated in the commedia dell'arte style in the early farces becomes channeled and disciplined. Reason and fixed notions are swept along before the movement and melody, and this is actually the concept of many of Molière's endings rather than an emphasis on the power of reason to triumph over eccentricity. But unless the interludes and spectacles had some function as expression of a theme, they would offer mere titillation of the senses and serve merely as unconnected adornment. Many writers could handle theater on this level; a Molière was necessary to infuse real life and meaning into plays composed with all of these varied parts.

Chapter Seven
Myth and Reality in Marriage
Amphitryon

Machines pictorial illusions, living tableaux, and splendid spectacle—these were the features sought after by the audiences composed of the courtiers of Louis. Molière could produce such things upon demand, but when he put his mind to it, he could add a lot of poetic and ironic truth to the play. Such a creation is his *Amphitryon*. Disparate parts like social satire and dazzling effects of nonreality merge together into a work with strong inner coherence and meaning.

In view of the fact that *Amphitryon* turns upon a plot of confusions of identity it is appropriate to consider just how baroque Molière was in his writing for the stage. The presence of such plots in the plays suggests that an author who ranges from simple works about misidentifications like those in *Le Dépit amoureux* to works of great sophistication about self-delusions, *Le Misanthrope* for example, must be part of a cultural current that seemed preoccupied with the tensions produced by questions of identity. The opposition of realities and appearances is another typical manifestation of baroque thought, and we are led to conclude that most of the creations of Molière tend to place him as an artist of this period. This seems true only to the extent that he wrote to please the taste of the age and found his materials in its literature and theater, and, in a higher sense, it is possible to say that his plots and themes are fundamentally comic rather than symptomatic of a movement. Theater that deals with man as a temporal creature subject to his limited illusions and to ambiguities imposed upon him is basically comic. When the characters self-consciously ponder and philosophize about their peculiar states, then such theater moves into a more baroque category, but Molière's figures are not accustomed to uttering monologues about their queer situations. If they could analyze them, they would not be comic. Arnolphe, in *L'École des femmes,* approaches such a state more than any other character in that he sees how he is split by conflicting tendencies of tyranny and tenderness; but intellectual self-assessment is seldom a strong point in the major figures we have observed. They are essentially doers, not musers, and the

misanthropic Alceste, to whom some critics lend great philosophical wisdom, is a man of action forced to function in a world of slippery words that he
prefers to thrust aside.

When Molière took as his subject the popular myth of Jupiter's assumption of mortal form to woo a woman, he had an excellent opportunity to give
a highly baroque treatment to the material, as had been done by Rotrou in his
Les Sosies. In this earlier work of the seventeenth century the author stressed
the pondering by the slave Sosie of his doubling by another Sosie, Mercury in
disguise.[1] The orientation in Molière's comedy remains wholly earthbound
in that there is no recognition of the possibilities of another realm of identity
and existence. Mythical material is humanized and "socialized," so that the
interference by gods in human affairs is turned into a satire about motives of
sex and control of others. It is an exploitation of spectacle and fantasy for purposes that are quite typical of Molière's plays. Given a case in which Jupiter
takes the form of Amphitryon to gain the bed of the man's wife, what would
the results be on the human level of practicality? When the great royal lover
preempted a lady of the court in this manner (and the audience was quick to
see the flattery of Louis and his amatory prowess), accommodation was essential. To see in *Amphitryon* a deep intellectualizing of a problem is as erro-
neous as to see nothing but court spectacle in it. The tendency in the plays of
this stage of the writer's career is toward a hearty affirmation in the endings of
the power of the collective social will. Eccentricity and folly are not permitted
to impede the orderly working of society that expresses its control by isolating
a miser or whirling a social climber off in a wild dance.

The way in which Molière changed the myth shows how he forced it to
serve his typical ends; the noble love affair is paralleled by the relationship between Sosie and his wife, Cléanthis, a character invented by the writer to permit this old scheme of comic routines. The subject of love and marriage, the
bread and butter of comic stage, is central in *Amphitryon*, yet this work is not
entirely like so many of the other comedies dealing in it. It is distinguished
not only by the use of spectacle with some poetic effect but also by the deep
tone of irony that pervades, a tone that gives this court entertainment a bite
surprisingly sharp, evocative of that of *Tartuffe*. The ancient myth of a god
descending to earth to sire a hero becomes debased to a resigned commentary
on human foibles in matrimony, and much of the ironic comment comes
from the "little man" caught up in the antics of his superiors. He has a prominent role and is given the curtain speech, so that analogies with Don Juan's
Sganarelle are apparent. There is no protesting bitterness by master or servant, let it be noted, nor is there any moral judgment on the abuse of power.
The facts are laid on the line ironically by their poetically lovely presentation,

and this is what makes the play so unique and effective. When Molière adds a realistic reflection of the main plot in having Mercury dally with Sosie's wife, all actions of gods are brought down to a very human level and satirized.

The theme of the comedy, then, can be expressed as an idea of acceptance, and, in matters of rule and love, life's realities require that one accept the power of status, conventions, and outward signs. The moral message is neither inspiring nor edifying, yet it is a strong affirmation of social stability and timeless truth of the type. Actually, *Amphitryon* is much more purely and traditionally comic than *Le Misanthrope*. Even gods are reduced to behaving like men and are subject to principles of human behavior and acceptance of the central idea because, despite being all-powerful, the very ruler of heaven must take on mortal form and play the mortal marriage game to satisfy his sexual desires. The irony inherent in the situation appealed to Molière, no doubt, who created a Jupiter dependent upon having the outward signs of Alcmena's husband in order to win her. Status lets Jupiter toy with people in this way but does not exempt him from the rules. It might seem to us that Louis could have been displeased by such an implication of his limitations. His affair with Mme de Montespan was reflected so gracefully by the form of the comedy (and he probably perceived his situation quite realistically) that he did not take the work other than as a fine compliment. The courtiers shared his enthusiasm.

The use of free verse as well as alexandrines in *Amphitryon* is notable. Such a form is all the more important when we consider the theme of the work, and the final words by Sosie on the situation sum up also Molière's skill in sweetening an ironic play: "My lord Jupiter knows how to sugar the pill" (3.10). The novel verses are *vers libres* which rhyme *abab* but which vary in length, and these are interspersed with the customary lines of twelve syllables. The effect of such verses in the mouths of a Mercury, a Sosie, or an Amphitryon can be very supple and varied, suiting the different personalities and stations in life. The similar excellence of the fables of La Fontaine comes to mind. The appeal of poetry is coupled with that of ingenious stage machines permitting appearances of Mercury on a cloud chatting with Night or a miraculous descent and departure by Jupiter. The official critic of the age, Boileau, found this work below *Le Misanthrope* in quality, but he displayed little sympathy for theatrical invention that could turn machines to good dramatic purpose. The coordination of imaginative staging with verbal poetry of a high order was with the aim of expressing the themes suggested above. Some résumé and excerpts will illuminate the work.

A prologue conversation between Mercury and Night, situated on a machine cloud, serves to set a tone of ironic debunking amidst the charming spectacle. Reality of ideas and nonreality of setting are cleverly combined. In a bantering exchange Night is asked to prolong darkness to favor the amours of Jupiter, but the subtlest suggestion of the tone of the work is in Mercury's recognition of the fact that he exists largely as an invention of poets and mythmakers, whom he treats very flippantly. Any lofty pretensions of meaning by the author seem punctured by the disrespect of the characters for their creator. The discussion of the many love affairs of Jupiter is done in elegant style, but the history of Don Juan related by Sganarelle is very similar. In act 1 Jupiter visits Alcmena and woos her with eloquence, declaring that conjugal love based on duty can be replaced by passion if she will look upon her husband as a lover. The god has the form of Amphitryon, but the words are not his, and there ensues a delicate argument on the nature of married love that is worthy of a precious novel; the lover, it is declared, "wants to obtain your ardor from a pure source" (1.3). The trickery involved to win Alcmena contrasts sharply with the noble words, and we see that Molière is constructing a play once more on themes of masking and role-playing. The entire work is self-consciously illusionistic, from the prologue's keynote to the final resolution of a plot about deceptions by appearances. The comedy seems to urge us constantly to remember that all is just stage play, yet this urging brings home to us the sharp implications of meaning.

The "comedy of errors" routine begins as Sosie encounters Mercury who has assumed his shape. Sosie has entered very full of his importance as a messenger from Amphitryon, and he rehearses and polishes his speech for great dramatic effect, a device that stresses the theatricality of the work. Mercury uses physical persuasion on Sosie to make him acknowledge that he is not himself: "It's true, up to now, I believed the matter was clear, but your stick has made me see that I was deceived in this" (1.2). The scene remains on the level of slapstick farce because Sosie does not indulge in any profound speculation as to his nature, reasoning later that obviously he must be himself. The slave is governed by physical laws of being and resorts to pinching himself to feel his reality. The stick of Mercury is a more potent argument, however, so Sosie accepts the dictates of the god. When two Amphitryons appear before him and give conflicting orders, he resolves the problem of identification by physical means again, deciding that the "real Amphitryon is the one where he gets his dinner" (3.5). This is the common man's sort of vital necessity, just as status and conformity to appearances are the essential things for the noble characters. His role is one of unquestioning acceptance, even though his observations are accurate and well expressed, for he has not sufficient status to possess truth and must be silent when so ordered. "All speeches are nonsense when they come from a person without lofty position. They would be exquisite words if a nobleman were speaking" (2.1). The expression of truth counts for nothing unless it is done in acceptable social forms, and Sosie is quite resigned to these conditions: "In such matters, the best thing is always to be silent" (3.10).

Jupiter announces his real nature to the mortals and declares that Alcmena shall bear his son Hercules. His departure on a cloud with conventional rattling of thunderbolts then takes place. The normal social order of the human world resumes, never having been threatened seriously by the incursion of the gods, for Jupiter could move among men effectively only by being one of them, and despite his glorious exit our impression of him is that he too must submit to the necessity of playing a conformist role. The ironic principle extends even to the all-powerful individual, be he king or god, and all the poetic and spectacular delight of the comedy does not erase the basic thought. If *Amphitryon* is not one of the greatest of Molière's works, it stands as a brilliant piece of theatrical experiment, a successful mixture of disparate parts. It surely never corrected any social evils by its satire, but the deflation of pretentious stage production by a master producer who set up his machines and then mocked them was highly effective. It served to put the theater of spectacle back into a proper comic focus.

As a companion piece Molière's *George Dandin* offered a more serious treatment of social forces with less deliberate comment on theatrical problems. It was written in 1668 and followed *Amphitryon* by a few months as a court entertainment, but, aside from the chronological relationship, the two plays form an interesting pair as comedies on marriage and status.

George Dandin, ou le mari confondu

The fusion of the realities of human society with illusionary, poetic theater was achieved in *Amphitryon;* in *George Dandin, or the Dumbfounded Husband* Molière continued to mix these elements but in different proportions. The original production was part of a court-ballet entertainment, yet the author did not attempt to deal in terms of charm and fantasy, proceeding rather to work in harsh satire baldly stated in prose. The gently ironic tone of the preceding comedy was replaced by a heavy one that farcical gaiety barely covered.

The plebeian Dandin makes a misalliance with the daughter of the noble Sotenville family, and the results of this folly are the bitter pill that he must swallow, quite unsugared by any Jupiter. The suggestion that "love can level ranks," as W. S. Gilbert says in *H.M.S. Pinafore,* would be unthinkable in the stratified and closed society of the 1660s, so Dandin is obliged to accept his

fixed identity, low of station and cuckold. No comic logic in a topsy-turvy
world can rescue him, and Molière ends his play with stress on the hopeless-
ness of the character's plight, caught in a situation that he thought he desired.
The desperate thought that suicide is the only way out is not very funny, and
"the dumbfounded husband" appears less a figure of humor to us than he did
to the seventeenth-century audience which could only agree that he was a fool
to go against rules of convention and status.

Thematically, this comedy turns about the idea of fixity, because the hero
is obviously fixed in his worldly position yet is deceived by the illusion of
changing it by taking on other forms and appearances. The action of the play
is to reduce him rudely to his original state; ruefully he faces the truth about
himself and repeats, "You asked for it" (1.7). The curious thing is that this
speech is in the first act, and we see that recognition of his state has taken
place before the curtain ever rises. The subject of the deceived husband puts
matters on a plane of farce or commedia, making Dandin into the typical
clownish sufferer of indignities. Refuge can be found only in flights of unreal-
ity, and this is seen in the final ballet into which he must be dragged against
his will. Sosie ends *Amphitryon* by making the best of things, but Dandin is
no patient slave who can accept his fate. Of all the abused clowns in Molière's
theater he elicits most real sympathy because his little dream of happiness is
destroyed so harshly. This is a comedy about fixity, and the title character
serves as a pivot about which all moves, very much to his awareness.

Knowing all that goes on, the duped husband is unable to defend himself,
recalling for us the situation of *L'École des femmes,* but *George Dandin* is a
rather devaluated version of the earlier play. A stupid servant tells him all the
activities of his unfaithful wife, and George tries to make his in-laws witness
to her conduct. The names of Sotenville ("stupid in town" for country nobility) and Angélique need little comment on their significance, nor is Dandin,
suggestive of "simpleton," very subtle. The crushingly evident characterizes
this comedy, as Dandin sees the flagrant infidelity of Angélique, abandons
all pretense at personal honor, and calls upon the Sotenvilles to bear witness
to his being cuckolded. All of this is unavailing, and we observe him squirm-
ing like an insect on a pin. From his first speech this is clear: "Ah! how strange
it is to have a noble lady for a wife, and how my marriage is an eloquent lesson
for all peasants who want to rise above their condition and marry, like me,
into a gentleman's family! The nobility is fine in itself, a great thing surely,
but it is accompanied by so many bad circumstances that it is well not to get
too cozy with it" (1.1). He says that he was accepted by the Sotenvilles for his
wealth and that he is husband in name only. "George Dandin, you have done
the stupidest thing in the world" (1.1).

Complete recognition of the truth is useless, so he is led about in a wild chase, always confounded in his efforts to combat his fate. Like the clown of *La Jalousie du barbouillé,* he is forced to go out of his own house or to hear Clitandre make love to his wife. A prisoner within the boundaries he himself has created, Dandin is constantly obliged to accept what must be and to be reduced to impotency. His very name is taken from him by the Sotenvilles, who want something more elegant, like "La Dandinnière," to cover his peasant origins. The round of activity going on about him emphasizes his forlorn loneliness, and, after the final deception when Angélique fakes suicide to get him out of the way, he can think only in terms of escape in death, "to jump in the water head first" (3.8). Such a somber touch is coupled with the harshness of the portraits of all the types, and were it not for the farce plot and style, the comedy would be bitter satire of social evils. The provincial nobility is shown as grasping and ignorant, their daughter as immoral and unprincipled, and the lover as a small-time Don Juan.

Is *George Dandin,* then, the blackest of comedies? It is important to observe the setting in which it was created, and the background of pastoral ballet leads us to think that the somber tones of the play were deliberately set in contrast to the gay brilliance of a royal *fête champêtre.* Rather than drown his sorrows in a pond, it is suggested that Dandin drown them in wine, and a dance of shepherds and shepherdesses then celebrates the joys of love and Bacchus. The two aspects of the entertainment should be kept in mind.

As a sort of parallel to *Amphitryon,* this comedy is obviously below it in artistic finish or experimentation, yet the comment it makes on the idea of acceptance of status and the rules of the game of love is probably stronger. Moral force, however, is not the criterion for judgment of a work of this sort, but rather effectiveness of handling of theatrical forms must be evaluated. Farce, the clown as patient, the social force as agent, the movement about the fixed pivot—all of these elements are handled with meaningful cohesiveness. The crudity and cruelty are appropriate theatrical tones adopted to communicate a strong affirmation of the collective values of a closed society and its ways. Social cohesion is to be accepted as the governing principle of temporal existence, and it is better to take it as an excuse for song and dance instead of courting disaster by trying to change the order. The path leading to the creation of *Le Bourgeois gentilhomme* lies clear ahead of Molière.

Chapter Eight
On Wealth and Happiness

The great number of *comédies-ballets* that Molière created for the delight of the royal court can only have confirmed in him the knowledge that any development of a "new comedy" in the style of a *Tartuffe* would have to be made on the Parisian stage. In one phenomenal success he was to integrate elevated satire and musical comedy, but the production of his last years, 1668 to 1673, was above all a return to his early farce techniques to which he gave a new heightening. In a prose theater of conventionalized farce and slapstick, the ailing author and director found his ultimate medium, reasserting the values of this stage as the true means of symbolic expression then available to the comic dramatist. The possibilities of poetic and illusionary theater were clear to him, we must conclude from *Amphitryon,* but a different and personal sort of stage poetry, that of hard, brilliant, and self-conscious theatrical illusion, gave free rein to his style. In his hands stock forms knew no limits of meaning.

L'Avare

Late in 1668 Molière returned to the stage of the Palais-Royal to put on *L'Avare* (*The Miser*) which had been planned for a year. This full-scale comedy in prose was not versified for good reason since it constituted a definite experiment in a new style, with a "low" technique of expression called upon to treat a "high" subject. Borrowing the material of Plautus's *Aulularia* and other miser plays, he set about creating a sharp satire of some ugly human traits and still retained his usual framework of farce routines and values. The merging of psychological realism with what amounts to stylized form of prose farce makes of *L'Avare* one of Molière's carefully conceived innovations. The use of prose in *Dom Juan,* it will be recalled, was called for by the haste of composition, but the writer must have been interested in seeing what could be achieved in this style.

The rather dark picture of corruption of the human spirit by gold may have disappointed a public eager for gay entertainment, and we must consider just why this play should be termed a comedy and not a moral drama.

The problem is the same as the one that confronted us in studying *Tartuffe* and *Dom Juan,* for thematically *L'Avare* repeats much found in the plays about the impostor and the seducer. Motives of sex and power come to the fore again, nor are we surprised to observe that Molière has got around to linking them to the theme of wealth and greed. The threat by the dangerous individual to the social order is contained, as usual, and there is a familiar contrived ending to settle matters. The play may thus be classed as one with great dramatic and moral potential that is kept from taking these directions by the author's vigorous use of heavy comic techniques. The apparent scheme of running through a series of variations on a theme will remind us of the nature of the work, so that the pernicious effects of gold upon human love do not overwhelm us with a moral lesson but rather serve as one variation of theme, the nature of possession in love.

The setting selected for the play is important. In a bourgeois living room of the period (what has become the "Molière room" of French theater) the unities of place and action take on a natural realism that may delude us into seeing the entire comedy in such terms. The transplanting of comedy into such a setting was observed first in *Les Précieuses ridicules,* and the device is to be exploited yet more. Let us recall that the standard locale for comedy was the street, reflecting both the medieval, popular tradition of farce on trestle stages and a learned, Italian notion of ancient comic set. *George Dandin* was set "in front of the house," and *Monsieur de Pourceaugnac, La Comtesse d'Escarbagnas,* and *Les Fourberies de Scapin* take place in generalized *place publique* settings of Paris, Angoulême, and Naples, respectively. The other works of the final period are played in the bourgeois salon. To this extent, Molière took advantage of the skill of the scenic decorators of his theater, using illusionary décor for the purpose of giving a visual comment on the in-tellectual or mental action of his comedy.[1] The appearance of "real life" is pure theatrical trick, however, for the real world is jammed by the comedy into a distorted and zany mold by the rigorous adherence to conventional farce and commedia patterns.

Harpagon, a wealthy widower, is in a dilemma caused by the conflicting desires to hoard his gold and to take a costly young wife. The standard plot is soon established, complete with a son, Cléante, in love with a poor girl, Mariane, on whom his father has marital designs. Harpagon, like Oregon, ruthlessly sacrifices the happiness of Cléante and of a daughter, Elise, in love with Valère. The girl is to be married off to a rich old man who will take her without cost of dowry to Harpagon. The miser is worried about his buried treasure in the garden, and a running gag is established as he trots out period-ically to check the hoard. When he suspects his servant of spying on the hoard, he fires him brutally. Misunderstandings multiply as Cléante finds that he is not only rival with his father for Mariane but also has been borrowing money at an outrageous rate of interest from his father, the unknown lender he had been put in touch with. A marriage broker comes in to promote the wedding of Harpagon and Mariane, but she stands truth on its head by flattering the old man.

The conflict of love for gold and the desire for the girl is the basis of a scene in act 3 in which Mariane must be entertained at dinner. The extremes of parsimony are wildly exaggerated as Harpagon instructs his household in economy for the banquet. Cléante takes a diamond from his father and presents it to her for him, causing the miser agonies, but Harpagon is no fool and perceives the love between his son and Mariane. A clownish butler, Maître Jacques, has a Gros-René sort of role in trying to make peace among his betters, confusing reason and getting nothing but buffets for his trouble. At the end of act 4 the chest of money is stolen by the discharged servant, eliciting the frantic plea by Harpagon to all, including the audience, to help him catch the thief. Molière, who called for a realistic stage setting, deliberately broke through the theoretical "fourth wall" of the room and had his Harpagon speak "across the footlights" to the people in the hall, shattering one theatrical illusion for the purpose of creating a higher one. The madness of the miser has illusionary powers transcending conventions of stage setting, as his speech shows:

Stop, thief! . . . (*taking his own arm*). Give me back my money, you wretch! Oh, it's me. My mind is disturbed and I don't know where I am, who I am, or what I'm doing. . . . Alas, my poor money . . . my consolation, my joy. . . . What a lot of people out there! I can't look at anyone without suspecting him, and everyone seems to be my thief. What are you talking about there? . . . I beg you to tell me. . . . Isn't he hidden among you? They all look at me and start to laugh. . . . Police, judges, hangmen! I want to hang everyone, and if I don't get my money back I'll hang myself! (4.7)[2]

Act 5 neatly resolves the problem of getting the young couples ready to marry. Valère and Mariane turn out to be the long-lost children of Anselme, to whom Harpagon wanted to marry Elise. The deus ex machina ending, outrageous as it is, serves a good functional purpose, for it permits the simultaneous joining together of the miser and his beloved, the chest of gold. It is as if comic principles had to triumph by any means over the threat to society in the person of the miser seeking domination; healthy love and youth are victorious over selfish possessiveness and aged sterility.

Neither as brilliant as *Tartuffe* nor as challenging as *Dom Juan*, *L'Avare* still commands our interest as an experiment in theatrical techniques that rely upon and reaffirm farce while suggesting the range of moral import possible in such theater. It has been observed that ideas of "identity, coincidence, duality, exclusion, incompatibility, tenderness, generosity, and vanity" are thematic, nor is the critic wrong in perceiving these things, but the analysis of the play's structure as a forceful juxtaposition of opposites that are calculated to split the work apart at its end seems overdrawn.[3] Fracture is threatened throughout the play (the stock Molière routine that parodies serious drama), but the strength of the ending is such in Molière's dramaturgy that it banishes the threat of a real split and imparts a sense of joyous physical assembling of all parties. Harpagon is not banished from the scene so that the others may resume a normal existence (Tartuffe's fate) but is very much present in the contrived denouement, and he has his share of happiness, warped as it is by his mania. The impression of traditional comic sense and significance is so great that we may go briefly through the play and see how its parts are organically structured to lead us to such an ending.

In *L'Avare* the title suggests a verb that serves to set forth the action: to possess. From start to finish the unifying idea is happy possession of the object desired, whether this is the loved person or the chest of money. Joy of lovers, parental love, and the avarice of the miser can be brought together in meaningful combination at the end, but the play may be termed successful only if the thematic relationships are clearly developed throughout. An expanded statement of the action of the comedy is necessary to cover the rapidly changing scenes of assorted mimetic activity, and the observation by Hubert that words of love and finance are neatly interwoven aids in elaboration of our definition.[4] Engagements in debt and in love may be means or impediments to happiness, so the characters all find themselves trying to get a clear way to touch the treasure desired. Motives of sex and avarice are mutually illuminating, and for them to be fulfilled certain obstacles must be surmounted. Bonds of obligation of various sorts are stressed heavily through the comedy, with claims of filial loyalty, financial debts, bonds of love, relationships between servant and master, and respect for human values posing problems for the characters. Elise and Cléante must liberate themselves from a tyrannical parent to marry; Cléante must also break free from the usurer; Valère and Mariane have to overcome social and financial barriers; and the servants must circumvent the restrictions of the miser to serve him properly. In all respects, the play and its parts emphasize "becoming free to possess one's desire"

The cases of all the figures are clear-cut, with the exception of that of Harpagon himself, and in this character Molière displays great skill in showing shifting planes of values and impressions of the world about him. When Harpagon wavers in treading the thin line between normal and abnormal desires, the playwright devises speeches and business to exploit the duality and yet show the unifying theme of effort to reach his true desire. Lack of accurate perception of his own nature leads him into the position of wanting a young bride while being unwilling to spend enough money to keep up a suitable home for her. His gentleman's household has been reduced to a "phantom" with a skeleton force of starving servants and horses. He does not know what he must free himself from, and because this basic action of cutting self free from things goes against the grain of the acquisitive miser, he is in a position of simultaneously grasping and deciding what to reject. The movement of the comedy is thus a function of his increasing clarity about what his true fetters are, that is, human concerns with paternal and sexual love, kindness, generosity, and respect for others. The comical hesitations and shifts which he goes through are the essential normal touch in the characterization that otherwise would verge upon the monstrous. W. G. Moore comments, "This man obsessed by money is shown in situations which do not stress, as they do not deny, his wickedness; they illumine the range and the limits of his obsession. His own energy (a significant point) drives him into situations in which he becomes a man like the rest of us."[5]

Thus, we are reminded not to put too much stock in the moral implications of the case of the miser, thwarted or not. He is a moral caricature, a stage figure, and the denouement and the broad farce style of scenes like the dinner indicate that all is in the realm of stage magic. Is the ending an evasion of the harsh realities of avarice and selfishness? It seems not, just because of the deliberate use of comic *lazzi* (the physical comic routines Molière learned from Italian comedy) that kill any pretense at serious dramatic effect and create a topsy-turvy world. Molière's aim is to put into motion a rapid series of staged actions, the sum of which is indicative of the meaning of the play. The sheer movement about a theme such as we have elicited is meaningful in itself, and the means employed in this movement are arrangements of analogies, symmetries, and repetitions on the subject of possession of property and love.

At the start of the play, in characteristic manner, the notion of deception by words is established as a structural element, and the deception of Cléante by his father, for example, is introduced naturally. Elise says: "All men are alike in their words, and it is only their actions that reveal them to be different" (1.1). Then, too, Molière will constantly show us Harpagon deceiving himself by his words, as he goes so far as to think that he "loves" Mariane in the conventional sense of the word. The repeated gag line in his mouth, "Without a dowry!," is a good sample of his substitution of cant for values. As the characters labor to see their ways clear to surmounting all the obstacles before them, they are hindered by the language in which the situations must be discussed. Polite verbal intercourse, for one thing, hardly illuminates truth, as the author stressed in *Le Misanthrope,* and Elise has trouble communicating sincerely with her Valère: "Do not assassinate me . . ." pleads the lover, and his mistress is not sure whether this is verbal smokescreen or sincere anguish. It is hard enough to possess truth about oneself without having matters obscured by meaningless verbiage.

The next element for expression of themes is that of "mask" as it is referred to by Valère. He complains that he must act in disguise as the maître d'hôtel in order to be near Elise, and he regrets his compromise with sincerity. But all the characters will play a false role to deceive others at some time in the comedy, with evil or good intentions. Maître Jacques's comic quick changes of costume from chef to coachman underscore in visual fashion this concept. Sincerity is played off against falseness, however, as Elise and Cléante declare their loves, and Harpagon is quite truthful with himself in his frenzy about guarding his gold. The general tone of falsehood and suspicion dominates the first act, and it culminates in a scene in which Valère finds himself obliged to praise the miser's scheme to marry Elise to Anselme "without a dowry."

The rest of the play does not bring in new techniques or ideas so much as it sets up developments of the material at hand, for we see Harpagon being a secret usurer to his own son behind the mask of his agent and deliberately trapping Cléante into admitting his love for Mariane. The playwright devises a series of variations on his theme and finally ties the whole business up in a neat comic package by the ending that has been described. Rather than creating an effect of disruption and breach at the end, Molière marries together the conflicting parts of his work, the ugliness of greed and the beauty of love, by presenting simultaneously a traditional comic ending and a caricature of the tragic ending, abnormal sterility and death of the soul. The young people embrace each other, while the miser treats his chest of gold like a virgin bride: "They did not take anything away from you?" (5.6). The use of the unnatural love in comic form is the master stroke that creates the ultimate unity of *L'Avare* as a work of art. The contributing elements of dupery, masking, and deceptive words are all brought to mind at the end, after they have created obstacles now swept aside. Through the medium of the clown, Maître Jacques, Molière recalls to us his essential building materials in the comedy: "They give me blows for telling the truth, and they want to hang me for lying" (5.6). Right up to the end he is a burlesque mirror of the essential ac-

tion, stumbling into the pitfalls now passed by everyone else, confusing matters, and failing to gain what he wants. The satire on desire and possession is
complete.

One is finally led to the conclusion that the play is so satisfactory because
of the poetic and theatrical fitness of all of its parts and their arrangement,
that is, the inevitability and the wholeness of the work show the hand of the
master maker of comedy. Much the same effect is produced by the court entertainment of 1670, which was hastily turned out to royal order. In the
comedy-ballet of *Le Bourgeois gentilhomme* the qualities of *L'Avare* are to be
found, but wonderfully augmented by the stage of spectacle and music.

Le Bourgeois gentilhomme

In many important ways *Le Bourgeois gentilhomme* (*The Would-be Gentleman*), written in 1670, exemplifies the essence of Molière's theater, and it is
highly significant as a stage in his late career. It marks a moment of some triumph, yet is embittered by a sense of frustration as the playwright demonstrates his genius in *comédie-ballet* and then is forced to admit that public
taste really wants something else. A play in the style of *L'Avare* was not necessarily the answer, for this was not an unqualified success, and our impression
of the works created during Molière's final years is that he ceased bold experimentation to repeat with brilliance his successes of his early period. Thus, *Les
Fourberies de Scapin* is an *Etourdi* masterfully reworked; *Les Femmes savantes*
is a full-scale *Précieuses;* and *Le Malade imaginaire* is a sharp satire with musical interludes. The biographers of the man give ample evidence of his weari-
ness, illness, and personal troubles at this stage, but our major interest is in his
attitude as it affected his creations. His works suggest a professional's bitterness at inventing a superior product and seeing it rejected; the "new comedy"
that he personally conceived and made did not set the pattern to be followed
by comic theater. The trouble was partly because he was too unique and in-
imitable, but it was small comfort to be a genius in a conformist world.

Le Bourgeois gentilhomme is all the more impressive when we reflect upon
how much the author packed into it in executing a specific royal command
for a musical entertainment to include some Turkish bits. The sultan's am-
bassador had visited the court, so *turquerie* was a current fad, and for a royal
fête at Chambord it was ordered that the official troupe entertain in this style.
Under the hand of Molière the performance joined humor, spectacle, and
sharp satire in a *comedie-ballet*. The ambiguity created by the introduction of
some ugly human traits into plays like *Tartuffe* is avoided, yet the serious import of the work is not less. This is achieved by the use of a thematic principle

wherein the title character pursues a powerful illusion, in this case the effort
to achieve self-fulfillment by extreme conformity to social status patterns.
Absurdly exaggerated social climbing takes on a certain serious tone as it becomes a harmful excrescence threatening the happiness of others. Society actually finds itself disrupted by an egoist who only wants to live up to its strict
forms. It is rather like a burlesque version of *Le Misanthrope* in which a theoretical virtue is a destructive force in worldly social intercourse.

The "would-be gentleman" is introduced by a series of danced or highly
stylized routines in which tailors, dancing and fencing masters, and a professor of philosophy converge upon the bourgeois to convert his exterior at least
into the simulacrum of a gallant nobleman. The audience of courtiers at
Chambord was used to seeing ballets with pastoral or mythical figures, so
that the appearance of tailor's apprentices in a dance took them a bit by sur-
prise. The inventiveness of the author in setting up a ritual of dressing and
training the socially ambitious merchant, Monsieur Jourdain, shows his ability to make ballet serve his ends as a meaningful part of a central "action." A
conventional plot of frustrated lovers who are finally affianced is the thread
upon which Molière strings a series of witty and significant scenes. The first
two acts are devoted to showing Jourdain's efforts at self-improvement, the
disruption of his household, and their need to curb his folly. The power of delusion by costume and ritual seems to be unbeatable, so the obvious course of
the suitor, Cléonte, and the daughter, Lucile, is to turn such power to their advantage. This they will do with the aid of the clever valet, Covielle, who will
convince Jourdain that he is to be honored by the Turkish sultan, Cléonte
being passed off as the son of the Grand Turk. The witty Covielle is paralleled by a pert servant, Nicole, who aids in defeating the plans of her master.
The roster of masking types is completed by two courtiers, Dorante, a nobleman who sponges on Jourdain's full purse, and a marquise whom Jourdain
thinks he must court. Real hollowness and sham are presented alongside the
playacting sort of business on which Monsieur Jourdain is building his life.

The perfect logic of the ending is what gives such a satisfying touch to the
comedy, for Jourdain is dealt with by leading him yet further into his world of
fantasy, all to protect the real world in which everyone else must continue to
exist. The classic denouement sees Lucile and Cléonte, Nicole and Covielle,
and Dorante and the marquise, Dorimène, joined as couples. The mad rejection of reality by the "would-be gentleman" is shown by his last words that he
will give his wife to whoever wants her. The great egoist is completely catered
to, as far as he can see, and yet he is effectively isolated into harmlessness by
the mock ceremony that makes him into a Turkish *mamamouchi* (a mock title
of nobility). The playing of a theatrical sort of role is the principle of his life,

so there is small wonder that a master of comic theater took this idea as thematic and used every means at his disposal to make a great stage production of such stagy material.

Le Misanthrope comes to mind at once as the major play about social accommodation, but this later comedy has a great ingenuity in the use of an exaggerated attempt to conform to social norms as the basis of an eccentricity. *Monsieur de Pourceaugnac* undoubtedly provided Molière with the framework on which to build, but the rather crude effects of the work of 1669 are far outshone by the ballet comedy that creates an impression of joy, wholeness, and gala masking, all the while it suggests its satirical meanings. The subtleties of the play lie in part in the nature of the comic hero who has an identity problem like that of Harpagon. Already in possession of as much happiness as money can buy, Jourdain yet feels compelled to strive for the achievement of a higher *gloire,* or personal standing, and as he works to clothe himself in the symbols of a higher status he aids society in keeping him at his proper level. The sophistication of the work emerges as we see the convoluted ways in which he is both agent and the person acted upon. The feeding of an ego's hunger for power is usually depicted by Molière as a process that consumes everything ruthlessly, but Jourdain's case does not have quite the malevolent tone of the others we have seen, and he presents the spectacle of a bumbling bourgeois easily duped by everyone around him.

With such a sound basis of character and organization Molière composed his scenes to give the entire production the stylized and formal quality of ballet, and what he truly created was a musical comedy or *opera buffa* with great artistic finish. Thematically and structurally it is so integrally conceived and executed as to have remarkable unity of "style," a quality of Molière at his best. Not only in formal dance patterns but also in speeches and gestures the stylized manner of expression produces an effect of self-conscious theater that is most useful to import the symbolic nature of each part. Critics have frequently observed the rhythmical balance of scenes such as the lovers' quarrel of act 3, scene 10, but the stagy quality of the entire work is apparent from the start when everything stresses the idea of acting a formal role in the world. Thus the entire play is drawn in terms of careful poses and maskings.

To assign to *Le Bourgeois gentilhomme* an "action" or organizing theme, we might try to summarize the elements as follows: Monsieur Jourdain (and all the other figures) want to assure themselves of their possession of happiness by playing suitable roles. The possibilities for confusions and ambiguities, for deceptions and ruses, for interplay of the real and illusory are so evident and familiar from Molière's earlier works that they bear little elaboration. Since this play is meant to exploit visual spectacle, maskings and disguises play a large role in the deceptions, but, as usual, language and its confusions are very important. The supposed possessor of command of language and meaningful expression, the professor of philosophy, is inevitably the stock pedant character who winds up by creating verbal confusion as he tries to explain ideas. While this figure holds forth the promise to Jourdain of creating an elevated image of himself by words, the dancing and fencing masters claim that their arts will give him the physical appearance of nobility. Each *maître* is convinced that his "pose" is the way to social success, and we are not surprised when their formal argument descends to a level of harsh words. Naturally, the polished speaker wins the quarrel with low invective, showing the false front being dropped to achieve practical results.

When Covielle contrives the ceremony of the *mamamouchi,* he simply reverses the process and erects a vast false front that Jourdain eagerly accepts as real and practical for him. The donning of the elegant costume seems to possess the greatest magic for Jourdain, both as he puts on his fine suit at the start and the Turkish outfit at the end. Intellectual or mental symbols are worthless to him (he rejects the learned lore of the philosopher), for he accepts only meaningless language in lieu of reasoned advice from his wife and Nicole. The "song and dance" that the others hand him is taken for reality, and Molière's crowning touch is seen in the burlesque ceremony that uses a mumbo-jumbo language supposed to be Turkish but is a sort of lingua franca quite intelligible to the others. When he believes he is at the pinnacle of status, he is receiving slapstick blows described as the "ultimate affront." The power of the status symbol, both visual and verbal, is emphasized throughout; Jourdain tips the apprentices who address him as "Highness." It is interesting to note that all that he himself tries to create in the way of forms of status fails miserably because his efforts to demonstrate his fencing skill to Nicole are disastrous and his presents to the marquise are appropriated by Dorante. Even his new title of *paladin* turns into *baladin* (mountebank) as he tries to explain it to his wife.

The two plays, *L'Avare* and *Le Bourgeois gentilhomme,* have analogous aspects, therefore, as treatments of notions of happiness and wealth. Both deal with problems of delusions of self and others, but the techniques Molière employs are appropriate in each case to the nature of the theatrical production. When he seems to work in terms of realism, as in *L'Avare,* the ultimate effect is one of fantasy, while a ballet comedy gives a surprising sense of life beneath its highly stylized series of dancelike routines. As a common structural basis we must note the dependence upon commedia or traditional farce, for the *lazzi,* or set routines, undergird both plays. The presence of a Covielle, a trickster type from Italian comedy, is indicative of Molière's resumption of a firm position in farce, the source and true location of his theatrical strength. The next play in personal style, *Les Fourberies de Scapin,* is to be a sort of apotheosis of the trickster.

Chapter Nine
The Power of Illusion

Les Fourberies de Scapin

If the theater of Molière had to be characterized in a word, one would probably pick "illusion" with the proviso that some elaboration of the term be
permitted. Not that this quality is not inherent in any good theater, for it is
an essential condition of the acceptance of the staged production as a meaningful illusion of some sort of reality by an audience, but in Molière's works
there is an evident grasp of the nature of stage illusion. He neither attempts
an exact imitation of ordinary reality nor tries to create sheer illusionary
spectacle that has nothing to offer but excitement of the senses; in Molière,
the illusion is always reminding us both of the illusory nature of its being
and showing us that such things are clearly symbolic of serious aspects of
human life. This is true theatrical sense, and it finds its most natural mode
of expression in theatrical forms that profit from long usage and accumula-
tion of meaning, conventionalized comedy, since Molière sees and functions
as a comedian.

The chapter title is thus chosen to emphasize this aspect of his work and
also to permit a distinction between the various sorts of illusion on stage. No
clearer distinction between the "illusionistic" and meaningful illusion could
be found than that apparent in the two plays of 1671, the ballet *Psyché* and
the farce *Les Fourberies de Scapin* (The tricks of Scapin). What is really lacking in a great machine spectacle like *Psyché* is the sense of the hand of the
master illusionist guiding gestures and words. We see Molière in the witty
Scapin, masterminding endless plots and schemes both as himself, the dramatist and director, and as the figure of the scheming valet. Scapin was played
by Molière, and the character functions like an author, scene decorator, actor,
and general impresario for the comedies he devises for the other characters. In
his successful, staged illusions Scapin epitomizes the triumph of farce and all
its means in Molière's theater. From the Mascarille who aided his clumsy
master in *L'Étourdi,* there is no great development in principle; Scapin represents the same theatrical concept as Mascarille, the central importance of a
meneur de jeu, or "action producer."

In speaking of "power of illusion" we recall the use made of the idea in works like *Dom Juan* which took on remarkable depth of meaning as the author pondered in his theater questions of "illusions of power." Scapin is devoid of other than a simple self-interest, however, when he acts as director of his comedies, and he seems to delight in leading people through mad pranks purely for a sense of accomplishment of skillful direction. The performance of the comedy is his great reward, and, as for the rest, a bit of food, drink, or cash suffices. The resources of the figure as creator of limitless illusions are what strike us particularly, and we wonder whether the human propensity for being duped by such showmanship is not as deep a commentary on man's behavior as the use of illusion to achieve personal power. The eagerness of all to accept the specious or the conventional for real values seems to be reiterated as strongly as in *Amphitryon,* for example. *Scapin* is not quite devoid of implications of the sense of mastery in the title figure, so Molière must have him tricked by fate at the end despite all his successes in arranging lives. He too must be a victim of illusion. Professor Hubert points out in his analysis that the effectiveness of Scapin's tricks proves to be illusory at the finish, and this is the properly artistic climax.[1]

The Harlequin ancestry of Scapin is clear as he whirls and bounces his way through his inventive slapstick routines. Masked and garbed in a traditional costume of gaily colored lozenges, he is the spirit of vitality, and as such he is the very stuff of comic theater. Entirely aware of his nature and function, Scapin regards the world as his stage and all persons as his cast in a manner strongly expressive of baroque thought. The sheer professionalism of the type is important also, for he has a great detachment and clarity about himself; he finds his work "a noble calling" just as his creator must have regarded his own career in the theater. From all standpoints, Scapin is that theatrical Molière we observed behind the small mask of Mascarille.

Satire of the power of intellectual illusion, which is the subject of *Les Femmes savantes,* is complemented by the direct, physical style of the humor and scheme of *Scapin.* The "learned ladies" will be motivated by abstract ideas, while the figures of the farce are driven by factors like imagined danger, profit, or pleasure. Motivation by love, desire, or power is familiar to us and is the foundation of the ruses of the valet. The obstacle of an old man's interference with the wedding of a young couple is the sine qua non of the standard farce, and once again it is used, yet the ending of happy marriage comes about almost automatically or as if fated, so that the sense of social accommodation is very strong. Scapin's methods of working toward such an end use not only visual deception but many verbal ruses, so that both miming and words are his materials in his little plays-within-the-play. Often an outrageous tale can convince, and indeed the more exaggerated the better, for the melodramatic and conventionally theatrical are highly successful. The whole business is truly so self-consciously trite that we see that this is in itself a purpose of the author. The stock characters (Géronte and Argante are the old men, of course) are old friends, nor do they fail to act as we expect. The two fathers have sons, Léandre and Octave, in love with girls unacceptable to the parents because Hyacinthe is an orphan and Zerbinette a Gypsy. Scapin is appealed to by both young men, and he undertakes to straighten out matters by way of complications. With his touch, mad activity ensues.

Scapin's first action is to convince Argante that a shotgun wedding has united Octave and Hyacinthe. Sylvestre, Scapin's assistant, comments, "There's a clever rogue" (1.4), and the master will soon have the pupil playing a role as the violent soldier, brother of Hyacinthe, to terrorize Argante. (*Le Mariage forcé* once again.) The illusionist coaches Sylvestre in lines and gestures so as to achieve theatrical effect: "Stand up a bit straighter. Pull down your cap like a tough guy, weight on one leg, hand on hip. Look furious. Stomp around like a king in a drama" (1.5). Scapin's own histrionic ability is put to the test when Léandre accuses him of betrayal and Scapin thinks that his thefts of food and wine have been discovered, and worse, his appropriation of a watch sent to Zerbinette. To explain the latter, he "came back with muddy clothes and bloody face" (2.3) claiming to have been robbed. The creative talent will now serve the masters, however, and Sylvestre will do his soldier routine and offer to get the marriage annulled for a price. Scapin follows this by a long tale to Géronte about Léandre's captivity aboard a pirate ship; more money is needed for ransom, as is the usual case in Scapin's schemes. The line, "What the devil was he going to do in that galley?" (2.7), repeated by Géronte, has become proverbial. The miser will not part with his gold, however, so the valet determines to get even, devising a ruse by which Géronte is induced to enter a large sack to hide from ruffians. Naturally, he gets a beating all the same as Scapin assumes the voices of various types who claim they are beating the valet. The business ends with the old man's realization of the trick as the foolish Zerbinette describes a man whom she knows deceived by a yarn about pirates and forced into a beating. The unwitting disclosure of the ruse is another customary feature of the farce, from *L'Etourdi* to *George Dandin*.

The ending is wildly improbable as it is revealed that Hyacinthe is the long-lost daughter of Géronte who wanted to marry the son of his friend Argante in any case. Zerbinette, to balance things neatly, can be no other than the long-lost child of Argante, thus negating all the ingenious efforts of Scapin. Not to be prevented by a stroke of fate from creating a dramatic illusion of artistry, Scapin feigns an accident to win sympathy and forgiveness from those he hoodwinked. The ultimate logic of this nonsense is that Géronte agrees to forgive Scapin if he promises to die. Argante remonstrates with his friend, so all ends happily, Scapin playing his role of invalid to the hilt: "Carry me to the end of the dinner table while we're waiting for me to die" (3.13). The comedy ends with another farcical playlet by the master of illusion as he pretends to be expiring while feeding his very lively self.

Les Femmes savantes

Although *Les Femmes savantes* (*The Learned Ladies*) had been planned for several years during which Molière was largely engaged in royal entertainments, it did not arrive on the boards until 1672. The thought and care that went into its composition are evident in the intellectual satire and the poetic form. As a companion to *Les Fourberies de Scapin,* this play, offered to the public in Paris, balanced the wild antics of the farce with brilliant verbal comedy, yet maintained the characteristic Molièresque pace and drive. It shows the author thoroughly in command of his art in one of its major forms, the combination of elevated style, psychological truth, and basic comic structure. As such, *Les Femmes savantes* is a worthy penultimate creation by the great comedian.

The idea of "tyranny of words" is hardly the exclusive province of the play being studied here, for it has been seen to be a deeply rooted part of Molière's subject matter and expression. Confusions and deceptions by verbal means form the basis of too many plays to be cited in detail, but one thinks of Alceste, among the other characters, deluding himself in literal misapplication of heroic words and deeds, or of Don Juan, controlling people by his crafty utterances. The concept of deliberate creation of a world of illusion by words, the enchanting world of romance, was the basis of *Les Précieuses ridicules,* and the author returns to this theme in *Les Femmes savantes* but mingling into the self-induced enchantment an infatuation with abstract learning and philosophy. The same theme of rejection of normal feminine nature appears, as does the rude return to reality or the insulation of the mad individuals from threatened society.

If the folly of ignorant and incompetent ambition is treated in *Le Bourgeois gentilhomme,* the informing idea here seems to be the folly of self-denial for the purposes of status-seeking in great learning. The pedantic scholar or doctor is a stock comic character, of course, but Molière creates female pedants who outrage their natures as women for the sake of abstract words. As a study of sexual motives the comedy takes on some depth of meaning, and it offers an additional case of the acceptance of the specious for the real, even on the part of the learned. The simple Monsieur Jourdain is thus paralleled by pedant, poet, and bluestocking lady scholars who are as eager to possess their forms of success in the world as he was. While the bourgeois admitted his ignorance and tried to learn forms and conventions, the characters of this comedy are fully convinced that they have the magic words of wisdom and status at their command. Conventional patterns of verbalizing are taken as having genuine significance, so Molière deals once more with language as noncommunication or obfuscation of meaning. To balance the madness of the ladies and their salon cohorts there must be some reasonable behavior, and thus we find direct and simple expression of feelings of love on the part of certain figures. Honest humanity finds itself hard-pressed by the persistent illusionists of ideas, however, and the bourgeois husband caught up in the pedantic salon life is really overwhelmed.

With such a collection of forms, at once intellectual, artistic, and theatrical, Molière launches into a blistering attack on the corrupters of human nature. The pattern of folly and that of the author in treating it are typical and well known to us, so our examination of the comedy centers upon the new means Molière finds for exploiting and arranging patterns. The scheme of tensions is evident in the title that asks, in effect, Can women be both women and learned? We are led to inquire whether love of knowledge is compatible with knowledge of love, Molière's idea of the area of feminine expertise. Does not a woman abandon her real power in assuming a spurious masculine command through science and letters? The play revolves about these conflicts of values. In the household of the honest bourgeois, Chrysale, the women are wearing the trousers, and he is helpless before his wife, Philaminte. Armande apes her mother in pedantry and self-assertion, while her sister Henriette is a maiden hopeful of marrying her Clitandre. Aiding the dominant female is a social lion of a poet, Trissotin, who introduces his friend, the scholar Vadius. The two salon habitués are necessary to Philaminte since she uses literary and intellectual superiority to browbeat Chrysale. Utterly deluded about her own nature is Bélise, sister of Chrysale and aged *précieuse ridicule*. The reasonable side of things is upheld by Ariste, brother of Chrysale.

The alignment of forces is customary, nor will plot vary greatly from the standard. The strength of the comedy lies in the simple reversal of the roles of the sexes, however, and this has been accomplished by the women in the interest of sheer power. "Tyranny through words" would be the conscious principle of Philaminte, and this is not mere farcical henpecking but intellectual mastery. An old scheme from medieval comedy is thus elevated to a new level as Molière writes a parody of the tyrant drama with women ruling men. The reprise of the *Tartuffe* situation is interesting, with Trissotin and Vadius acting as low-grade Tartuffes to aid Philaminte's tyranny of her family. As religion brought no grace, learning brings no liberation of the spirit to a Philaminte.

The sting of Molière's lash fell directly upon some personal enemies easily recognized under Trissotin and Vadius, but the author did not let this sort of attack vitiate the principle of his comedy, for he shows these figures, the Abbé Cotin and Ménage, as subject to being deluded by their own words. Their actual speeches are the basis for some of the characters' lines, and the direct, personal satire becomes part of a whole. Paradox and perversion of values in the name of high principles are the framework of the play, and we perceive that love turns into egoism, knowledge produces error, and the grotesque is called beautiful. In the structure there is a sort of vertical axis with "lowness" of spirit at one end and "elevation" at the other, these being the standards against which all is measured by the savantes. Whether a thing is intellectual, artistic, or simply physical, it is held up to the yardstick of fixed values, and the recurrent words of lowness and elevation are noteworthy as they qualify all. Armande thus starts the play by chiding her sensible sister for "having a mind on a low level and playing a small role in the world" (1.1), but Armande is shown to be confused in her assignment of value, mixing up the mental and the physical by applying precious terms of love to the delights of science. "Love of study" brings "charming sweetness" to the heart; she would "marry philosophy which raises us above the human race" (1.1). Henriette reminds her of the facts of life, the physical reality of marriage, a "lowness to which you owe your clarity" (1.1). The exposition stresses heavily the supplanting of sex by abstract ideas; Orgon's distortion of love for a peculiar faith is restated.

Clitandre is coveted by Armande, although she rejects the idea of marriage, and the attentions paid to Henriette make her jealous. Says her sister, "Where is the ethic which can control our animal side and restrain anger?" (1.2). When Clitandre tries to get the aunt, Bélise, to help him win the hand of Henriette, the old fool assumes that he is making a confession of love to her. The addled distortion of reality in her mind is a neat counterpoint to the willful distortions by the other women. When Philaminte arrives in act 2, we are prepared by her treatment of her husband, but Molière gives her a scene of wildly exaggerated character as she fires a servant girl for smashing language like crockery. Obviously, she suffers from the tyranny of the words that are her key to power; the sacred verbal talismans rule her life, nor can she function any longer on a simple, natural level. Trissotin enters to exploit the situation, being the great master of language, the poet. With the aid of

Trissotin, Philaminte weaves her spells of words about her poor husband, holding him like a Circe or Medea. She speaks in terms of Cartesian philosophy and physical theory, but the incantatory power of the words lifts her to another realm high above the world of men. The physically oriented Chrysale seems outclassed badly, but he gathers his courage and resolves to fight at the end of the act. "I'm going to be a man right to their faces" (2.9). The French phrase *la barbe* (the beard) is used, being just the right thing to show the reversal of the roles of the sexes.

When the poet prepares to read one of his works, the women demonstrate all the symptoms of sexual excitement, further showing the transferral of behavior patterns from the physical to the abstract. Armande: "I'm burning to see them." Philaminte: "Don't keep such pressing desires languishing" (3.1). The scheme is carried on by Trissotin, who calls the poem his "new-born babe" and says, "Your approval can serve as its mother" (3.1). The introduction of Vadius as a great scholar of Greek is the cause for similar manifestations: "Please, sir, let me embrace you for the love of Greek" (3.3). The are in ecstasies over new linguistic thrills, but the intellectual heroes descend to a verbal slugfest rather than edifying the women with noble words. The scheme of the quarrel of the *maîtres* of *Le Bourgeois gentilhomme* is employed to puncture the poses of superiority of Trissotin and his friend. The deluded Philaminte is not deterred from planning to offer Henriette in marriage to the poet, however, and the conflict that sums up the play's themes is set forth at the end of act 3 when Chrysale promises Henriette to Clitandre. The next act shows us Philaminte in a rage at such defiance of her authority, and Molière brilliantly has her express herself in a weird mixture of raw feelings and abstract terms: "I'll show her to which one of the two laws of reason she must make her desires subject, and which must rule, mother or father, mind or body, form or matter" (4.1). The parallels are most eloquent.

Armande still has designs on Clitandre while denying her interest in physical existence, and the young man expresses a reasonable viewpoint in arguing with Trissotin. The latter is exposed as a materialistic opportunist, but Philaminte will not be thwarted in her plans. The final act sets things to rights, but the interesting feature here is the retreat by the mother into her own world of verbal magic and fantasy. She is more concerned with the beauty of the vocabulary of a marriage contract than with its meaning, asking whether Greek money can be used to set the sum of the dowry. Martine, the servant who was discharged, has been rehired, and her peasant wisdom on the roles of the sexes is intended to stress the madness of the *savantes*. A stratagem on the part of Ariste leads Trissotin to think the family bankrupt, a condition that his philosophy cannot accept, but even the complete unmasking of the hypocrite does not cure Philaminte. She tells the disappointed Armande to console herself with lofty thoughts, while Béliste remains convinced that Clitandre cares for her.

The power of ideas, or rather of the verbal symbols of them, has led the women to erect an elaborate structure of illusion in which they are determined to live, hopelessly neurotic and denatured. The menace to the social system (love-marriage-family) has been contained, as always in the Molière comedy, but we are left with a strong impression of the malignancy of their malady. In comparing this play with *Les Fourberies de Scapin,* it is clear that the playwright perceives the tyranny of abstract notions to be structurally identical with the control by crude, physical means, but the tone of the later work seems bitter. Delusion by tricks makes for a triumph of farcical theater; delusion by elevated ideas produces some moral shock, no matter how burlesque the style and conventional the material.

Chapter Ten

Death in a Musical Comedy

Le Malade imaginaire

As a culmination of a theatrical career devoted to the creation of an illusion of living action, Molière's final comedy, *Le Malade imaginaire* (The imaginary invalid), could not have struck a more fitting note. In a farce about a hypochondriac intent upon achieving an illusion of vitality and health, the doomed playwright wrote the last of his works, which would give him his only triumph over death, the immortality of the great artist.

This comedy caps a series of "medical" plays in which the doctor is portrayed as the destroyer of life and health, a figure whose verbal and material magic give him a peculiar power over the gullible. The character was ideally suited to the purposes of an author who delighted in exploiting the acceptance of such illusory notions for reality, so from 1659 on medicine and doctors are frequently satirized. *Le Médecin volant* was followed by *L'Amour médecin* (1665), *Le Médecin malgré lui* (1666), and by the part of *Dom Juan* in which Sganarelle is disguised as a doctor. Then too, *Monsieur de Pourceaugnac* (1669) has heavy satire of medicine, so that the final comedy is very much a reprise of earlier material. Extending the satire in depth and resuming so many things observed throughout his works, *Le Malade imaginaire* moves far beyond its predecessors in medical farce and stands as a remarkable example of the style of noble farce.[1]

It is so great an irony that the playwright-actor should have died in the role of the hypochondriac that one cannot help commenting on this supreme instance of the interplay of truth and fancy, yet it is not justifiable to conclude that this indicates an extension of showmanship into his very existence and that he planned to exploit his own fate. All hint of the macabre is driven in flight before the affirmation of health, life, and love in this "comedy mixed with music and dance," as the writer described his play. Undoubtedly, a premonition of an early end must have been with this longtime victim of a lung condition, but his cough was simply made into part of his characterizations. The most direct connection between his condition and his works was in the evident reaction to slander that mocked his physical infirmities as well as attacking his morals. The early nonsense about medical quackery takes on bitterness as Molière projects a personal resentment of inept and ignorant medical practice into his farce.

Other personal factors enter into the formation of the last play, a musical entertainment in his own style which had to be given in Paris despite the intention to offer it before the king at Versailles. The decline of royal preference, and with it the taste of the court, for Molière's type of musical was coupled with and partially caused by the rise of the popularity of lavish opera produced by Lully. The professional rivalry between the erstwhile collaborators had become sharp. Molière countered as best he could, attempting to please Louis by combining his farce with music by Charpentier and ballet by Beauchamp, but a simple scene change from bourgeois interior to a "public place" for a ballet interlude did not make for much spectacle.[2] It is almost despite this gesture toward illusionary theater that *Le Malade imaginaire* succeeds, drawing its true strength from the combination of the author's best techniques, a combination that can be called the result of his sense of "style." This we feel in his ordering of characteristic theatrical elements that are both in the common domain and yet bear his imprint. The impression of a personal style emanates from such things as stock routines that he has somehow made his own.

This comedy, like the others, is predicated not upon originality of subject or handling but upon a regrouping of essential parts, and thus we see a plot framework of deluded egomaniac, the tyrant father, threatening and disrupting his family for his own ends. The customary young couple is prevented from marrying until an ingenious ruse conceived by a witty servant controls the title figure. The old friends are all on stage, for Argan is the father, Toinette the maid, Angélique the daughter, and Cléante the gallant suitor. Not to be forgotten are the reasoning brother, Béralde, the scheming second wife, Béline, and they are joined by the farce types of doctors and lawyer, the Diafoirus, father and son, Monsieur Purgon, and Maître Bonnefoi. The ironic names, suggesting "purges" and "good faith," are completed by that of Fleurant, the apothecary, whose "flowery" name belies his chief function as enema giver. The stock types immediately place us in the world of commedia dell'arte in which such business as repetition of humorous lines and gestures is fundamental. With the rules of the game clearly established, Molière can then proceed to devise analogies and variations on his theme, and his control through style will make for an impression of rightness and balance. Music and dance will have integral functions expressive of the central idea, and there is little from his repertory of techniques that does not come into play. The comedy is in prose, but by now we perceive that the true poetry of his theater is not dependent upon the use of alexandrine verses but rather upon the poetic expressiveness with which the various parts are used in relation to each other and to the whole effect. The production of symbolic sense by all means at the command of the dramatist is the touchstone for judgment of the poetic worth.

The informing idea toward which all aspects of *Le Malade imaginaire* should direct our attention must obviously involve illusions about health or some similar neurosis. The key verb would be "to live" and furthermore, in the notion of Argan, "to live forever" by medical magic. The typically Molièresque twist is that the character who is so intent upon living should dwell as if in suspended animation, bound to his rest and cures. In contrast to this idea, the true magic life—joy in the present moment—is stressed by the young lovers and by Toinette. The message of natural happiness is presented by Béralde as well, and the grasping Béline also expresses her version of present joy through her wish for gold to buy happiness. The wife is a transitional sort of character, thematically speaking, since she is one of the group of leeches who live by exploiting illness and death, the doctors and lawyer. They profit from Argan's mania that has made living a hollow mockery by purging and medicating the body until he is nothing but an evacuating, embalmed bag of flesh, to use Béline's terms of description. To go on living, he feels he must limit himself to a deathlike imprisonment, chaining himself to a cane, chair, or toilet. The morbid preoccupation with the chance of demise has led him to reject his true healthy nature and take on the stench of death. Molière shows occasional flashes of normal strength on the part of Argan, in order to illuminate the aberration.

So consistently does the author develop a theme in this manner that one may say that an aspect of his style is the use of great paradoxes of the sort, the endless, striking contrasts of truth and its distortions, of fact and fancy, of knowledge and ignorance. There can be no greater paradox than a light comedy about fear of death, but the mastery of Molière comes to the fore as he creates this very thing. He starts the comedy with the title character ruminating (he is visceral in his mode of thought) upon his medical treatments even as he is waiting for a purge to take effect. He uses his wealth to buy health through medication, but he remains an economical bourgeois and tallies his bills carefully. The reading aloud of prescriptions "to refresh the entrails of Monsieur" (1.1) has an incantatory effect upon him, but he is still fastened to his toilet chair and must call for the servant to rescue him. When there is no answer, he rings and shouts for her in despair, exclaiming as if to announce the theme of the work: "They are going to leave me to die here!" (1.1). Toinette counters this by outyelling him, showing her nature as healthy and vigorous, and she resorts to physical actions both to mock him and ultimately to show him some sense. Action is the proper means to combat Argan's absurd fixity of mind and body, not to mention the languishing surrender of the daughter to her father's tyranny. Argan has decided to marry Angélique to Thomas Diafoirus to have a doctor in the family, hypochondria and bourgeois thrift being thus wed.

The death-life contrast is extended throughout all parts of the play, and to it may be connected analogous thematic contrasts. Love should be life at its fullest, but the romance of Angélique and Cléante is pretty feeble until aided by Toinette. Forced marriage to Thomas has given the word a fatal connotation for the girl, and she is furthermore threatened by her stepmother with banishment to a deathlike existence in a convent if she disobeys. The static must be fought by the active, and Toinette constantly tries to rouse ire if not good sense. Toinette: "I know you. You are naturally good." Argan: "I'm not at all good, and I'm mean when I want to be" (1.5). Nature asserts itself when she provokes her master into chasing her briskly around the chair, brandishing his cane in wrath. Another paradox is the strange combination within Argan of will to command with desire for protection, for from Béline he wants to hear, "Come, come, my poor little boy" (1.7) and to be coddled in a sort of infantilism. The process of paradoxes and twists of nature will be continued as the notary discourses on how to flout justice and do the children out of the inheritance and the doctors work harm with their supposed cures.

Act 1 was originally followed by an interlude of song and dance in which a merry Polichinelle routine restored some tone of healthy gaiety after the introduction of the mentally sick Argan and his morally sick household. Act 2 begins with a series of "bright" and "dark" scenes designed to express alternately hope and despair in keeping with the theme and plot of the play. Toinette introduces Cléante as a substitute music master for Angélique's singing lesson, and the couple exchange vows while singing a pastoral under the nose of Argan, a ruse like that of *Le Sicilien*. This light note counters the "dark" one of the entrance of the black-robed doctors who suggest vultures around the dying man, yet the patent idiocy of Thomas Diafoirus and the pride of his father are hilarious despite the blackness of the medical satire. The young people sing of their determination "to die rather than consent to separation" (2.5), giving a light bit of counterpoint on the ideas of life and death. Much of the scene is structured on contrasts between words and actions, a familiar process, and this is summarized by the speech of Toinette, mocking Thomas: "It will be wonderful if he cures as well as he talks" (2.5).

There follows a scene in which Argan pries from his young child, Louison, the fact that a young man has been visiting Angélique, and the inclusion of this, Molière's only use of a child character, is significant. The contrast of warped age and natural youth is basic, of course, but the little girl is an accomplished faker who uses the most effective weapon against her father by playing dead when he hits her. He is immediately reduced to abject self-pity by her sham, then furious at being tricked. The efficacy of the ruse has been shown, and it will be repeated later with Argan playing dead to deceive Béline and hear her reactions. Stage illusions on life and death could not be embodied more succinctly. The second act ends on a bright note as Béralde introduces a troupe of Gypsy dancers who do a Moorish ballet to help cure the hypochondriac, singing of the joys of youth and love.

Le Malade imaginaire has but three acts, a fact that may make for increased unity of action. At the start of act 3 Argan seems to have responded to the treatment by his brother, and he even forgets to walk with his cane, but any attempts to combat his mania with reason are met with resistance. Through Béralde Molière expresses the idea that nature is the sure guide and cure, defending his comedies as just making fun of the "ridiculousness in medicine" (3.3). The brother keeps the apothecary from administering a treatment to Argan with the result that the doctor, Purgon, enters in a rage to warn and curse the patient for disobedience. Like a witch doctor he condemns the victim to suffer a series of diseases and death, "lientery, dysentery, dropsy, and deprivation of life" (3.5). Argan, completely reduced by such an incantation, says, "Good Lord! I'm dead," but Béralde counters, "You are mad . . . Pinch yourself a bit, come to yourself, and don't let imagination run away with you. . . . The principle of life is within you" (3.6).

The last act is composed of scenes that bring together violent extremes like the folly of Argan at the curse and the lively vigor of Toinette's ruses, for the servant next enters to announce the arrival of a distinguished doctor, to be played by herself. The robe and title suffice to fool the hypochondriac who solemnly ponders the medical advice from Toinette to cut off an arm to give vigor to the other. Pretense and disguise will be turned to good advantage as Argan is persuaded to simulate death in order to see the faithful grief of Béline, criticized as avaricious by Béralde. Death, or the feigning of it, thus becomes the means for restoration of Argan to some contact with real life: "Isn't there any danger in playing dead?" he inquires uneasily (3.11). Béline's delight at his "demise" opens his eyes to her schemes, and the genuine grief of Angélique, fooled by the same trick, shows her real love for her father. The corpselike Argan springs to life and agrees to the marriage of his daughter and Cléante, apparently showing that light has returned to his darkened mind, but the hypochondria is incurable. Since the external features of medicine work the magic he craves, it is suggested that he himself become a doctor and minister to his ills. The mad logic appeals to him, so the play ends in a burlesque ceremony of the conferring of the degree of doctor. Comic ballet brings together words, music, and dance to sum up Argan's fantastic illusions, and Latin doggerel serves the same purpose as the "Turkish" language of the *mamamouchi* ceremony. The title character is duped for his own good and that of everyone else, since there is no other means to save him.

The final dance is introduced by the statement that carnival time authorizes such revelry and masking, so the play ends on a note of joyous freedom and vitality that contrasts with the closed, sick-chamber atmosphere of the start. It is as if Molière were reminding us that "it is always Mardi Gras before Lent" and that life's pleasures should be celebrated before one gives attention to death. The device is not "memento mori" or "think of death" but rather "remember to live." The sense of the play is so basic that these common expressions are not out of place as statements of theme, nor can there be any other real theme in true comedy. *Le Malade imaginaire* is a full development, by the best theatrical means at Molière's command, of the concept of joyous living and of the "imaginary" obstacles to such living erected by men's fancies.

During the fourth performance of this comedy, on 17 February 1673, Molière was seized by a paroxysm of coughing in the final ballet, but he insisted upon completing the show. Carried to his home, he was dead within an hour. His final physical efforts, like his whole existence, had been dedicated to the service of his art.

Chapter Eleven
Molière's Legacy

The profession of theater in which Molière had lived, struggled, and triumphed, was a poor one in which to die. Church authorities were only barely persuaded to permit the burial in hallowed ground of the body of an actor, the creator of *Tartuffe*. The unconfessed soul of Molière (no priest had been willing to come in time to administer the last rites) was entrusted to God, but the funeral cortege moved through Paris by night to cloak the spectacle. Eight hundred people gathered to follow the great comedian as he made his peace with a convention that he had not wanted to offend. The irony strikes us, but, in truth, this ending was in keeping with the life of a man who sought not to rebel against his world but to seek new ways of understanding its involved tensions between individual passions and social norms.

The disappearance of the dominant figure from the stage of the Palais-Royal was not the only blow that had been dealt the royal troupe of players. The beautiful Du Parc had followed Racine to a rival troupe and died in 1668, and Madeleine Béjart, mother of Armande and Molière's companion of the old Illustre Théâtre and provincial tours, died in 1672 after retiring from the stage. The king's taste for splendor led him to favor Lully's opera, and a number of actors left Molière for the Hôtel de Bourgogne. The death of the master of comedy left the way open for Lully to obtain the Palais-Royal for musical shows, so that Armande and the faithful La Grange were obliged to move their players to the Guénégaud hall and join forces with the Marais troupe. By royal decree in 1677 this company was merged with that of the Hôtel de Bourgogne, and thus the Comédie-Française was created.[1]

The repertory of this official theater included the works of Corneille, Racine, and Molière, as well as those of lesser lights, but the theater was definitely "the house of Molière." And he lived on in his theater so forcefully that no other spirit could so fully and naturally dominate the French repertory. In the first three years of its existence the Comédie presented twenty-one works by Molière, eight by Racine, the same number by Corneille, and an assortment of other plays. This preponderance of the great comic works was to continue, keeping his spirit perennially on the boards after he had coughed and mimed his last in 1673. The building of the structure of a major national repertory theater single-handed was an unparalleled feat.

The career and the achievements of Molière have been examined in some detail, yet we still mull over the question: Just how did he do it? Given the existence of the theatrical genius, it seems most pertinent to observe that he flourished at precisely the right moment for full development. Aided by the wisdom of historical hindsight, we can not only review his career and creations but also place him in a broad context of theatrical history. With our knowledge of the lines of growth in drama before and after Molière, we can assign to him his true role as a great inventor. He came to the fore at a timely moment for a theatrical innovator, an intellectually restless and experimental age that provided him with both his material and a stage upon which to project it. His original and formative function in his cultural world can be compared with that of Descartes in philosophy and that of Corneille in tragic theater. The time was ripe for a comic dramatist to bring to fruition the labor of centuries that had gone into the formation of theatrical techniques.

By the middle of the seventeenth century in France there existed an avid, critical, and cultivated audience that had been conditioned to look for brilliance amidst the wealth of entertainments offered for court and city. Native and foreign talent had worked since early in the century to perfect theater of conscious artistry and various effects of illusion, and the amassing of physical resources for theater was matched by the mental resources. We know of the rapid change from makeshift playhouses in tennis courts to proper theaters, and the simple act of bringing public theater in off the streets and trestles to covered halls was a great step. The influx of examples and ideas from Italy about scenic design had a powerful effect upon the regularizing of stage techniques, both in the visual illusions and in the dramaturgy. Corneille, Hardy, Rotrou, and others perceived what theater could mean and achieve, nor were their experiments insignificant as they played with manners of using conventions of the art and techniques of staging. The great *farceur* was to come and profit from the groundwork because he could see how basically theatrical and expressive this developing sort of playing could be. At their best, the predecessors struck a note of true symbolic theater; Molière characteristically worked in this mode.

The debt of Molière to traditional French and Italian comedy has been dwelt upon, and we comprehend how French theater could never be quite the same again after the creation of examples of the "new comedy" like *L'École des femmes* and *Tartuffe*. What must be stressed, however, is Molière's far-reaching vision and foreshadowing of the directions to be taken by theater in the decades and centuries after his death. A foreboding of things to come would be a more exact term, it is true, for the breakdown of his noble comedy into literal, realistic satire on the one hand and into sheer visual spectacle on the other was already visible and disheartening to him. Those who sought to imitate the surface effect of a *L'Avare* would produce plays of harsh realism, Lesage's *Turcaret* of 1709, for example, while the court ballet grew into an overblown, rococo excrescence. The "bourgeois" tragicomedy of the eighteenth century would become a "tearful" comedy and seek sentimental effect in lieu of the intellectual elevation of a Molière work. This seemed to be a likely development of the play set in a middle-class interior, in the hands of a nontheatrical writer. The most worthy successor of Molière on the French comic stage was Marivaux, whose delicate comedies of love give to early eighteenth-century theater a real flash of brilliant technique and perceptive symbolic suggestion. But Molière was his clear precursor in such a style.[2] Beaumarchais's Figaro is Scapin rejuvenated.

What sort of forecast for the development of theater beyond the eighteenth century can we discover in Molière's works? The costume drama with exotic stage sets, the poetic evocation of heroism, and touching melodrama dear to romantic theater—are they Molièresque? We think of *Dom Juan,* and the spectacle of the fascinatingly depraved and fated hero surely forecasts much that romanticism was to create. The swing from this type of illusionary theater to that of the psychological realism of the later nineteenth century does not carry us far from Molière, and we seem to see the stage peopled by Tartuffes played straight and tragic. At its best, this style is nobly symbolic, but so was the master comedian's "new" style. At the risk of dashing through theatrical history and falsifying through haste, we may observe that the current trend in drama is toward the theater of "non-illusion," or that which does not imitate reality. Beckett and Ionesco achieve their greatest effects by rejecting illusions of reality for an abstract and conventionalized style expressive of some higher meaning than the literal, and we realize, upon seeing modern productions of Molière, that this is his very forte. The modernism of the seventeenth-century playwright is striking, and current sophistication about symbolic theater can only lead to increased understanding of the nature of Molière's work. In short, no matter which direction theater seems to take, the great comedian has been there before, seeing the possibilities of various techniques, experimenting with them, and making them serve his ends.

The master trick of all poetic, symbolic theater was his. The capturing of human vitality in the forms of the art shows a comprehension and control of theatrical illusion in its best sense, and for maximum vital effect Molière compressed great psychological and intellectual tensions into forms that present a warm, familiar surface. The violent contrasts and paradoxes lurking beneath the fun, the mixtures of reality and fantasy, the interplay of the mad and the sane—all of these are characteristic of his style. When the lid flies up on the jack-in-the-box of a Molière farce, we realize that it is the result of a contrived compression of human forces, but we are always pleased to be able to reset the mechanism and see the performance again. The spring cannot be worn out because, for one thing, it has a basic elasticity and suppleness; the possible combinations of forces under tension can vary greatly within the artistic boundaries. In one play, *L'Avare,* for example, a miser may be seen and played as a brutal monster or as a clown, or the production may stress stylized fantasy in lieu of realism. A director or actor is provided with the essential, compressed charge of natural vitality by Molière, and the inherent dynamism can be projected in many ways in a staged production.

A comic theater remains staunchly nontranscendent, that is, its charge of human energy never arcs upward to superhuman, celestial realms of experience but inevitably discharges itself in its terrestrial contacts. We recall that Don Juan never understood the role of the supernatural in his life. The limits accepted by comedy require that even a great spiritual impulsion, which could suffice to elevate a tragic hero into a transcendent consciousness, should lead a comic hero only into a world of illusion while the temporal world closes ranks to reject or render him harmless. Transcendence becomes a figment of a diseased imagination and social accommodation is the guiding principle, but there is never any suggestion that man can or should give up trying to exceed himself. Yet such efforts will not succeed in the world of comedy, so the ultimate effect is paradoxical in the highest Molièresque sense. Man is at once a creature of unrealized potential and a humble cog limited by his worldly circumstances, and this basic tension is at the heart of the dynamism of Molière's theater.

The repeated cocking and releasing of such tensions is one essential part of humor, and the deliberate utilization of the method has been observed in the comic techniques analyzed. We are induced into a kinetic response by the comic device and thus we say that the plays are funny, but we are told by Henri Bergson that laughter also expresses a sense of superiority over the object mocked. There can be found no more typical cases of looking down on the folly of others than in the Molière plays, both as the sane characters handle the mad ones and as the audience feels superior to all these frantic puppets. Again the author induces an important tension as we both observe condescendingly and see ourselves clearly in the foolish stage characters. Thus Molière gives a brilliant external form in the theater to a highly interior phenomenon, the "laughter of the soul" in which we ponder our follies and accept them in a grateful self-awareness.

As a central theme of French writing in the seventeenth century, W. G. Moore has proposed simply "the limits of humanity."[3] With the energy and inventiveness of this age Molière pushed his exploration beyond supposed limits of the comic mode and into a previously uncharted area, but he always maintained the conventions of his art to link him to practicality. The great entertainer who never lost touch with his audience was at once the classical writer on the nature of man. It we can accept him on his own terms, as the entertainer on the boards, and try to understand his works as living theater, then we shall follow the surest route to an understanding of his greatness.

Recent Views on Molière

During the past two decades interest in Molière has not diminished. Critics and theatrical producers have interpreted and analyzed his plays in some new ways, giving us the opportunity to see how contemporary thought might illuminate the man and his works. As we have observed, some past ages have made his image over to suit their tastes or rejected him as irrelevant for their times. Examination of recent works on Molière reassures us that such is not the case now, for critical studies and staged productions leave no doubt of the current regard for his greatness as a master of theater. Inevitably, some strained interpretations are produced in every age, yet the overall impression gained is that the modern age finds Molière ever pertinent and vital. This overview of recent handlings of the playwright and his works can in no way claim to be comprehensive, so it is organized into areas of interest and subject matter, with evaluations of books and articles that seem most stimulating and productive of understanding of Molière's theatrical genius.

In 1975 was published a monumental volume marking the tercentenary of the death of Molière (1973), *Molière and the Commonwealth of Letters: Patrimony and Posterity.*[4] A compendium of articles and references then existing on the playwright, this book's broad scope demonstrates worldwide interest. Included are studies of Molière among his contemporaries and in the context of world literatures. Articles from scholars of note appear as well as information on the staged and filmed versions of the plays in many languages. The comprehensive bibliography is impressive and of greatest value, and one wishes that a similar work were now available. With a concept of the sheer number of treatments existing in 1975, it is possible to grasp what exists almost fifteen years after. We can only build upon this foundation.

A few figures will back up these generalizations. For the thirty-year period prior to 1972, 1,363 items of bibliography are listed and nearly five hundred translations. The rate of production of Molière studies thus averaged about forty-five per year, including books and articles. The yearly bibliographies published by the Modern Language Association of America[5] confirm that from 1972 through 1986 the average number of works per year has remained close to the previous level. Six hundred thirteen items directly concerned with Molière are noted, plus many other references. A high point was hit in 1973, the tercentenary of Molière's death, with one hundred fifteen items, and the next year had seventy-four.

Among these critical studies, only a few of which can be examined in detail, it is useful to see how they group themselves into trends and approaches. The criteria for evaluation of the works will be their clarity and effectiveness in aiding understanding of how the playwright wrote his classics of living theater and how they live for the modern world. Critical concepts and fashions come and go, and the past twenty years have witnessed a steady parade of ideas regularly applied to classic texts in the hope of illuminating old corners. Thus the New Criticism, archetypal theories, structuralism and its poststructuralist forms, and semiotic approaches have all been put to work on Molière. Aside from representative studies from these schools, it is useful to classify works as to general type. One finds biographical studies, those that set Molière among his contemporaries and cultures, articles on sources and references in the plays, and comparisons with other plays. Writers stress characters, plot, dialogue, types or structures. Others formulate theories of religious, philosophical, historical, or psychological meaning in the plays, while current interest in the nature of language and communication is evident in a number of studies. No matter what the tack taken, the most productive works are, in my opinion, those that focus upon the playwright's ultimate reason for being, the creation of theater.

How to sort through the wealth of material of the last twenty years? With so many lines of thought coming into play, each with merits, one cannot state that one approach or another has dominated. The very fact that Molière has elicited so many studies is more a tribute to his vitality than to the value of any particular interpretations of his plays. It sounds a bit ironic when a scholar lays claim to revitalizing Molière, when a study is just tapping into a flowing source. For a helpful introduction into the state of Molière studies and controversies one can turn to two excellent summaries.[6]

Laurence Romero furnishes a clear statement of the issues debated in reference to Molière in his "Molière's Morale: Debates in Criticism" of 1975. Despite the date of the article, it is a valuable overview of the timeless question of the moral or philosophical significance of the comedies. The effort to assign intent or meaning to the plays has engaged writers on "morale" since the seventeenth century, from the condemnations by churchmen through the ideological interpretations of the Enlightenment and the romantic versions of the nineteenth century. Molière's "morale" has strongly resisted any pigeon-holes, and critics have inevitably used Molière as a mirror for their own beliefs, imputing meanings to the plays. Thus we have a Molière anticlerical, seriously philosophical, free-thinking, and upholder of bourgeois values, a skeptic, an ironist, and a pure aesthete. The modern debate narrows down to discussion of the position held ably by Moore and Bray,[7] that Molière was above all a man of the theater and not a conscious promoter of philosophical views. Lionel Gossman remains the strongest proponent of the idea that the reasoner characters in the comedies truly express Molière's belief in good sense in a world full of masking and deceptions.[8] The issue is still debated, but the general trend is to look upon the comedies not as statements of moral positions but as a complex and personal body of theatrical creation. The mastery of theater by Molière can be agreed upon, and the book by Jacques Guicharnaud[9] effectively projects the career in the theater of the master as a personal exploration by a subtle mind of the human condition. Jules Brody[10] suggests that the aesthetics of the comedies and the moral stance are not incompatible because the basis of the laughter is the inability of a character, even with virtuous aspects, to live successfully in human society.

Critics will now impute to Molière fixed moral positions at their own risk. H. Gaston Hall's "The Present State of Molière Studies"[11] adds to Romero's study a valuable summary of important works that have established details of the life and works of Molière. Hall calls for studies that may "deepen our perception of how Molière received a rich cultural heritage at an exciting time of new developments in French sensibility, at once captured and transcended in his unique achievements."[12] The fundamental task of the scholar is to understand Molière as a creator of plays of comic genius, for his world and for ours.

A healthy note of caution about expectations to arrive at a total truth about Molière was sounded by Ralph Albanese,[13] who declared that the task of the critic is to take the text, our only possession, and to elaborate a coherent interpretation but without hope of finding historical verification. The realities of the seventeenth century must elude us, so let us concentrate on how the texts mean for us. Albanese moves toward the position that every critical assessment, however idiosyncratic, has its validity. This being said, one yet looks for thoughts that tell more of the subject than of the article's author. Modern criticism in French letters justly decries efforts to impute a particular intent to an author studied, but, by the same token, often claims the right of the reader to rewrite a text to his fancy. Equal validity of both versions is declared, and a Molière text might be the subject for a intellectual construction of great interest but quite removed from Molière. Such studies have their own brilliance of self-illumination, and one looks at them in the context of all that is being said currently in the wish to gather a consensus of perceptions on the original subject, Molière. Amidst the extremes of critical ideas it is not difficult to find a common stance assumed by most thinkers today who ponder Molière.

Since the publication in 1949 of W. G. Moore's *Molière, a New Criticism* scholarly opinion has generally recognized that the comedies must be considered as theater and not autobiography or philosophy. In addition to the critics who seek to elucidate the plays as such there exists a body of Moliérists who truly reach a much wider public than the academic specialist, and these are the theatrical producers and directors. It is important to consider their work on stage, and in film and television as well, as we try to see how Molière is faring in the modern world. Attention will be given to directors' interpretations of the comedies.

For a résumé of the types of studies being produced in the mid-seventies we are indebted to Harold Knutson's book, *Molière: An Archetypal Approach*.[14] Before beginning his own analysis of the plays in the light of archetypal theory, he remarks on the paucity of studies using such ideas as they were set forth by Northrop Frye in his *Anatomy of Criticism* of 1957.[15] Knutson notes the work of Charles Mauron, *Psychocritique du genre comique*,[16] which is Freudian in its basis but which approaches some archetypal theory. We are already aware of the psychological treatment by Guicharnaud, and Knutson points out that this study stresses the endings of the major plays in which "order triumphs over corruption."[17] The concept is rather archetypal, for the contrived endings posit an ordering of the world as sanity would wish it to be, a common feature of myth. Marcel Gutwirth is concerned with comic types in his book of this period,[18] while Francis Lawrence stresses the importance of Molière's early work with farce and *comédie-ballet* as the foundation of his other plays.[19]

When one adds to these major studies some of the others in this time frame, the focus upon Molière as a creator of theater is clear. With Knutson there is the treatment of this theater "as if on the timeless living stage of enduring drama."[20] The eternal verities of the human condition are always present in the form of the ironic comic myth that has a vision of harmony in the face of perennial disruptive forces in life. In the study by Alvin Eustis, *Molière as Ironic Contemplator*,[21] all elements of the comedies are seen to contribute to an ironic view of life, with heroic and pathetic modes having no place. The playwright himself is not exempt from this irony, as ideological messages from the writer are only suggested in order to be mocked in ironic laughter.

In 1974 Jacques Scherer offered a second edition of his *Structures de Tartuffe*,[22] noting that in eight years the conception of theater and ways to treat its classics had changed. He added an appendix on the comic Tartuffe to evaluate the character as comic rather than menacing,[23] making him one of the many critics who would wrestle with this problem of interpretation. He sees Tartuffe as a rustic in Paris, as an obvious sensualist, and as a fraud in his ostentatious pietism. Most important, he sees the ambiguity of this figure, a point to which we will return with other scholars.

A key problem in interpretation presents itself in the question of how to understand and play the comedies that have this ambiguous quality of seriousness and broad comedy. Is there an "authentic" Molière, true to his own intentions? Discovery of this is beyond hope, and critics who lay claim to such discovery must be discounted. The bulk of the studies and productions now to be considered is deliberately oriented to focus upon those that get down to cases with the key problem.

In 1982 W. D. Howarth asked, "*Tartuffe*: Satire or Comedy?" in a section of his book, and he decides that "a certain degree of realism" existed in Molière's setting but that Orgon and Tartuffe reminded the audience that they were in the tradition of Sganarelle and Mascarille.[24] The nature of *Dom Juan* is characterized similarly as "having some measure of contradiction between the comic and the dramatic content of the play."[25] In his conclusion Howarth touches upon problems of modern interpretations. Modern or period settings and costumes? He notes that Jean Anouilh produced a *Tartuffe* in a décor of 1900, with a tone of serious comment on eternal human follies. The Roger Planchon *Tartuffe* of the mid-seventies was a solemn social commentary devoid of much humor, and a like treatment of *Dom Juan* was given by the Comédie-Française in 1979. The entire problem of modern interpretation is thoughtfully discussed by Howarth. Molière's text must certainly not be tampered with to set forth a social or moral doctrine, and the very notion of laughter's purpose to castigate vices is questioned. Comedy simply makes us confront "a comic exaggeration of faults latent within ourselves."[26] Comedy's firm ground is human society, and Molière's plays, through laughter, never let us forget our universal virtues and vices. These ideas may well be kept in mind when we evaluate modern interpretations of the comedies.

More formal academic studies were being written in this period, as critics explored the texts in the light of current theories. A notable example is Suzanne L. Relyea's *Signs, Systems and Meanings: A Contemporary Semiotic Reading of Four Molière Plays*.[27] Analyzing concepts of language in the seventeenth century, particularly the ideas of Descartes and the Port Royal thinkers, Relyea points out that meaning in that age was conceived as deriving from divine essence, clearly expressed in words. Drama, however, is not merely spoken dialogue but a performance through signs as well, the whole producing meaning. *L'École des femmes, Tartuffe, Dom Juan,* and *Amphitryon* are examined to show the important role of signs, with language often functioning as noncommunication. That language has a disruptive or perverting role in human relations is scarcely a new concept, however, and it is as if contemporary semiotic theory has caught up with what Molière knew full well.

In 1980 Gérard Defaux wrote *Molière, ou les métamorphoses du comique*[28] with the thesis that physical gestures communicate as importantly as words, and that the *comédie-ballet* liberated Molière from the cerebral plays of his middle period, *Tartuffe* et al. The essential role of the physical in comedy has been understood since the article by Gustave Lanson in 1905 that emphasized Molière's nature as a creator of farce. Defaux does well to treat this aspect of Molière but not at the expense of denigrating the serious side. The book is flawed first by its traditional approach, the assumption that the comedies sought to instruct society and to moralize. Defaux believes that the playwright reached an impasse with the rejection of *Tartuffe,* failing to get his message across, and that his final period was a breakthrough into pure frivolity in theater. The study appears to perceive Monsieur Jourdain's madness as a triumph and a liberation, surely an injustice to the subtleties of this *comédie-ballet.*

Claude Abraham performs a greater service to Molière studies in his *On the Structure of Molière's "Comédies-ballets"*[29] in which he demonstrates the effective structuring of these plays and how they add to our understanding of the "serious" comedies. Theme and structure are masterfully interwoven in all of his works, the playwright applying his skills in any theatrical mode. Ronald Tobin concurs in this and treats *Les Fâcheux* and *Le Bourgeois gentilhomme* in two articles that show the clever construction incorporating music, dance, and ideas.[30]

While scholars such as these were underscoring the need for examining all aspects of a Molière play, the physical as well as the intellectual, a number of prominent critics ably defended the positions they had taken in previous books. Lionel Gossman, whose *Men and Masks* is a benchmark work for the understanding of Molière in the context of the mental climate of his age, commented that critics and the public have always escaped from the uneasiness of *Dom Juan* or *Le Misanthrope* by resorting to pure theatricality.[31] In the nineteenth century Gautier admired the commedia dell'arte side of Molière, as did Copeau in the mid-twentieth century. They thought Molière needed to be removed from solemnity and moralizing, and so emphasized sheer exuberance. The fundamental problem of interpretation of these ambiguous works has always existed, and a modern echoing of Gautier offers no real solution. Gossman wisely notes that Monsieur Jourdain must be seen as a prisoner of his own fantasies and not free in his madness as Defaux suggests. Paradox and antitheses must be acknowledged in Molière because these elements give true human scale to his comedies.

To gain some perspective on Molière studies at the start of the 1980s one may turn to a valuable issue of *Oeuvres et critiques* that appeared in 1981.[32] Several noted scholars contributed articles to assess the current state of work in the area, and Marie-Odile Sweetser's "Domaines de la critique moliéresque" offers a summary of the types of studies being produced, tallying closely with those we have just discussed. A companion article by Maurice Descotes outlines the many stage interpretations of the period, a resource of great importance on the French stage's handling of Molière. Not surprisingly, the burden of these articles is that much more remains to be done to illuminate the comedies in the light of scholarship and modern thought. Work is done on Molière in the comic tradition, in the climate of his times, as a commentator on the human condition, and as a creator of theater. Sweetser concludes that all must seek "a more complete, more just, more balanced view of the work and genius of Molière."[33]

Le Tartuffe

In an effort to cover every facet of the work of Molière scholars there is a risk of fragmenting this chapter. It seems practical and pertinent to concentrate on what has been written about the core of the Molière problem, how to understand and appreciate the "serious" comedies, *Le Tartuffe, Dom Juan,* and *Le Misanthrope.* All elements of his work and all sorts of critical approaches must be brought into play in any consideration of these pivotal comedies.

Judd Hubert's "Molière: The Playwright as Protagonist"[34] expands upon his valuable book of 1962, *Molière and the Comedy of Intellect,* treating many of the plays, although here we shall focus upon his study of *Tartuffe.* Hubert sees a constant self-conscious and self-referential theatricality in all the plays, and in the case of *Tartuffe* this theatricality emerges through the use of hackneyed plots (the preaching of salvation, tyranny of the father, generation gap, thwarted love, etc.). The characters use this sort of framework and create on it roles for themselves and scenes with others that they act out with vigor. The effect is highly theatrical, reminding the audience that this is not a slice of life but pure stage show. Tartuffe's act as a "dévot" is actually obvious and lazy, as he must convince only his dupes, Orgon and Mme Pernelle. Mariane and Damis emote in exaggerated fashion, while Elmire devises scenes that she has difficulty in playing out. The play is composed of "reactions to perform-ances"[35] among the characters. The playwright has no need to function as a protagonist here, manipulating affairs or speaking through one figure. His job has been to assemble the characters and to turn them loose on one an-other, or, at least, this is the masterful effect produced by the comedy.

Such remarks are helpful to a director of a stage production who may struggle to decide how much realism and theatricality to work into the ver-sion being presented. Unfortunately, Hubert is not of assistance on how to stage the difficult fifth act of *Tartuffe,* the rex ex machina bit in which Tartuffe is suddenly arrested at the moment of his triumph. For ideas on this we may consult an article by Michael Spingler, "The King's Play: Censorship and the Politics of Performance in Molière's *Tartuffe.*"[36]

Spingler suggests that this play is a subtle critique of the monarch's heavy-handed rule of all, including theater. In the article the principle action of the comedy is called "intervention," with Tartuffe apparently the winner until the king intervenes. The denouement is essential if Tartuffe is to be foiled, but the last scene is awkward to produce in a comedy. Orgon and his family have been defeated and are not ready for a conventional happy ending. A meta-theatrical effect is created, says Spingler, by having Louis, through his officer, appear and show that he has let the characters go through their puppetlike actions always under his eye. The true ruling force then snatches them back from a deserved fate. Spingler suggests that Molière thus subtly mocks om-nipotence, despite the surface flattery of Louis. Absolutism seems rather vac-uous when it stoops to making happy endings of comedies.

With such an interpretation, a production would do well to put heavy em-phasis upon the royal presence at the end. As to the characterizations and style of playing, a director has yet to create a comic or a villainous Tartuffe. Tone is all in a staged production, and it is revealing to observe a wide range of tones achieved in a number of staged Tartuffes. It will be clear that no one interpretation dominates in current theater, the ambiguous nature of this comedy stimulating many different versions.

Marie-France Hilgar comments upon this very issue in "Modern and Post-modern Interpretations of *Tartuffe.*"[37] She points out the various ways in which the comedy has been interpreted, from the versions by Louis Jouvet in the 1930s up to those of 1980. In 1978 a Vitez production tried to repro-duce Molière's original, while in 1980 the Comédie-Française went to the other extreme in a J. P. Roussillon production that modernized things to a point where Tartuffe is shot by police at the end. Orgon was done as a virtual madman, and Tartuffe as a seductive character leading a family to destroy itself. This was *Tartuffe* in tragic mode, and not well received. In the same year in a version directed by Jean Périmony the play was performed in fairly classical style, with an innovative twist at the end. Laurent, Tartuffe's servant, stops him with a blow, suggesting that the servant was truly an agent always watching his employer for the police. This would reinforce an impression of the royal power pervading all of life. Hilgar asks what version represents our age's interpretation of Molière. Some other critical studies and staged versions may help one decide.

Sound advice on the interpretation of Molière's plays is found in Robert McBride's book *The Sceptical Vision of Molière: A Study in Paradox*.[38] The title contains his concept, that multiple and conflicting elements are always in Molière. The characters consist of three basic types, the Fool, the Trickster, and the Wise Fool,[39] of which only the first really believes in anything. Orgon thus is the Fool, Tartuffe the Trickster, with the *raisonneur* Cléante as the third type. McBride correctly emphasizes that the second two types are consciously playing roles, that they are "comédiens"[40] acting out roles to influence others. The reasoner sagely accepts the paradoxes of life and seeks to find practical compromises. The interplay of all these types is not designed to send a message but to stimulate laughter at our own follies. The sum of critical opinions on the nature of Molière's theater, as we have reviewed them here, is the recognition of the theatricality and the ambiguity of the comedies. Have the staged productions of the period taken advantage of these perceptions?

The excellent Richard Wilbur translation of *Tartuffe* was used in a New York production in 1977, under the direction of Stephen Porter.[41] Tartuffe was played as a frenzied maniacal type, menacing yet wildly comic, eliciting critical acclaim. It is interesting to read the advice of Wilbur in an introduction to his published translation: "The best of the stage productions have repeatedly proved the verbal sufficiency of Molière's serious comedies. In short . . . trust the words . . . to convey the point and persona of comedy, and trust them also to be sufficiently entertaining."[42]

A lack of trust was evident in a German production of *Tartuffe* directed by Ingmar Bergman in 1979. The version was solemnly keyed to a theme of human alienation, with a pervading sense of helplessness. Orgon was played as longing for love, making the task of Tartuffe simple. The chief energy in a doomed world came from Tartuffe, while Cléante was depicted as an impotent invalid. Dorine's lucid comments were delivered ineffectually. In the final scene Bergman undercut Molière's rex ex machina resolution by having the Exempt deliver his long speech in French, in the German language production. One way to deal with a problem of production is to pretend that it does not exist.

Two years after this unhappy experiment the comédie-Française undertook the re-creation of a three-day royal fête of 1664, *Les Plaisirs de l'ile enchantée*. Director Maurice Béjart put on *Le Mariage forcé*, *La Princesse d'Elide*, and *Le Tartuffe* in Molière's original sequence. The underlying theme was variations on love. The director, however, moved the date of the fête to the end of the reign of Louis XIV, and *Tartuffe* reflected the gloom of the court under the sanctimonious influence of Madame de Maintenon. The final scene had Louis himself, as a doddering caricature of the regal portrait by Rigaud, enter to arrest Tartuffe. Life and art were intermingled, with solemn delivery of lines and costumes of black veils suggesting the aura of the court in 1715. Tartuffe was played as an inspired zealot whose religion meant death in life.

The sexual side of this comedy was stressed in Brian Bedford's 1982 production in Washington, D.C. Critic Ramond LePage reported that a destructive erotic force powered the production, the lustful Tartuffe almost raping Elmire on the table.[43] Scenes were cut or shortened, and the role of Cléante was greatly diminished. The famous "The poor man!" line was removed, and the whole effect was neither tragic nor comic. This production showed a sick mind mixing sex and religion, to the detriment of Molière's comedy.

In a London production of 1983 Tartuffe was played as a Rasputin-like fraud, coarse and farcical, while an Edinburgh version in 1986 used a Lowland Scots translation to suggest the kinship of Molière with Robert Burns in his mockery of human foibles. The possibilities for interpretation seem endless, indicating the depth and power of the Molière wellspring.

The most important interpretation of recent years must be the French version of 1985, a film by Gaumont based on the stage production of *Tartuffe* at the National Theater of Strasbourg. Gérard Depardieu directed and played the title role in a manner termed "an act of daring" by a critic.[44] The setting was sparse and bare, not just a filming of a stage production. Depardieu stressed the Molière text in a classical rendition, having the actors "erect the text as a structure within which the film happens."[45] A probing camera lets the director focus closely on effects not available because of distance between players and public in the theater. Imaginative use of the medium opens up great possibilities for more illumination of Molière's comedies, and diffusion through television to a wide audience is an exciting prospect. The direction of the Comédie-Française was well aware of all this, and in 1986 undertook to contract with six major European film directors to create video versions of Molière plays. Successful productions could have worldwide impact, as evidenced by the British video of *Nicholas Nickleby* by Dickens.[46]

Dom Juan

What have critics and directors made of *Dom Juan* in recent years? Barbara Woshinsky examines this play in regard to the "question of the nature and function of language,"[47] which she sees to be a central feature. Language is used for noncommunication and deception, as signs and referents are nimbly juggled by Don Juan. Words are the material with which he creates roles for himself and others, as I and other critics have remarked. For the rest of the characters in the comedy words have some objective meaning, but for the Don words are just tools to be manipulated. This article reflects an interest in semiotics in recent criticism, an example of which we saw in the book by Relyea. Woshinsky is correct in seeing *Dom Juan* as a reflection of a process going on in the seventeenth century, the gradual divorce of language from a divine order of things signified. Our impression of the power of this play is reinforced by such a study that shows Molière's awareness of the intellectual phenomenon of his age.

The structure of *Dom Juan* has frequently given rise to critical comment, for the problem of its apparently loose construction is not easy to solve. Where is the unity of this freely flowing piece that jumps from one incident to another? Franco Tonelli in his "Molière's *Dom Juan* and the Space of the Commedia dell'arte" of 1985[48] addresses this matter, seeing the development of the play in the spatial rather than temporal dimension. The actions of the Don are more parallel than sequential because he moves in a world of commedialike encounters. We have drawn attention to the importance of mobility and fixity in this present study, equating movement in space with success and fixity with defeat. It is good to see the development of these ideas in a work by Janice Berkowitz, whose dissertation analyzes *L'École des femmes, Le Tartuffe,* and *Dom Juan* as they create meanings through words, space, and scene.[49] The significance of the movement and of the scenes in the forest and on the shore is well presented in "actantial" terms, the mastery of space by the Don as he acts and exploits it. The immobility and containment of the later scenes lead to his failure and damnation.

The *Dom Juan* of current critical opinion, at least that which deals with relationships between meaning and structure, emerges as a play of strong construction, innovative and challenging to analyze but potent as theater. When critics ponder the work as a problem play, however, they err in trying to assign one philosophical meaning to it. Such an approach seems outmoded in an article by David Ball and Frank H. Ellis.[50] Their "Molière's *Dom Juan*: Form, Meaning, Audience" depicts the play as a comedy about "absolute freedom from self,"[51] essentially a tragic conflict between individual and society. They see the Don as "playacting" for an audience (an idea already well established in criticism by my article of 1962[52] and Jean Rousset's *Le Mythe de Don Juan*)[53] both in the play and in the theater. They conceive that Molière is stating the philosophical idea that that individual's need for freedom undergirds all the tensions within society. This idea is seen to be the basis of the comedy. The argument falls before the observation that the Don is prisoner of his own persona, doomed to unhappiness in his compulsion to disrupt the joy of others in love. Ironic bondage rather than freedom dominates.

In Marcel Gutwirth's sound article "Don Juan et le tabou d'inceste"[54] he reiterates the comic nature of the play, in concert with Moore, Guicharnaud, and H. Gaston Hall. He notes the uniqueness of the play among Molière's works but rejects any classification of it as tragic. The essentially absurd concept of possessing all of womankind is a bizarre exaggeration of a taboo elucidated by Claude Lévi-Strauss in his studies of myth,[55] the idea that it is incestuous to insert oneself universally between legitimate husbands and wives. The Don plays a game of capturing women to a point at which all of his existence consists of "having" rather than "being."[56] He becomes a victim of an illegitimate obsession, falling away at the end to perdition.

The complexities of this comedy remain a challenge to critics and stage directors alike. Stephen Porter, whose *Tartuffe* staging was noted, did *Dom Juan* in 1972 in New York, the title character being played as rather ineffectual in true relations with others. The humanizing of the Don made for an existential interpretation, and one wonders how the final scene was handled since this was not recorded in a review. A London production of 1981, directed by Peter Gill, used an interesting setting for the descent into the inferno. Against a backdrop of a medieval painting of the torments of the damned, the Don is surrounded by a ghostly chorus. The production sought to show the viability of the characters in the modern world, the Don being played as at once appealing and evil. The text was played in straightforward fashion in front of a projected painting for each act, a scene of odalisques, a Dutch landscape, a Georges de la Tour skull and candle, and the inferno. The device was brilliant to suggest the space and movement of the Don.

In the "House of Molière" at the Comédie-Française, Jean-Luc Boutté directed a *Dom Juan* in 1979, assisted by Philippe Kerbrat. Abstract setting was carried to an extreme, with Don Juan and Sganarelle depicted marooned on a desert island. The title figure appeared through a trapdoor, but garbed as a seventeenth-century nobleman. He was played with brutal sensuality and allure. The abstract setting permitted the commander to be represented by a helmet and sword floating in air, with a skull materializing in the helmet. Realism was abandoned to remove the impediment to understanding of the comedy at the end.

It is interesting to compare an American production of the same year on the Arena Stage in Washington, D.C. Directed by Liviu Ciulei, this version employed a two-level circular set with transparent floor. Early twentieth-century costumes and décor gave a tone of the world of the idle rich. Sganarelle's broad comedy was eliminated, so, treading a line between tragedy and comedy, the play seemed without much life or focus. The inference from these various interpretations of *Dom Juan* must be that one should choose a consistent approach in producing the play.

A successful job was done in 1981 at the Guthrie Theater in Minneapolis by Richard Foreman. His direction of *Dom Juan* called for a set much like the original, but he had the actors create a Brecht-like strangeness. The figures moved in rectilinear paths and often posed as if framed. The Don always held and used a hand mirror, observing his own performance, and in the final scene he was carried off in a cage of mirrors. Against this character whose focus was totally reflected to self, Sganarelle was played as a comic Everyman. The stone guest was made almost real to heighten the mingling of reality and fantasy in this version, and the director used a chorus and musical accompaniment.

The resources of the stage, knowingly exploited, can assist us in seeing this problematic comedy in helpful ways. There is no one correct interpretation but rather a challenge to innovate in the theater to create a Molière for our times. The depth and dynamism of the text invite this. New paths through cinema technique now open up for the interpreter of Molière, and they have not been ignored. Theater and film are two different modes, with the floating omnipresent eye of the camera having dreamlike capabilities, in contrast with the fixed viewpoint of the audience in the hall, present but removed from the bit of life being re-created on stage. For a play having elements of reality and fantasy, the film seems an ideal choice for interpretation, and it is gratifying to find a French television version of *Dom Juan* that succeeds in many ways.

Marcel Bluwal created a totally televised production of the comedy and not merely a filming of a stage version. Verisimilitude is strong at the start as we see the Don dressed as a nobleman of the early nineteenth century, inhabiting a vast château. Close shots reinforce the power and soberness of his delivery of Molière's lines, dominating by a glance the compliant but uneasy Sganarelle. The mobility of the character is asserted through scenes done on horseback in the first parts of the comedy. The Don rides away from Elvire and, after the scene on the beach, gallops off through great stretches of pine forest. The speeches on personal freedom are delivered while at a full gallop, while Sganarelle tumbles from his horse when expostulating with his master. The production fails to use the facilities of the medium, however, when the Commander is presented as a massive statue with lumbering tread. All the supernatural parts of the play are done in a manner lacking in imagination, for the camera and its tricks could suggest the unreal rather than simply photograph the devices necessary for a stage production, statue or trapdoor. We still await a great film interpretation of *Dom Juan*.

Le Misanthrope

The third of Molière's problematic plays, *Le Misanthrope*, has received the frequent attention of critics. The dimensions of this greatest of social comedies invite all sorts of analyses, so we must limit our attention to but a few articles that deal with questions of basic interpretation. Should *Le Misanthrope* be read and played as sober drama or as a comedy? Roger W. Herzel goes to the heart of the matter in "Much Depends on the Acting: The Original Cast of *Le Misanthrope*,"[57] which aims to show how Molière's company must have done its version. He writes not in expectation that all interpretations will mimic the original but rather to give a healthy reminder that the playwright created plays tailored to the abilities of his own acting company. A modern director would do well to remember that *Le Misanthrope* was written for actors and actresses with almost stereotyped personas. We know that the play was received as a comedy in 1666, and Herzel deplores a long tradition of stage versions that were somberly moralistic. A 1977 Comédie-Française production, for example, continued this tradition with a rather humorless version that showed a broken-hearted Célimène crushed at her loss of Alceste. Righteous anger at society's corruption is also a message frequently worked into productions, but did the originator play it this way? Herzel establishes the typical roles and stage personalities of the entire troupe, then envisages how each member would have fit into the *Misanthrope* cast. With Molière as Alceste there is no doubt about the comic quality of the interpretation, for he was renowned for his virtuoso comic playing and held to be poor at tragic roles. Grimace and miming must have opened this play of which the first lines are Philinte's reaction to Alceste's expression: "What is it? What's the matter with you?" Each member of the company is then characterized by his or her stage strengths and weaknesses, and the total effect of their playing the roles in *Le Misanthrope* is logically conjectured. La Grange, for example, always did the roles of the capable person in charge of the situation (Don Juan, Philinte) while Molière played the troubled characters. Du Croisy, heavy and unctuous, played Oronte with broad comic effects. Molière had a full gamut of comic acting opened up for him between the straight man and the clown. The feminine roles were equally determined by the women who played them in set styles of acting. Herzel's conclusion is that Molière must have done *Le Misanthrope* with an Alceste characterization that simultaneously won respect for his truthfulness about society and merited laughter for his own embracing of falsity when it was convenient. The best productions of this play will do well to suggest this mixture of the moralist and the comic misfit, paradoxical and challenging understanding but always laughable.

In this vein we turn to Patrick Henry's 1986 study, "Paradox in *Le Misanthrope*."[58] Henry declares that in this comedy "the aesthetics of stimulation prevails, and it is consequently impossible to locate an authorial voice, much less establish a coherent philosophy that would supposedly satisfy a seventeenth-century audience."[59] No petit bourgeois values can be imputed to Molière, a poet of struggle channeled through the comic mode. Echoing Gossman, Henry notes that the society in which the play was set offered no firm values to play against. Each character, as the present study has stressed, creates his own values or an image of them, then works to project them convincingly upon others. So paradox prevails, even among the "good" characters of Philinte and Eliante who demonstrate inconsistencies, both revealing and concealing themselves. Molière's dialectical method makes the reader scrutinize and question what is going on within the characters. Henry likens Molière to Rabelais and Montaigne in their probing of the ambiguities of human nature.[60]

In 1982 Lionel Gossman writes in "Molière's *Misanthrope*: Melancholy and Society in the Age of Counterreformation"[61] that his assessment of the play in his *Men and Masks* still has validity despite opinions that he emphasized too much the serious and antithetical nature of the play. He agrees that all evidence shows that "Alceste is and should be played as a comic figure."[62] Yet audiences have had trouble with this interpretation of a basically melancholy character. Comedy in the shallow and empty salon world is indeed prone to bitterness, and the effect is much like that achieved by La Rochefoucauld in his sharp maxims about this world. Melancholic types were all to often found in such a society, a fragile veneer over violently changing modes of life and values. Gossman says that critics and public have always sought to escape from the uneasiness of all this through resorting to pure theatricality, but such an approach merely sidesteps a confrontation with the paradoxical nature of the play and thus debases it to a frivolous level. *Le Misanthrope* demands both laughter and serious consideration in its all-too-human antitheses.

Have the staged versions of this comedy dealt adequately with these questions? A lackluster version was staged at Britain's National Theatre in 1973, when a Gaullist Paris setting made the play into a brittle drawing-room drama without humor. Happier results were achieved in an APA Repertory production in New York in 1968. From the audience I agreed with *New York Times* critic Clive Barnes that this version, using the Wilbur translation, was "a mixture of humor and humanity so skillfully blended that anyone wanting to know what a comedy really is could well study it."[63] The antitheses and paradoxes were all evident, wrapped in comic playing and wonderful verse. Stephen Porter directed this, then returned to do another *Misanthrope* in 1983 at the Circle in the Square. Nothing seems to have been lost in this production, for one reads that "*The Misanthrope* remains an entirely contemporary version of the price thinking people can pay for either accepting or abusing the restrictive coordinates of what we call civilization."[64] The critic also noted how well the actors, in concert with the author, "ask us to contemplate the troubling and often hidden ambiguities of the heart." Alceste was called "a mystery man" in this review.

Also worthy of note is a production of *Le Misanthrope* directed by Garland Wright at the Guthrie Theater in Minneapolis in 1987. Innovative in staging but grounded in paradox, this version is available on tape.[65]

The French theater did not neglect Molière, of course, and Marcel Descotes gives a quick critique of interpretations of *Le Misanthrope* in a useful article.[66] No spectacular versions of this comedy emerged "since it is so true that they very long history of the role of Alceste seems to have almost exhausted the gamut of possible variations." Fresh ideas may come from elsewhere, as we have seen. In 1975 a version featured a sinister Alceste in an interpretation that violently dramatized things, yet Molière's masterpiece remained "unmoveable." In 1977 the play was presented in traditional manner, with Alceste as a sad, romantic figure. Humor came only from the roles of the marquesses.

This sampling of scholarly studies and stage productions of *Le Tartuffe, Dom Juan,* and *Le Misanthrope* has hit only a few high spots of the period, but a clear trend is toward demanding real depth of interpretation, the sincerest tribute to the importance of Molière and his works. No great critical breakthrough has emerged, despite a lively interest in theories of criticism in recent years. Concentration on these three great plays has been just a device to make possible some evaluation of the work being produced that gives thoughtful consideration to the real nature of Molière's theater. The challenge to define and illuminate comic genius cannot be denied by anyone who deals with the major problematic comedies. Equally responsive have been several scholars who have chosen to handle other aspects of the Molière legacy. There follows a review of some studies and productions that focus upon different sorts of plays, as well as some works that can be characterized as grouping themselves around critical approaches or topics.

Plays about Women

It is not surprising to find great interest in Molière's plays dealing with the nature and role of woman in society. The comedies most directly concerned are *Les Précieuses ridicules, L'École des femmes,* and *Les Femmes savantes,* yet these do not form a homogenous whole but vary between broad farce and the problematic. Marcel Gutwirth analyzes these plays in an article of 1982, "Molière and the Woman Question: *Les Précieuses ridicules, L'École des femmes, Les Femmes savantes,*"[67] and gives a fairly conventional reading of the first two plays, echoing his book, *Molière ou l'invention comique.* He singles out *Les Femmes savantes* for criticism, however, finding this play to be a weak source of comedy in its unevenness. The women are caricatures and the men are depicted as weak and stupid. There is no real affirmation of the superiority of one sex over the other, both displaying equal amounts of folly. The feminine stereotype of Henriette is hardly a heroine for the supporters of women's liberation, and the pretentious pedantry of the other female characters is a gross parody of the learning being sought and obtained by women in Molière's times. Gutwirth considers *L'École des femmes* to be the playwright's "enduring statement on the subject of woman"[68] as Agnès follows her healthy instincts to undo the schemes of her self-deluding guardian Arnolphe. This seems to be saying that the message of Molière is simply to follow nature's guidance.

At the other extreme one finds a study of the women characters in *Tartuffe*[69] that deplores the stereotyping of women by Molière as basic Freudian types, imputing to him a fear of creating too strong a female character. Psychocriticism is the basis of this article that purports to analyze the author's psyche on evidence within his plays.

Barbara Johnson writes perceptively in "Teaching Ignorance: *L'École des femmes*"[70] that the pedagogy of Arnolphe, his instruction of Agnès, is not designed to educate her but to perpetuate ignorance. The intentional problem of the author's own position arises in such a study because, again, one attempts to put ideas into Molière's head because they occur in his play. Johnson is justified, however, in linking Arnolphe's teaching to a long tradition of male domination of education that kept woman untaught and subordinate. She points out that modern editors of the text are guilty of the same glossing over of touchy matters such as specific sexual references, continuing to "teach ignorance." The woman question in Molière is thus placed in historical context.

These two studies show how Molière's works may function as a mirror from which many ideas are reflected, suggesting that more understanding of the nature of woman in the seventeenth century is to be sought. *L'École des femmes* is now perceived to be more and more of a difficult play to interpret.

An article by Larry W. Riggs[71] focuses on the use of precious speech by the women in *Les Précieuses ridicules* and *Les Femmes savantes,* and Riggs says that the women are not as much perpetrators of linguistic abuses as they are victims of society. They are truly just enthusiastic followers of a widespread linguistic trend of the period, the use of an accepted language formed to communicate the exaggerated norms of the salon world. The women become ridiculous, to be sure, but it is the ridiculous nature of the whole social system that Molière is attacking. The use of language that is supposedly clear and reasonable, but in fact highly strained, creates serious illusions in the users. The officially accepted meanings for words, when unquestioningly accepted by all, are a political tool that serves to make people think of reality through a linguistic veil. The abuse of language is knowingly mocked by Molière, and characters such as those in *Les Femmes savantes* are his vehicles for showing the extremes of absurdity.

As critics pondered such aspects of the plays centered on women, theatrical productions, particularly of *L'École des femmes,* were being created. In 1973 the Comédie-Française production of this comedy was done with two different actors taking the role of Arnolphe. One was "a monster blinded by passion"[72] while the other was a fanatic full of self-righteousness. The Agnès role was handled so as to play to both male interpretations, evidently a tour de force by the actress. The setting and mood were generally somber, under the direction of J. P. Roussillon. Within one production it was demonstrated that a number of different readings of Molière is most valid.

Two American stagings, both in 1985, used the Wilbur translation. The Indiana Repertory of Indianapolis gave a fairly conventional interpretation of the play, while the other, by the Actors' Theater of Louisville, Kentucky, featured an innovative setting. The director, Laszlo Marton, called for a dark fortress to suggest the imprisonment of Agnès. Against this background the play opened with what represented an erotic dream of Arnolphe, vague figures miming an orgy as Arnolphe dozed. A modern psychological tone prevailed in the interpretation of Arnolphe's problems.

In 1987 a British production showed a remarkable new departure. Di Trevis directed the comedy in a set depicting the grounds of an opulent French country house. Ethereal music accompanied the appearance of Agnès at a window. The effect of an elegiac pastoral was created, but its appropriateness was not clear. Arnolphe, at the end, was met by a goddess at the top of a heavenly stairway. The lines were delivered almost mechanically, producing an overall bizarre effect.

The door for innovative productions remains wide open in Molière at present, an important indication of the ongoing vigor of his comedies. An outstanding example of a novel approach is found in a Swedish version of *Les Femmes savantes* created in Stockholm in 1985. In a furiously physical mode, jazz, farce, and break dancing kept up constant motion. Philaminte was played by a seven-foot man in female attire. The frenetic action was designed to show the rejection by the women of their physical beings in their desire for intellectual existence.

This comedy, with its echoes of questions of women's rights, has not been popular in France, and, when played in 1978 at the Comédie-Française, it was done as a sober family conflict and an attack on bourgeois mediocrity. One arrives at the conclusion that the plays about women resist integration into the current scene, the problem lying not with the author but with our society.

Farce and *Comédie-Ballet*

No problems stand in the way of work with the farces, and we find a successful musical adaptation of *Les Fourberies de Scapin* having long runs as *Scapino*. As a foundation of Molière's theater, the farce, evolving into the comic ballets with music and dance, constitutes a vital part of his heritage. What has been made of comedies such as *Le Malade imaginaire* and *Le Bourgeois gentilhomme?* We have noted the critical studies by Defaux and others, and now let us see what theater has done with the plays. Do they impress us as embodying the essence of Molière as opposed to the problematic plays? Or can we perceive how the various styles of comedies relate to each other in the corpus of his theater?

Le Bourgeois gentilhomme was directed by Jean-Louis Barrault in 1972 in a production much like a modern musical. The airs of Lully were played as rock music, and the entire version emerged as a gigantic joke, a riotous diversion for the court. In 1986 this *comédie-ballet* again appeared on the boards of the Comédie-Française directed by Jean-Luc Boutté. Jourdain was played as full of childlike wonder at his new knowledge, and the Professor of Philosophy showed tenderness for his naive pupil. The setting was spare, stressing the creation of a world of imagination in the mind of Jourdain. The costumes, dances, and dinner brightly enlivened a drab world when they were called into being by Jourdain. The other characters fool him but cannot keep from being swept up in the joyous *mamamouchi* dance. The essential so well expressed by Ronald Tobin,[73] that there be total integration of theme with music and dance, seems to have been achieved in this stage production.

Le Malade imaginaire

In 1978 the Théâtre National de Marseille did *Le Malade imaginaire* under the direction of Marcel Maréchal. He chose to present an Argan truly ill, but uncertain of the nature of his malady. He truly suffers from melancholy in this version, and the set reinforced this with somberness. The limits to living space emphasized his own limitations of access to a real life. The reference to the dying Molière was evident, and the production was a tribute to him.

Reference to the death of Molière while playing Argan is handled with grace in a production of the Théâtre Marigny, which was taped for television. The presentation of *Le Malade imaginaire* is framed by having all the company on stage ready to go on with the show, standing in fixed poses. The ill Molière insists upon playing his role. A harlequin and a polichinelle begin the action with song and dance. Apothecaries then fumigate the bed chamber, creating a depressing effect. Harlequin reappears at a brightly lighted window, however, bringing the spark of life. The original interludes of music and dance are thus preserved, and farce is underscored in the playing. At the end, during the doctoral ceremony, Molière collapses on stage. The camera shows the dying man, then shifts back to a joyous curtain-call routine by the troupe. This is not Molière's play, but the drama of life and death makes for highly effective theater.

The capacities of the stage were well used by a Guthrie Theater production of *Le Malade imaginaire* in 1988. Director Garland Wright worked with a set that was a manifestation of the mind of Argan. For example, a ticking clock without hands occasionally stopped to the terror of Argan, so unsure of his allotted time. Wright's notes on the production reveal a perceptive grasp of the nature of this comedy, with its reflections back and forth between reality and fantasy. The dying actor Molière played a well character who plays at dying. The production's modernity came from its suggestion of the prevalent self-obsessions in our society, beset by doubt and fear and longing for an authority to solve problems. Argan's clinging to medicine is just one version of the problem. Molière wrote a farce about deep anxieties that can reduce a well man to dependency upon a crutch. This farce contains more reality than a well-made play, Wright contends, for life has not neat linear flow. The play starts as a comedy of character, is successively a comedy of ideas, a melodrama, a farce, and a song and dance. He says that "this oddly deconstructed form is utterly right for the play's subject and ambitions."[74]

Conclusion

What one hopes for in a stage production of Molière does take place now and then. A director reads the text and reacts with sensitivity to give physical substance to its turnings and paradoxes. Such handling gives a glimpse of the work of a master playwright, simultaneously comic and profound. The most stimulating treatments of Molière thus sometimes are found not in the probings of scholars but in readings by those who seek the theatrical nature of a play in order to put it on stage. One should be open to innovative suggestions for staging as well as to studies of academic origin. In selecting among so many interpretations, of various sorts, the present study has tried to define the legacy of Molière as a vital force that continues undiminished to delight and to challenge modern readers and audiences. The works that seem to enhance best our appreciation of Molière in his roles as classical writer and creator of great comic theater have been chosen with personal predilections for those pertinent to the major issues in Molière studies. The question always posed has been that of whether or not one grows closer to the life spark that Molière kindled and passed on to us, whether or not an interpretation shares a bit of that spark.

Keeping in mind the nature of the playwright as a working creator of theater, who discovered himself to be an author in print, does any study stand out that aids us to sense how this genius may have created his comedies? I award the palm to the article by Judd D. Hubert that was cited earlier.[75] In writing of "the playwright as protagonist" Hubert reminds us that the comic and the intellectual, the literary and the theatrical are indissolubly bound together in Molière, mutually nourishing each other. The comedies can come alive for us as we participate in a remarkable process of viewing or reading them, with the driving power commanding our attention now located in ideas, now in broad comic play. The author is at once visible and invisible. We think of Molière in the midst of acting out a role he wrote. Is he an author or a vehicle of the author's thoughts? Being physically present on stage in one's own comedy immediately suggests that the actor-author is voicing his personal ideas. Far from this, the author effaces himself so that it is Alceste or Arnolphe who shapes the action, creates the scenes. It is a process we have observed constantly, the forging of plays within plays by the characters set into movement by the script. Once launched, the play gains momentum from the force within the characters, as Hubert observes.

At the start of his Paris career Molière writes *Les Précieuses ridicules* about literary and verbal delusions. The women then create their own fantasy world and act out the roles they make. Ordinary reality immediately falls away before the onslaught of theatricality. The play seems self-generating. The writer is the "hidden protagonist," vicariously playing out the scenes though the persons of the actors and actresses who seem to function autonomously. The case of *Le Misanthrope* is especially noteworthy in this respect, for all of the characters compose scenes and personas for selves and others. It is "essentially the confrontation between antithetical types of role playing."[76] Who, we ask ourselves, is protagonist, who playwright? Hubert notes that in *Dom Juan* the title character is protean in playing roles that suit him until the end when he undertakes one beyond his abilities as a protagonist. In *Le Bourgeois gentilhomme* it is Jourdain who composes a script for himself, generating a veritable theater for his own life. He then moves happily into the role composed by the others who become protagonists. One forgets that the original Jourdain was the playwright himself, ultimately the source of the entire comedy. Hubert observes that all the plays have what he terms a more or less "occulted or sunken script which serves as a prop." The playwright posits a phenomenon of the social world and lets his play seem to "unfold in a constant relationship"[77] with it. The very conventionality of the script's basis lets all the characters have a part in creating a piece of theater rather on their own. The originator of the whole thing seems to remove his hands from it and enjoy participating in the stage production as just one of the creative players on the boards. Perhaps Hubert guides us to some comprehension of how the genius of Molière functioned. He sets up some guidelines for a game of human relations, gives the characters an initial nudge, and lets them play themselves. In such a way the playwright may be able to make an audience participate, seeing human beings in action in a situation of common truth. It is at once theatrical and contrived but also a means to get people to see honestly their own virtues and failings mirrored in the words and actions on stage. It is comic in scope because it approaches no cosmic or transcendental concerns. Laughter may be inner or boisterously on the outside, but, in all cases, when one reacts to a Molière play, it is a recognition of the human follies that we all share. Molière has left for us a means by which any age can know itself. It is a fact that the plays seem to be ever prepared to go on stage, revealing to new audiences new meanings about themselves. An ongoing process of creation was set in motion by Molière more than three centuries ago, and this is his real legacy.

Jacques Copeau, a mid-twentieth-century practitioner of French theater, said these words about Molière, and they make a fitting final salute:

Molière is the great man alive on stage. He is more than a genius. He is a great soul who exhibits himself and sacrifices himself for the theater.

By his presence, by his example, by his personal devotion the art of the theater changes in meaning, nature, and scope. It rediscovers a principle of life, it becomes a true art in which the spirit of creation and the means of realization are intimately mingled and in which the principles of the craft are as one with the inspiration of the creative artist.

"Discours au public pour le Trois centième Anniversaire de la naissance de Molière." (*Revue d'histoire du théâtre,* 5:4)

Notes and References

Chapter One

1. Biographies range from Grimarest, *La Vie de M. de Molière* (Paris, 1704) to Ramón Fernandez, *La Vie de Molière* (Paris: Gallimard, 1930). For Molière's early life, see Gustave Michaud, *La Jeunesse de Molière, Les Debuts de Molière à Paris, Les Luttes de Molière* (Paris, 1923–25). For facts of his life, I draw on these.

2. For theater history, W. L. Wiley, *The Early Public Theater in France* (Cambridge: Harvard University Press, 1960).

3. Fernandez, 41, English translation by W. Follett, *Molière, the Man Seen Through the Plays* (New York: Hill & Wang, 1958).

4. J. Huizinga, *Homo Ludens, A Study of the Play Element in Culture* (Boston: Beacon Press, 1955), passim.

Chapter Two

1. On the history of the editions of Molière's works, Maurice Rat, preface to *Molière, Oeuvres complètes* (Paris, 1956) ix–xiv.

2. Ibid., 1:868.

3. J. D. Hubert, *Molière and the Comedy of Intellect* (Berkley: University of California Press, 1962), 2.

4. Numbers in parentheses refer to act and scene and are cited hereafter as such.

5. See Jean Rousset, *La Littérature de l'âge baroque en France* (Paris: Corti, 1954). On the novel, Jacques Ehrmann, *Un Paradis désespéré, l'amour et l'illusion dans L'Astrée* (New Haven: Yale University Press, Presses Universitaires de France, 1963).

6. Hubert, *Comedy of Intellect,* 23.

Chapter Three

1. F. Baumal, *Molière, auteur précieux* (Paris: Renaissance du livre, 1924).

2. Hubert, *Comedy of Intellect,* 52.

3. See H. C. Lancaster, *Le Mémoire de Mahelot, Laurent, et autres décorateurs de l'Hôtel de Bourgogne* (Paris: Champion, 1920).

4. The *Avertissement* of *Le Fâcheux* is the printed explanation prepared by Molière to describe the circumstances of the creation of the play and the way in which it was performed first.

5. Blaise Pascal, in his *Pensées,* a series of religious and philosophical writings

first published in 1670, comments on the human search for diversion to avoid thinking of grave issues.

6. The use of games structure is to be observed in this play. The pursuit of an object through obstacles will be a structure used by Molière notably in *Le Misanthrope*. See my article in the Bibliography.

Chapter Four

1. See chapter 5 on *Le Misanthrope*.

2. Fernandez, *La Vie de Molière*.

3. Hubert, *Comedy of Intellect*, 66–67.

4. Cf. R. J. Nelson, *The Play within the Play* (New Haven: Yale University Press, 1958), passim.

5. The fête's marvels are described in the text accompanying *La Princesse d'Élide* in the Pléiade edition (Paris: NRF Gallimard, 1933).

6. Cf. Baumal and Ehrmann.

Chapter Five

1. On the background, see H. G. Hall, *Molière: Tartuffe* (London: Arnold, 1960). 7–30.

2. Rat, *Molière, Oeuvres Complètes* 2:889.

3. Hall, *Molière*, 24.

4. Erich Auerbach, in "The Faux Dévot" essay in *Mimesis*, trans. W. Trask (Princeton: Princeton University Press, 1953), stresses these aspects.

5. One list of stage properties calls for a stick. Lancaster, *Le Mémoire de Mahelot*, 118.

6. See J. Cairncross, *New Light on Molière* (Geneva: Droz, 1956).

7. A summary of opinions is given by L. Gossman in his *Men and Masks, a Study of Molière* (Baltimore: Johns Hopkins University Press, 1963), 65. Professor Gossman's analysis probes the philosophical implications, 37–65.

8. Cf. Hubert, *Comedy of Intellect*, 115–18.

9. Fernandez, *La Vie de Molière*, 29.

10. See F. Gaiffe, *L'Envers du Grand Siècle* (Paris: Michel, 1924), 237–47.

11. Hubert, *Comedy of Intellect*, 117.

12. James Doolittle, "The Humanity of Molière's *Dom Juan*," *Publications of the Modern Language Association* 68 (June 1953):509–34.

13. James Doolittle, "Human Nature and Institutions in Molière's Plots," in *Studies in Seventeenth-Century French Literature* (Ithaca, N.Y.: Cornell University Press, 1962), 153–64.

14. Professor Gossman examines this theme but concludes differently.

15. The general theme of classical literature in W. G. Moore, *Molière, a New Criticism* (Oxford: Clarendon Press, 1949).

16. A broad range of interpretations if found in R. Jasinski, *Molière et le Misanthrope* (Paris: Librairie Nizet, 1951) and in the other general Molière studies cited.

17. J. Doolittle, "Human Nature and Institutions in Molière's Plots," 160 (see note 13, chapter 5).

18. Baumal, *Molière*, 133–46.

19. Roger Caillois, *Les Jeux et les hommes: le masque et le vertige,* revised and updated edition (Paris: Gallimard, 1977).

20. Eric Berne, *Games People Play: The Psychology of Human Relationships* (New York: Grove Press, 1964).

21. Ibid., 48, 163.

22. F. de La Rochefoucauld, *Maximes* (Paris, 1665–78). On the moralists of the age, P. Bénichou, *Morales du Grand Siècle* (Paris: Gallimard, 1948). A. J. Krailsheimer, *Studies in Self-Interest from Descartes to La Bruyère* (Oxford: Clarendon Press, 1962), 81–97 and 152–72 on La Rochefoucauld and Molière.

23. Jasinski, *Molière et le Misanthrope,* 283.

24. Quentin Hope treats this aspect of Molière in "The Scenes of Greeting in Molière," *Romanic Review* 50 (1959):241–54.

25. J. Guicharnaud, *Molière* (Paris: Gallimard, 1963), examines these plays intensively.

Chapter Six

1. Hubert, *Comedy of Intellect,* 157.

2. See T. E. Lawrenson, *The French Stage in the XVIIth Century* (Manchester: Manchester University Press, 1957), on the influence of the Italian order. "The net result, socially, is the diminution of the theatre performance as a significant occasion, and dramatically, of the power of entrance" (181).

Chapter Seven

1. Gossman, *Men and Masks,* 30–32, compares the Rotrou and Molière treatments.

Chapter Eight

1. The set for *L'Avare* as played in 1668, is described in Lancaster, *Le Mémoire de Mahelot,* 118. "Théatre est une salle, et sur le derrière, un jardin." The frequent exits by Harpagon to check his hoard require the garden set behind the room.

2. The speech is greatly cut here and occupies a full page.

3. Hubert, *Comedy of Intellect,* 215 and 210.

4. Ibid., 205–10.

5. Moore, *New Criticism,* 109.

Chapter Nine

1. Hubert, *Comedy of Intellect,* 240.

Chapter Ten

1. On farce sources and Molière's treatment, see René Bray, *Molière, homme de Théâtre* (Paris: Mercure de France, 1954), 215–17.
2. Lancaster, *Le Mémoire de Mahelot,* 123–24, gives the setting used at the Comédie-Française in 1680. "Théâtre est une chambre et une allecove dans le fonds. . . . Il faut changer le théâtre au premier intermède et représenter une ville ou des rues, et la chambre paroist comme l'on a commancé. Il faut 3 piece de tapisserie de hautte lisse et des perches et cordes" (original spelling preserved).

Chapter Eleven

1. The history of the Comédie-Française may be read in a work like John Lough, *Seventeenth-Century French Drama. The Background.* (Oxford: Clarendon Press, 1979).
2. Marivaux's debt to Molière is discussed by P. H. Nurse in "Molière, précurseur de Marivaux," *Revue des Sciences Humaines,* fasc. 100, 379–84.
3. For a treatment of Molière in intellectual history of seventeenth century and after, see Gossman, *Men and Masks,* chapters 6 and 7. On Molière as a dramatist, Louis Jouvet, "Molière," *Conferencia* (September 1937).
4. *Molière and the Commonwealth of Letters: Patrimony and Posterity,* ed. Roger Johnson, Jr., Editha S. Neumann, Guy T. Trail (Jackson: University Press of Mississippi, 1975).
5. *MLA International Bibliography,* vol 2, European, Asian, African, and South American literatures, 1972–1987.
6. In Johnson, Neumann, Trail, *Commonwealth of Letters,* 706–27, 728–46.
7. See Moore, *New Criticism,* and Bray, *Molière, homme de théâtre,* annotated in the Bibliography.
8. Gossman, *Men and Masks,* in the Bibliography.
9. Guicharnaud, *Molière, une aventure théâtrale,* in the Bibliography.
10. J. Brody, "Esthétique et société chez Molière," in *Dramaturgie et Société au 16e et au 17e siècles* (Paris: Centre National de Recherche Scientifique, 1968), 316–17.
11. H. Gaston Hall, "The Present State of Molière Studies," in Johnson, Neumann, Trail, 728–746.
12. Ibid., 745.
13. Ralph Albanese, in *Oeuvres et critiques* 6, no. 1 (19   ): 57–68.
14. Harold Knutson, *Molière: An Archetypal Approach,* (Toronto: University of Toronto Press, 1976).
15. Northrop Frye, *Anatomy of Criticism: Four Essays,* (Princeton: Princeton University Press, 1957).

16. Charles Mauron, *Psychocritique du genre comique* (Paris: José Corti, 1970).

17. Knutson, *Molière*, 9.

18. Marcel Gutwirth, *Molière, ou l'invention comique: la métamorphose des thèmes et la création des types* (Paris: Minard, 1966).

19. Francis Lawrence, *Molière: The Comedy of Unreason* (New Orleans: Tulane Studies in Romance Language and Literature, no. 2, 1968).

20. Knutson, *Molière*, 173.

21. Alvin Eustis, *Molière as Ironic Contemplator* (The Hague and Paris: Mouton, 1973).

22. Jacques Scherer, *Structures de Tartuffe, deuxième édition revue et augmentée* (Paris: Sociéte d'édition d'Enseignement supérieure, 1974).

23. Ibid., 253–58.

24. W. D. Howarth, *Molière: A Playwright and His Audience* (Cambridge: Cambridge University Press, 1982), 195, 204.

25. Ibid., 212.

26. Ibid., 250–54.

27. Suzanne L. Relyea, *Signs, Systems, and Meanings: A Contemporary Semiotic Reading of Four Molière Plays* (Middletown, Conn.: Wesleyan University Press, 1976).

28. Gérard Defaux, *Molière ou les métamorphoses du comique: de la comédie morale au triomphe de la folie* (Lexington, Ky.: French Forum Monographs, 1980).

29. Claude Abraham, *On the Structure of Molière's Comédies-Ballets* (Paris: Papers on French Seventeenth Century Literature, 1984).

30. Ronald Tobin, "Le Chasseur enchâssé: la mise en abyme dans *Les Fâcheux*," *Cahiers de Littérature du XVIIe siècle*, no. 6 (1984), and "Fusion and Diffusion in *Le Bourgeois gentilhomme*," *French Review* 59, no. 2 (December 1985): 234–45.

31. Lionel Gossman, "Molière's *Misanthrope:* Melancholy and Society in the Age of Counterreformation," *Theater Journal*, October 1982, 322–43.

32. *Oeuvres et critiques* 6, no. 1 (1981).

33. Marie-Odile Sweetser, "Domaine de la critique moliéresque," *Oeuvres et critiques* 6, no. 1 (1981): 25.

34. Judd Hubert, "Molière: The Playwright as Protagonist," *Theater Journal*, October 1982, 361–71.

35. Ibid., 367.

36. Michael Spingler, "The King's Play: Censorship and the Politics of Performance in Molière's *Tartuffe*," *Comparative Drama* 19, no. 3 (Fall 1985): 240–57.

37. Marie-France Hilgar, "Modern and Post-modern Interpretations of *Tartuffe*," *Theater Journal*, October 1982, 384–88.

38. Robert McBride, *The Sceptical Vision of Molière* (New York: Barnes & Noble, 1977).

39. Ibid., 213.

40. Ibid., 215.

41. Stage productions are listed in *N* *Theater Critics, Plays and Play-* ers, *Theater Journal,* and *Drama* for the yea 88. Other sources used are play- bills of productions.

42. Richard Wilbur, trans., *Tartuffe* (New York: Harcourt Brace, 1968).

43. Raymond LePage, "Tartuffe," *Theater Journal,* October 1982.

44. Stanley Kauffmann, in *New Republic,* 18 March 1985, 26.

45. Ibid.

46. Bethany Haye, "Molière for the Masses," *American Film* 11 (September 1986): 10.

47. Barbara Woshinsky, "Discourse of Disbelief in *Dom Juan,*" *Romanic Review* 62, 4, (November 1981): 401–8.

48. Franco Tonelli, "Molière's *Dom Juan* and the Space of the Commedia dell'Arte," *Theater Journal* 37, 4 (December 1985): 440–67.

49. Janice Berkowitz, "Systèmes de signification verbale, spatiale et scénique dans trois pièces de Molière," Ph.D. diss., University of Michigan, 1980.

50. David Ball and Frank H. Ellis, "Molière's *Dom Juan:* Form, Meaning, Audience," *Modern Philology* 81 (November 1983): 146–58.

51. Ibid., 146.

52. H. Walker, "The Self-Creating Hero in *Dom Juan,*" *French Review* 36, no. 2 (December 1962): 167–74.

53. Jean Rousset, *Le Mythe de Don Juan* (Paris: Armand Colin, 1978).

54. Marcel Gutwirth, "Don Juan et le tabou d'inceste," *Romanic Review* 77, no. 1 (January 1986): 25–32.

55. Claude Lévi-Strauss, *La Pensée sauvage,* rev. ed. (New York: Adler, 1985), among his many other works.

56. Gutwirth, "Don Juan," 32.

57. Roger W. Herzel, "Much Depends on the Acting: The Original Cast of *Le Misanthrope,*" *PMLA* 95, no. 3 (May 1980): 348–66. See also his "Problems in the Original Casting of *Les Femmes savantes*" in Francis L. Lawrence, *Actes de New Orleans,* and "Molière's Actors and the Question of Types," *Theatre Survey* 16 (1975).

58. Patrick Henry, "Paradox in *Le Misanthrope,*" *Philology Quarterly* 65 (Spring 1986): 187–95.

59. Ibid., 188.

60. Ibid., 195.

61. Gossman, "Molière's *Misanthrope.*" 335.

62. Ibid., 335.

63. Clive Barnes, *New York Times,* 10 October 1968.

64. Frank Rich, *New York Times,* 28 January 1983.

65. In the Theatre Collection, New York Public Library at Lincoln Center.

66. Marcel Descotes, "Nouvelles interprétations molièresques," *Oeuvres et critiques* 6, no. 1 (1981): 36–37.

67. M. Gutwirth, "Molière and the Woman Question: *Les Précieuses ridicules, L'École des femmes, Les Femmes savantes*," *Theater Journal*, October 1982, 345–59.

68. Ibid., 359.

69. Patricia F. Cholakian, "The Itinerary of Desire in Molière's *Le Tartuffe*," *Theater Journal*, May 1986, 165–79.

70. Barbara Johnson, "Teaching Ignorance: *L'École des femmes*," *Yale French Studies* 63 (1982): 165–82.

71. Larry W. Riggs, "La raison de la plus folle est toujours la meilleure: Synthetic Language and the Hallucination of Reason in *Les Femmes Savantes*," *Symposium*, Fall 1987, 214–26.

72. Descotes, "Nouvelles interprétations," 38.

73. Tobin, "Fusion and Diffusion in *Le Bourgeois gentil-homme*."

74. Garland Wright, *The Guthrie Theater Program Magazine*, 1988. Program for *The Imaginary Invalid*, p. 14.

75. Hubert, "The Playwright as Protagonist."

76. Ibid., 365.

77. Ibid., 371.

Selected Bibliography

PRIMARY WORKS

Important Editions

Les Oeuvres posthumes de Monsieur de Molière. 2 vols. Paris: chez Denys Thierry, Claude Bardin et Pierre Trabouillet, 1682. The first complete edition (of plays available at the time). Prepared under the direction of Molière's associates, Lagrange and Vinot. Biography.

Oeuvres complètes de Molière. Edited by Despois and Mesnard. 13 vols. Paris: Hachette, 1873–1900). Collection "Les Grands Ecrivains de la France." A standard edition.

Oeuvres de Molière. 10 vols. Paris: Cité des livres, 1926–29. Notes by Jacques Copeau, a director of productions that revitalized the plays as modern theater.

Oeuvres de Molière. 2 vols. Paris: NRF Gallimard, 1933. Thorough and handy edition in the Bibliothèque de la Pléiade series.

Oeuvres complètes de Molière. 3 vols. Paris: Club du Meilleur Livre, 1954–56. Edited by René Bray and Jacques Scherer, both major scholars.

French Editions Published in the United States

Les Oeuvres complètes de Molière. Preface by P.-A. Touchard. New York: Macmillan, 1963.

Le Bourgeois gentilhomme. Edited by C. Abraham. Englewood Cliffs, N.J.: Prentice-Hall, 1967.

Le Tartuffe. Edited by H. Walker. Englewood Cliffs, N.J.: Prentice-Hall, 1969.

Le Tartuffe and Le Médecin malgré lui. Edited by J. Guicharnaud. New York: Dell, 1962.

Translations

Six French Plays. Edited by E. Bentley. New York: Doubleday, 1961. Contains *Le Misanthrope.*

The Actor's Molière. Translated by Albert Bermel. Vol. 1, *The Miser* and *George Dandin;* vol. 2, *The Doctor in Spite of Himself* and *The Bourgeois Gentleman;* vol. 3, *Scapin* and *Don Juan.* New York: Applause Theatre Books, 1987.

Eight Plays by Molière. Translated by M. Bishop. New York: Modern Library, 1957. Contains *Le Médecin malgré lui, Les Précieuses ridicules, Le Tartuffe, Le Mis-*

anthrope, *L'École des femmes, La Critique de l'École des femmes, L'Impromptu de Versailles, Le Bourgeois gentilhomme.*

Classical French Drama. Translated by W. Fowlie. Contains *Les Femmes savantes.* New York: Bantam, 1962.

Don Juan. Translated by W. Fowlie. Great Neck: Barron's, 1964.

The Miser. Translated by W. Fowlie. Great Neck: Barron's, 1964.

The Misanthrope and Other Plays. Translated by Donald Frame. New York: New American Library, 1968.

The Learned Ladies. Translated by R. Wilbur. New York: Dramatists Play, 1977.

The School for Wives. Translated by R. Wilbur. New York: Harcourt, Brace, 1972.

The Misanthrope. Translated by R. Wilbur. New York: Harcourt, Brace, and World, 1955. A distinguished poetic translation.

Tartuffe. Translated by R. Wilbur. New York: Harcourt, Brace, and World, 1963. A distinguished poetic translation.

The Miser and Other Plays. Translated by J. Wood. Baltimore: Penguin, 1953. Contains *L'Avare, Le Bourgeois gentilhomme, Les Fourberies de Scapin, L'Amour médecin, Dom Juan.*

The Misanthrope and Other Plays. Translated by J. Wood. Baltimore: Penguin, 1959. Contains *Le Misanthrope, Le Sicilien, Le Tartuffe, Le Médecin malgré lui, Le Malade imaginaire.*

SECONDARY WORKS

Bibliographies

Edelman, Nathan, ed. *The Seventeenth Century* ("Molière" pp. 226–43), vol. 3 of *A Critical Bibliography of French Literature,* edited by D. Cabeen and J. Brody. Syracuse: Syracuse University Press, 1961.

Jurgens, Madeleine, and **Elizabeth Maxfield-Miller.** *Cent ans de recherches sur Molière.* Paris: Archives Nationales, 1963.

Biographies

Fernandez, Ramón. *La Vie de Molière.* Paris: Gallimard, 1930. Translated by W. Follet as *Molière, the Man Seen through the Plays.* New York: Hill and Wang, 1958. Good psychological interpretation.

Grimarest. *La Vie de Monsieur de Molière.* Paris, 1704. Edited by G. Mongrédien, in *Publications de la Société d'Histoire du Théâtre.* Paris: Michel Brient, 1955. The first biography.

Meyer, Jean. *Molière.* Paris: Librairie académique Perrin, 1963. An actor's view of Molière.

Mongrédien, Georges. *La Vie privée de Molière*. Paris: Hachette, 1950. Scholarly study.

Background

Adam, Antoine. *Histoire de la littérature française au XVIIe siècle*. 5 vols. Paris: Domat, 1948–56. Exhaustive and authoritative treatment.
Durant, Will, and Ariel Durant. *The Age of Louis XIV*. New York: Simon & Schuster, 1963. Cultural and intellectual currents in the period.
Lancaster, H. C. *A History of French Dramatic Literature in the Seventeenth Century*. 9 vols. Baltimore: Johns Hopkins University Press, 1929–42. All known works of the period studied against historical background.

Critical Studies

Arnavon, Jacques. *Notes sur l'interprétation de Molière*. Paris: Plon-Nourrit, 1923. A director's ideas on staging.
Audiberti, Jacques. *Molière, dramaturge*. Paris: L'Arche, 1954. Analysis of the works as theater.
Bray, René. *Molière, homme de théâtre*. Paris: Mercure de France, 1954. Important study of Molière as author, actor, and director.
Cairncross, John. *New Light on Molière*. Geneva: Droz, 1956. The order of creation of parts of *Le Tartuffe*.
———. *Molière, bourgeois et libertin*. Paris: Nizet, 1963. The plays' ideas and values as derived from Molière's background.
Chancerel, Léon. *Molière*. Paris: Presses Littéraires de France, 1953. Illustrated. The staging of the plays, with sets, costumes, etc.
Conessa, Gabriel. *Le Dialogue moliéresque, étude stylistique et dramatique*. Paris: Presses Universitaires de France, 1983. A close analysis of verbal techniques in plays.
DeFaux, Gérard. *Molière ou les métamorphoses du comique: de la comédie morale au triomphe de la folie*. Lexington, Ky.: French Forum Monographs, 1980. Molière's career is seen as a progression toward a final stance in farce and comedy-ballet.
Döring, U., Lyroudias, A., Zaiser, R., eds. *Ouverture et Dialogue: Mélanges offerts à Wolfgang Leiner à l'occasion de son soixantième anniversaire*. Tübingen: Narr, 1988. Contains five articles on Molière with varied approaches.
L'Esprit Créateur 6, 3 (Fall 1966). Issue devoted to Molière, with excellent articles by W. G. Moore et al.
Eustis, Alvin. *Molière as Ironic Contemplator*. The Hague–Paris: Mouton, 1973. A good analysis of ironic technique in comedy, with many examples.
Gossman, Lionel. *Men and Masks, a Study of Molière*. Baltimore: Johns Hopkins University Press, 1963. Analysis of themes and structures in philosophical context.

Guicharnaud, Jacques. *Molière, une aventure théâtrale.* Paris: Gallimard, 1963. Important study of the psychological depths of *Le Tartuffe, Dom Juan,* and *Le Misanthrope.*

———, ed. *Molière, a Collection of Critical Essays.* Englewood Cliffs, N.J.: Prentice-Hall, 1964. Good collection of essays for an introduction to critical work.

Gutwirth, Marcel. *Molière ou l'invention comique. La Métamorphose des thèmes et la création des types.* Paris: Minard, Lettres Modernes, 1966. Traditional themes and types in theater are seen taking on human depths with Molière.

Hall, H. Gaston. *Comedy in Context: Essays on Molière.* Jackson: University Press of Mississippi, 1984. The cultural and literary contexts illuminate the plays.

———. *Molière: Tartuffe.* London: Arnold, 1960. A penetrating study of all aspects of this play.

Howarth, W. D. *Molière, A Playwright and His Audience.* Cambridge: Cambridge University Press, 1982. The plays viewed against a background of seventeenth-century theater.

———, and M. Thomas, eds. *Molière, Stage and Study. Essays in Honour of W. G. Moore.* Oxford: Clarendon Press, 1973. Nineteen essays on Molière's techniques, themes, and import.

Hubert, Judd D. *Molière and the Comedy of Intellect.* Berkeley and Los Angeles: University of California Press, 1962. A study of intellectual themes as sources of unity in each play.

Ikor, Roger. *Molière double.* Paris: Presses Universitaires de France, 1977. A playwright views Molière as both comic and tragic.

Jasinski, René. *Molière, l'homme et l'oeuvre.* Paris: Hatier, 1969. A thorough and insightful study of importance.

Johnson, R., S. S. Neumann, and G. T. Trail, eds. *Molière and the Commonwealth of Letters.* Jackson: University Press of Mississippi, 1975. Sixty-five essays of wide scope and exhaustive bibliography.

Jouvet, Louis. *Molière et la comédie classique.* Paris: Gallimard, 1965. A master actor's courses at the Paris Conservatoire (1939–40).

Knutson, H. C. *Molière, an Archetypal Approach.* Toronto: University of Toronto Press, 1976. Psychological constants underlying recurrent themes in Molière.

Lanson, Gustave. "Molière and Farce," translated by R. Cohen. *Tulane Drama Review* 8, 2 (Winter 1963): 133–54. Originally appeared as "Molière et la farce" in *Revue de Paris* (May 1901). The pioneer study of the theatrical essence of Molière.

Lawrence, Francis L., ed. *Actes de New Orleans.* Paris: Papers on French Seventeenth-Century Literature, 1982. Molière is the subject of nine contributions to the meeting of the North American Society for Seventeenth-Century French Literature; a valuable source of studies.

———. *Molière, the Comedy of Unreason.* New Orleans: Tulane Studies in Romance Language and Literature, 1968. The early comedies and career of Molière.

McBride, Robert. *The Sceptical Vision of Molière, a Study in Paradox*. New York: Harper & Row, 1977. Molière's ideas are compared with those of the philosopher La Mothe Le Vayer.

Moore, W. G. *Molière, a New Criticism*. Oxford: Clarendon Press, 1949, and New York: Doubleday, 1962. A landmark study of the thematic coherence of the works.

Revue de l'histoire littéraire de la France 72, no. 5–6 (September–December 1973). Issue devoted to Molière contains valuable studies, from critical analyses to lists of films.

Scherer, Jacques. *Structures de Tartuffe*. 2d ed. Paris: SEDES, 1974. Detailed study of all aspects of the play.

Simon, Alfred. *Molière par lui-même*. Paris: Editions du Seuil, 1957. Inventive blending of Molière's life on and off the stage.

Van Baelen, Jacqueline, and David Rubin, eds. *La Cohérence intérieure. Etudes sur la littérature française du XVIIe siècle, présentées en hommage à Judd D. Hubert*. Paris: Jean Michel Place, 1977. Contains three good studies of Molière, including one by W. G. Moore.

Vedel, Valdemar. "Molière" in *Deux classiques français vus par un critique étranger*. Translated from the Danish by E. Cornet. Paris: Champion, 1935. Concise assessment of Molière's creations in context of his life and times.

Wadsworth, P. A. *Molière and the Italian Theatrical Tradition*. N.p., 1977. A detailed study of Molière's debt to the Italian comic theater.

Walker, Hallam. "*Les Fâcheux* and Molière's Use of Games." *L'Esprit Créateur* 11, no. 2 (Summer 1971): 21–33. The game structure of *comédie-ballet* is studied in major plays.

Index